SMP 16–19

Pure 1

Functions and calculus

D0231723

CAMBRIDGE
UNIVERSITY PRESS

Much of this book is based on earlier SMP books to which the following people contributed.

Simon Baxter
Chris Belsom
Stan Dolan
Doug French
Andy Hall
Barrie Hunt
Lorna Lyons
Paul Roder
Jeff Searle
David Tall
Thelma Wilson

PUBLISHED BY THE PRESS SYNDICATE OF THE UNIVERSITY OF CAMBRIDGE
The Pitt Building, Trumpington Street, Cambridge, United Kingdom

CAMBRIDGE UNIVERSITY PRESS
The Edinburgh Building, Cambridge, CB2 2RU, UK
40 West 20th Street, New York, NY 10011–4211, USA
477 Williamstown Road, Port Melbourne, VIC 3207, Australia
Ruiz de Alarcón 13, 28014 Madrid, Spain
Dock House, The Waterfront, Cape Town 8001, South Africa

http://www.cambridge.org

First published 2001
Reprinted 2002

Printed in the United Kingdom at the University Press, Cambridge

Typeface Minion and Officina   *System* QuarkXpress®

A catalogue record for this book is available from the British Library

ISBN 0 521 78797 1 paperback

Acknowledgements

The authors and publishers would like to thank the following for supplying photographs:

page 21   © R. Sheridan/Ancient Art & Architecture Collection
page 30   © Hulton–Deutsch Collection/CORBIS

Cover photograph: Telegraph Colour Library/F.P.G. © A. Montes de Oca
Cover design: Angela Ashton

Contents

Using this book

Each section within a chapter consists of work developing new ideas followed by an exercise for practice in using those ideas.

Within the development sections, some questions and activities are labelled with a **D**, for example **2D**, and are enclosed in a box. These involve issues that are worth exploring through discussion – either teacher-led discussion in the whole class or discussion by students in small groups, who may then feed back their conclusions to the whole class.

Questions labelled **E** are more demanding.

At the end of some chapters there is support material. This is referred to at the point in the chapter where some students may need it to consolidate a basic idea or technique before moving further with the main flow of the work.

Proof

The examination specification for this module refers to proof. Proof permeates mathematics and it is not helpful to separate it from particular topics. The best way of building students' confidence in this area is by drawing their attention to short chains of deductive reasoning throughout the course. This book and *Methods*, which precedes it, provide ample opportunities for the teacher to encourage students to 'show how ...' or 'explain why ...', to learn to set out mathematical arguments correctly and to follow and criticise deductive chains that they have been presented with.

1 Functions and graphs

A Function notation (answers p. 143)

A scientist performs an experiment to investigate the absorption of light by a liquid. Light is shone through a coloured solution and the intensity of light emerging is measured.

She finds that if she varies the concentration of the solution her readings are as follows.

Concentration (mg cm^{-3})	c	0	0.2	0.4	0.6	0.8	1.0
Intensity (lux)	L	20.0	17.4	15.2	13.2	11.5	10.0

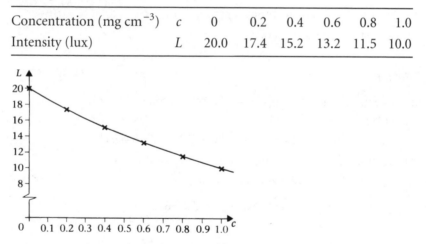

The two variables are related by the formula $L = \dfrac{20}{2^c}$.

This is an example of Beer's law of absorption.

The formula can be used to calculate the value of L for any given value of c.

It is often helpful to consider a formula as a device which generates an **output** for any given **input**. In this case the input is c and the output is L.

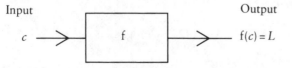

Input

c ⟶ ☐ f ⟶ f(c) = L

Output

In other words, if the scientist inputs any value of c into her formula she will get a corresponding output which tells her the value of L. This dependence on c can be emphasised by use of the **function notation** $L = f(c)$, where the function f is given by

$$f(c) = \frac{20}{2^c}.$$

This gives a convenient shorthand, since you can immediately write $f(0) = 20$, $f(1) = 10$ and so on.

1D | Compare the notations

$$f(c) = \frac{20}{2^c} \quad \text{and} \quad L = \frac{20}{2^c}.$$

What are the advantages and disadvantages of each notation?

Example 1

Consider the function $f(x) = 2x^2 - 3x$.

(a) Find $f(1)$ and $f(2)$.

(b) Find a simplified algebraic expression for $f(x+2)$.

(c) Solve the equation $f(x) = 0$.

Solution

(a) The function of f is applied to 1, so x is replaced by 1 in $2x^2 - 3x$. This gives the value -1.

$$f(1) = 2 - 3 = -1; \text{ similarly } f(2) = 8 - 6 = 2.$$

(b) To apply f to $(x+2)$ replace x by $(x+2)$ in $2x^2 - 3x$.

$$f(x+2) = 2(x+2)^2 - 3(x+2)$$
$$= 2(x^2 + 4x + 4) - 3x - 6$$
$$= 2x^2 + 5x + 2$$

(c) $f(x) = 0 \Longrightarrow 2x^2 - 3x = 0 \Longrightarrow x(2x-3) = 0$
$$\Longrightarrow x = 0 \text{ or } x = \tfrac{3}{2}$$

Exercise A (answers p. 143)

1 Given $f(x) = x^2 + 3$ find these values.

(a) $f(0)$ (b) $f(1)$ (c) $f(\sqrt{2})$ (d) $f(-1)$

2 Given $g(t) = \dfrac{5}{3^t}$ find these.

(a) $g(2)$ (b) $g(1)$ (c) $g(0)$ (d) $g(-1)$ (e) $g(x)$

3 (a) Given $f(x) = x^2 + 3x + 2$, find these.

(i) $f(1)$ (ii) $f(-2)$ (iii) $f(0)$ (iv) $f(-1)$ (v) $f(n)$

(b) Given $f(y) = y^2 + 3y + 2$, find these.

(i) $f(1)$ (ii) $f(-2)$ (iii) $f(0)$ (iv) $f(-1)$ (v) $f(n)$

(c) Does $f(x)$ differ from $f(y)$?

4 Consider the functions $g(x) = (x+1)^2$ and $h(x) = x^2 + 1$.

(a) Find simplified algebraic expressions for these.

(i) $g(x-3)$ (ii) $h(a+2)$

(b) Solve the equation $g(x) = h(x)$.

(c) Solve the equation $g(x-3) = h(x-3)$.

5 Consider the functions $g(x) = x^2 + 2x + 1$ and $f(x) = x + 1$.

(a) Show that $\dfrac{g(x)}{f(x)} = x + 1$.

(b) Find simplified algebraic expressions for these.

(i) $g(2x)$ (ii) $g(x-1)$

B Relationships between functions (answers p. 143)

The graphs of $f(x) = x^2$ and $y = x^2 + 6x + 5$ are given below.

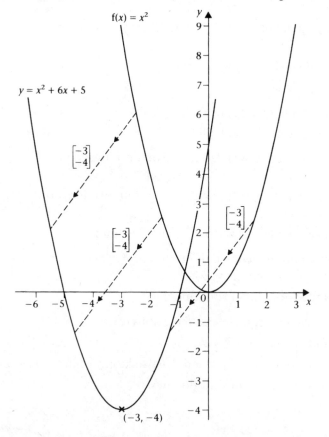

The expression for y can be written in completed square form:
$$y = (x+3)^2 - 9 + 5 = (x+3)^2 - 4$$
Notice that this is the same as $f(x+3) - 4$.

Considering the two graphs, you can see that the graph of $y = x^2 + 6x + 5$ is translation by $\begin{bmatrix} -3 \\ -4 \end{bmatrix}$ of the graph of $f(x)$.

Function notation provides a convenient and useful way of describing the relationship between functions and their graphs. This idea is explored more fully in the following questions.

1 (a) Sketch the graph of $f(x) = x^2$.

(b) Rearrange the expression for $f(x-2) + 5$ into the form $ax^2 + bx + c$.

(c) Superimpose the graph of $f(x-2) + 5$. How is this related to the graph of $f(x)$?

2 For each of the functions below,

(i) sketch the graph of $g(x)$

(ii) write down the expression for $g(x-2) + 5$

(iii) what translation of the graph of $g(x)$ do you expect to give the graph of $g(x-2) + 5$?

(iv) superimpose the graph of $g(x-2) + 5$ and check your answer to part (iii).

(a) $g(x) = x^3$ (b) $g(x) = 2^x$ (c) $g(x) = \sqrt{x}$

3 (a) Sketch the graph of $f(x) = |x|$.

(b) Without using a graph plotter, sketch the graph of $|x+3| - 4$.

(c) Check your answer using a graph plotter.

4 (a) For any function f, what is the relationship between the graphs of $f(x)$ and $f(x+a) + b$?

(b) Illustrate your answer to part (a) by choosing your own function and values for a and b.

(c) Will what you have described be true for any function?

5E (a) Describe the relationship between the graphs of $g(x)$ and $g(x+a) + b$ when $g(x) = \sin x$.

(b) Write an illustrated account of your findings.

6E (a) Investigate the relationships between the graphs of
$$h(x) \qquad \text{and} \qquad ah(bx+c) + d$$
where h is any function, and a, b, c and d may take any values.

(b) Write an illustrated account of your findings.

Any function of the form $f(x + a) + b$ has a graph which is a translation by $\begin{bmatrix} -a \\ b \end{bmatrix}$ of the graph of $f(x)$.

Defining functions

You saw in Section A that an example of Beer's law of absorption is

$$f(c) = \frac{20}{2^c}.$$

It would not be sensible to calculate $f(-2)$, for example, because a concentration of -2 mg cm^{-3} would have no meaning. When defining a function you must be specific about the values to which it applies.

The precise **definition** of a function consists of two parts.

The **rule**　　　This tells you how values of the function are assigned or calculated.

The **domain**　　This tells you the set of values to which the rule may be applied.

For example, $f(x) = \sqrt{x - 5}$, $x \geqslant 5$ defines a function f, where

* the rule is $f(x) = \sqrt{x - 5}$
* the domain is $x \geqslant 5$.

In describing the domain of a function, the following notation is a useful shorthand for defining important sets.

$\mathbb{N}$ – the natural numbers $1, 2, 3, \ldots$

$\mathbb{Z}$ – the integers $\ldots, -3, -2, -1, 0, 1, 2, 3, \ldots$

$\mathbb{Q}$ – the rational numbers (or fractions, including, for example, $\frac{6}{2}$)

$\mathbb{R}$ – the real numbers (irrational, such as $\sqrt{2}$ and $-\pi$, as well as rational)

This notation can be extended using $^+$ and $^-$ signs. Thus $\mathbb{R}^+$ means the positive real numbers, $\mathbb{Z}^-$ means the negative integers.

You can use the symbol $\in$ to mean 'belongs to'. Thus $x \in \mathbb{Q}^+$ means 'x belongs to the set of positive rationals'.

Note that $\mathbb{N}$ is a subset of $\mathbb{Z}$, which is itself a subset of $\mathbb{Q}$, which is a subset of $\mathbb{R}$.

When a function is written down, both the rule and the domain should be given. However, in practice the domain is often omitted and the function is assumed to be defined for all values that are valid in the rule. This is a common 'misuse' of the description of a function.

Exercise B (answers p. 143)

1 Consider the function $f(x) = \dfrac{1}{x+2}$.

(a) Find these.

(i) $f(0)$ (ii) $f(-1)$ (iii) $f(a)$ (iv) $f(a-2)$ (v) $f(-2)$

(b) What is the largest possible domain for f?

(c) Sketch the graph of $f(x)$.

2 (a) Given $h(x) = \sqrt{x}$, find these values.

(i) $h(2)$ (ii) $h(9)$ (iii) $h(\sqrt{2})$ (iv) $h(\pi)$ (v) $h(\pi^2)$

(b) What is the largest possible domain for h?

(c) Sketch the graph of $h(x-3)$.

3 Write down the largest possible domain for g in each of the following.

(a) $g(x) = \dfrac{1}{x+5}$ (b) $\dfrac{1}{\sqrt{x-3}}$ (c) $g(x) = \sqrt[3]{x}$ (d) $g(x) = \dfrac{1}{\sqrt[3]{x+2}}$

4 The modulus function $|x|$, meaning 'the magnitude of x', is defined as

$$|x| = \begin{cases} x, & x \geqslant 0 \\ -x, & x < 0 \end{cases}$$

(On some calculators it is called abs(x), which is an abbreviation for 'the absolute value of x'.)

(a) Write down these values.

(i) $|5|$ (ii) $|-7|$ (iii) $|\sqrt{2}|$ (iv) $|-\pi|$ (v) $|0|$

(b) What is the largest possible domain for the function?

(c) Sketch these graphs.

(i) $y = |x|$

(ii) $y = |x-2|$

(iii) $y = |x-2| + 4$

C Graph sketching and dominance (answers p. 144)

In Sections A and B you looked at many different functions. Now you will investigate the general properties of graphs of functions and techniques used for obtaining these graphs. You will be *sketching* graphs rather than *plotting* them. You can illustrate why sketching is often better than plotting if you use the plotting method to draw the graph of the function

$$y = 4x + \frac{1}{2x-5} \qquad \text{for } x \in \mathbb{R}^+$$

This gives the table of values and plotted points as follows.

x	1	2	3	4	5
y	3.7	7.0	13.0	16.3	20.2

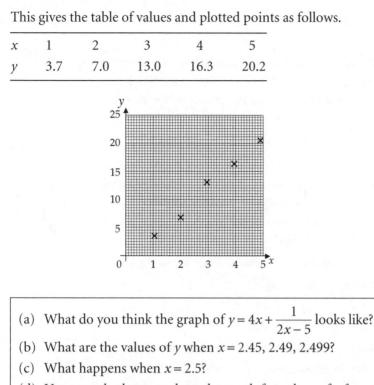

1D   (a) What do you think the graph of $y = 4x + \dfrac{1}{2x - 5}$ looks like?

(b) What are the values of y when $x = 2.45, 2.49, 2.499$?

(c) What happens when $x = 2.5$?

(d) Use a graph plotter to draw the graph for values of x from 0 to 5.

You have seen that drawing a 'smooth curve' through selected points can lead to major errors. In general, for functions it helps to have an idea of what the graph will look like before you attempt the sketch.

> Sketching a curve is about giving a good overall impression of its shape without the need for detailed plotting of points.

To obtain the overall shape of a graph you only need to consider some of the major features.

2 (a) Plot on the same screen and thus superimpose each of the following graphs.

(i) $y = x^2$ (ii) $y = x^3$ (iii) $y = x^4$ (iv) $y = x^5$

(b) What points do all the graphs have in common?

(c) Which function increases most rapidly, and which increases least rapidly, as x becomes large?

(d) What are the main differences between the graphs of the even powers of x and the graphs of odd powers of x?

3 (a) Plot on the same screen the following graphs.

   (i) $y = x^2$ (ii) $y = 4x$ (iii) $y = x^2 + 4x$

   (b) What do you notice about the graphs of $y = x^2$ and $y = x^2 + 4x$ when x is a large positive or negative number?

   (c) What do you notice about the graphs of $y = 4x$ and $y = x^2 + 4x$ when x is a small positive or negative number?

4 (a) Plot on the same screen the following graphs.

   (i) $y = x^3$ (ii) $y = -4x^2$ (iii) $y = x^3 - 4x^2$

   (b) What do you notice about the graphs of $y = -4x^2$ and $y = x^3 - 4x^2$ when x is a small positive or negative number?

   (c) What do you notice about the graphs of $y = x^3$ and $y = x^3 - 4x^2$ when x is a large positive or negative number?

5 (a) Plot the graph of the function $y = x^3 + x^2 - 2x + 1$.

   (b) Superimpose these graphs.

   (i) $y = x^3$ (ii) $y = -2x + 1$

   (c) Compare the three graphs for

      (i) large positive and negative values of x

      (ii) very small positive and negative values of x.

6 Plot the graph of the function $y = 3x + 2x^2 - x^3$.
   What are the zeros of this function; that is, where does the graph cross the x-axis?
   Which term do you think determines the shape for

   (a) large positive and negative values of x

   (b) very small positive and negative values of x?

7 (a) What term is suggested by the shape of this graph when x is large?

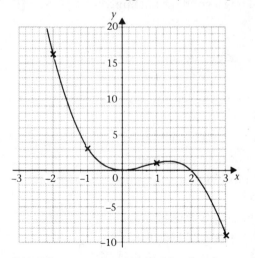

   (b) What term is suggested by the shape of the graph when x is small?

(c) (i) Suggest an equation for the graph on page 8.

(ii) To confirm your suggestion, plot the graph of your equation.

(d) If necessary repeat part (c) until you have found the equation of the graph.

In the questions above, you developed some of the ideas that can be used to build up an impression of a graph of a polynomial function.

> For a general polynomial function of the form
>
> $$y = ax^m + \ldots + bx^n + c \qquad (a, b \text{ are non-zero})$$
>
> where m is the highest power of x and n is the lowest non-zero power of x, the graph will look like $y = ax^m$ for very large x, look like $y = bx^n + c$ for very small x and will cross the y-axis at $(0, c)$.

Example 2

Sketch the graph of $f(x) = 4x^3 - 6x^2 - 11x + 18$.

Solution

(i) For large x the graph behaves like $y = 4x^3$. This is the **dominant** term.

(ii) For small x the graph behaves like $-11x + 18$.

Using just these features, you can draw part of the graph.

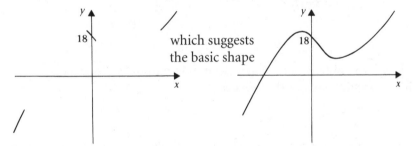

which suggests the basic shape

However, the graph of Example 2 might take any of these forms.

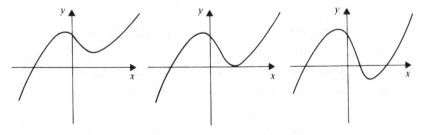

You need more information to establish which is the correct form. For example, you may be able to find the points of intersection with the *x*-axis, or the coordinates of the turning points (i.e. points where the gradient changes sign).

When a polynomial function is given in factorised form, the roots give you extra clues to help determine the shape of the graph.

When sketching the graph of a function always put down as much information as you can, such as the coordinates of intersections with the *x*-, *y*-axes and turning points.

Example 3

Sketch the graph of $f(x) = (x - 2)^2(2x + 7)$.

Solution

(i) $f(0) = 28$.

(ii) For large *x*, $2x^3$ is dominant.

(iii) The zeros of the function are at $x = 2$ and $x = -3\frac{1}{2}$.

The available information is plotted as shown.

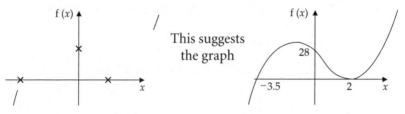

8 How can you obtain facts (i) and (ii) in the solution to Example 3 *without* multiplying out the brackets?

9 Why is   not possible in Example 3?

You can get a good idea of the main features of the graph of a polynomial function, f(*x*), by

(a) knowing the zeros, the *x* value(s) where it cuts the *x*-axis

(b) knowing f(0), the *y* value where it cuts the *y*-axis

(c) applying the principles of dominance.

It is only necessary to apply those principles that allow the essential features of the curve to be drawn.

Exercise C (answers p. 145)

1 The function $f(x) = (x-2)(x+3)(3x-7)$ may be written in expanded form as
$$f(x) = 3x^3 - 4x^2 - 25x + 42.$$

(a) On a partial sketch

(i)   mark any zeros

(ii) mark the value of $f(x)$ when $x = 0$

(iii) use dominance to sketch parts of the graph.

(b) Complete the sketch.

2 Consider the function
$$f(x) = -5x^4 + 28x^3 - 33x^2 + 2x + 8 = -(x-1)^2(x-4)(5x+2).$$

(a) Use dominance to sketch parts of the graph.

(b) Complete the sketch.

3 Sketch the graph of the function
$$y = x^3(x+4)(x-7).$$

4 A girl standing on the edge of a cliff throws a stone. The height of the stone above the point of release, after t seconds, is given by
$$h = t(12 - 5t) \text{ metres.}$$

(a) When is the stone level with the point of release again?

(b) The stone hits the sea after 4 seconds. Estimate the height of the cliff above sea level.

(c) Sketch a graph of height against time.

D Graph sketching using derivative functions (answers p. 145)

Information about the essential features of a curve should always be given in a sketch. In Chapter 7 of *Methods* you learnt of the importance of stationary points, and in this section we look more closely at turning points and other features of curves.

For a function $f(x)$ the notation for the gradient function is $f'(x)$.

Hence if $y = f(x)$ then $\dfrac{dy}{dx} = f'(x)$.

1   For $f(x) = -x(x+2)^2$, differentiate to find the gradient function $f'(x)$.

f'(x) gives useful information about the shape of f(x). For example, if
f'(x) is positive we know f(x) is increasing. If it is zero we have a
horizontal gradient.

The rate of change of the gradient of a function allows you to
determine what the curve looks like for particular values of x. This
involves finding the differential of f'(x) or the **second derivative of
f(x)**, which is denoted as f''(x), and if $y = f(x)$ then

$$f''(x) = \frac{d\left(\frac{dy}{dx}\right)}{dx} = \frac{d^2 y}{dx^2}.$$

If $y = f(x)$ then $\dfrac{dy}{dx} = f'(x)$ and $\dfrac{d^2 y}{dx^2} = f''(x)$, where f'(x) is the

differential or gradient function of f(x) and f''(x) is the second

derivative of f(x), or rate of change of f'(x).

These diagrams show how f''(x) can indicate how the graph of f(x) is
bending as x increases.

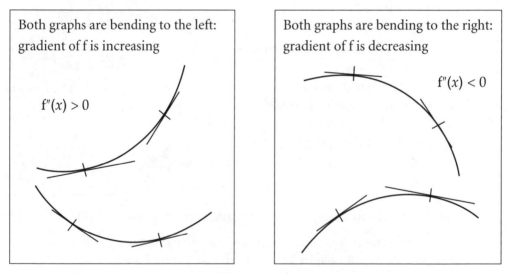

Both graphs are bending to the left:
gradient of f is increasing

$f''(x) > 0$

Both graphs are bending to the right:
gradient of f is decreasing

$f''(x) < 0$

2   For the function $f(x) = -x(x+2)^2$ in question 1, find the second
derivative f''(x), and give the values of x for which f'(x) is
(a) increasing   (b) decreasing.

The second derivative indicates whether a stationary point is a maximum (negative $f''(x)$) or minimum (positive $f''(x)$).

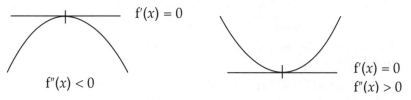

$f'(x) = 0$

$f''(x) < 0$

$f'(x) = 0$
$f''(x) > 0$

3 Find the stationary points for $f(x)$ and use $f''(x)$ to decide whether each is a maximum or a minimum.

As well as stationary points we are also interested in when a function changes the direction in which it is bending. These are called **points of inflexion**.

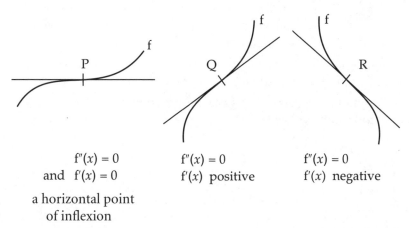

$f''(x) = 0$
and $f'(x) = 0$

a horizontal point
of inflexion

$f''(x) = 0$
$f'(x)$ positive

$f''(x) = 0$
$f'(x)$ negative

At both P and Q, f changes from bending to the right to bending to the left.

4 (a) Calculate where there is a point of inflexion for $f(x) = -x(x+2)^2$ and describe it fully.

(b) Sketch the graph of $f(x)$.

Example 4

Sketch the graph of $g(x) = x^3 - 9x^2 + 15x$.

Solution

x^3 is dominant for large positive and negative values of x, and the curve goes through the origin.

The other zeros are more difficult to find since $g(x) = x(x^2 - 9x + 15)$ and the quadratic factor $(x^2 - 9x + 15)$ will not factorise.

$g'(x) = 3x^2 - 18x + 15$ and $g''(x) = 6x - 18$

To find stationary points solve $g'(x) = 0$.

$$g'(x) = 0 \Longrightarrow 3x^2 - 18x + 15 = 0$$
$$\Longrightarrow (x-1)(3x-15) = 0$$
$$\Longrightarrow x = 1 \quad \text{or} \quad x = 5$$

To find the nature of these stationary points determine whether $g''(x)$ is positive or negative.

$g''(1) = -12$ The negative sign shows there is a local maximum at $x = 1$.

$g''(5) = +12$ The positive sign shows there is a local minimum at $x = 5$.

Look for points of inflexion.

$g''(3) = 0$ This suggests a point of inflexion.

$g'(3) = -12$ This confirms that at $x = 3$ there is a point of inflexion where the gradient of $g(x)$ achieves a local minimum.

There is now sufficient information to sketch a graph of the curve. You can then find the value of $g(x)$ at the key x values.

Local maximum: $g(1) = 7$ Local minimum: $g(5) = -25$
Point of inflexion: $g(3) = -9$

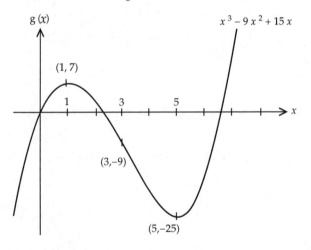

Exercise D (answers p. 146)

1   Find the second derivatives of these.

(a) $f(x) = 5x^3 - 3x^2 + 2x - 1$

(b) $h(x) = x^5 + 3x^3 - 4x$

(c) $y = 5x - 3x^2 + 2x^4$

2   Find and describe the stationary points for these functions.

(a) $f(x) = 5x - x^2$

(b) $f(x) = x^3 - 12x^2$

(c) $f(x) = 3x^5 - 10x^3 - 2$

3 For each of these functions, find $f(2)$, $f'(2)$ and $f''(2)$ and sketch the portion of the graph near the point where $x = 2$.

(a) $f(x) = -2x^5 + 5x^4 - 8x$

(b) $f(x) = x^5 - 10x^4 + 40x^3 - 60x^2 - 10$

4 Sketch the graph of the following functions, clearly showing the coordinates of any stationary points and points of inflexion.

(a) $f(x) = x^3 - 3x^2$

(b) $h(x) = x^4 - 2x^3 - 1$

5E Sketch the graph of $g(x) = (x-1)(x-5)^3$.

E Differentiating and integrating inverse functions and x^n
(answers p. 147)

You know how to differentiate x^2 but not the inverse of this function, $\sqrt{x}$.

For the locally straight curve shown, $\dfrac{dy}{dx} = \dfrac{b}{a}$ at P.

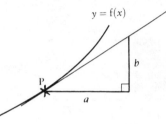

The graph of the inverse function is a reflection of the graph of $y = f(x)$ in the line $y = x$. Its gradient at the equivalent point in P will be $\dfrac{dx}{dy}$.

Since, in the reflection, the x- and y-coordinates are interchanged,

$$\frac{dx}{dy} = \frac{a}{b}$$

Hence, $\dfrac{dx}{dy} \times \dfrac{dy}{dx} = \dfrac{a}{b} \times \dfrac{b}{a} = 1$

This result may be written as

$$\frac{dx}{dy} = 1 \div \frac{dy}{dx}$$

Example 5

Find the derivative of $y = \sqrt{x}$.

Solution

$$x = y^2$$

$$\Rightarrow \frac{dx}{dy} = 2y \Rightarrow \frac{dy}{dx} = \frac{1}{2y} = \frac{1}{2\sqrt{x}} \qquad \text{or} \qquad \frac{dy}{dx} = \frac{1}{2}x^{-\frac{1}{2}}$$

You already know that if n is a positive integer, then

$$y = x^n \implies \frac{dy}{dx} = nx^{n-1}$$

The working above shows that the rule is also applicable when $n = \frac{1}{2}$. In fact the result is generally true.

> If $y = x^n$ then $\dfrac{dy}{dx} = nx^{n-1}$ for all values of n.

The fundamental theorem of calculus you met in Chapter 9 of *Methods* says that the process of differentiation (e.g. finding gradients) is an inverse process to that of integration (e.g. finding areas).

Thus if $y = \dfrac{1}{2\sqrt{x}}$ then $\displaystyle\int y\,dx = \int \dfrac{1}{2\sqrt{x}}\,dx = x^{\frac{1}{2}} + c$.

integrate

$3x^2$ x^3

differentiate

> If $y = x^n$ then $\displaystyle\int y\,dx = \dfrac{1}{n+1}x^{n+1}$ for all values of n.

Example 6

Find the integral of $y = \sqrt[3]{x}$.

Solution

$$y = x^{\frac{1}{3}}$$

$$\int x^{\frac{1}{3}}\,dx = \tfrac{3}{4}x^{\frac{4}{3}} + c$$

Exercise E (answers p. 147)

1 (a) Show that the derivative of $\dfrac{1}{x^2}$ is $-\dfrac{2}{x^3}$.

   (b) Find the derivative of $(1 + x)\sqrt{x}$.

2 Differentiate these.

   (a) $\sqrt[3]{x}$ (i.e. $x^{\frac{1}{3}}$)   (b) $\dfrac{1}{x}$ (c) x^{-3} (d) $\dfrac{1}{x^2} + \sqrt{x}$

3 Find the derivative of $\sqrt[n]{x}$ (i.e. $x^{\frac{1}{n}}$) with respect to x.

4 Find the integral with respect to x of these.

(a) $5\sqrt{x}$ (b) $\dfrac{2}{\sqrt[3]{x}}$ (c) x^{-3} (d) $\dfrac{1}{x^2}+\sqrt{x}$ (e) $(1+x)\sqrt{x}$

5 Find the integral of $\sqrt[n]{x}$ (i.e. $x^{\frac{1}{n}}$) with respect to x.

F Decimal search (answers p. 148)

In earlier work you have looked at techniques for solving polynomial equations. Although you found a formula that works for **all** quadratic equations, the method that you used for cubic and quartic equations will only work if the factors can be found easily. In fact there are general methods of solving both of these types of equation, but they are beyond the scope of this book.

The first step for an approximate method is to **locate the roots of the equation**, and this can be accomplished by plotting a graph.

Consider the equation $x^2 - x - 1 = 0$ which has an alternative arrangement of $x^2 = x + 1$.

1D

(a) In each arrangement, what graphs should you draw to solve the equation, and which points give the solutions?

(b) Sketch the graphs and find inequalities (**bounds**) for the roots.

(c) Use the 'zoom' facility of a graph plotter to find the roots to 3 decimal places.

(d) What are the advantages and disadvantages of the two arrangements?

Example 7
Find bounds for the solutions of

$$x^2 = 1 + \frac{1}{x+3}.$$

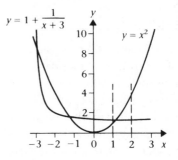

Solution

From the graph, it can be seen that roots lie between -3 and -2, between -2 and -1 and between 1 and 2.

Graphs can be drawn very easily using a graph plotter, but care is needed to ensure that all the intersections representing solutions are displayed on the screen.

2 For each of the following, sketch appropriate graphs and find bounds for all the possible solutions.

(a) $x^2 - 1 = 5\sqrt{x}$ (b) $x^3 + 3x^2 - 2x - 2 = 0$

(c) $2^x = 5 - x$ (d) $10 - x^2 = 2|x|$

Once you have located approximate roots there are a number of alternative ways of finding approximate solutions to equations. These techniques do not give **exact** solutions to an equation, but will often give **good approximations** in cases where exact methods break down. You will meet more powerful and accurate techniques in later books.

The first method is a numerical one called **decimal search**. This is introduced by looking at the **golden ratio**.

Consider the following problem. Given a square, can a rectangle be 'added' ...

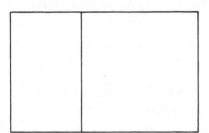

... so that the shape of the new rectangle is the same as that of the added rectangle, as shown below?

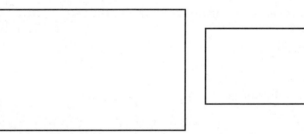

A rectangle with this shape is called a **golden rectangle** and the ratio of the lengths of its sides is called the **golden ratio**. Later you will see that there is only one possible value for this ratio. It is denoted by the Greek symbol ϕ (phi) in honour of the great sculptor Phidias who used it in his work. Like other famous mathematical constants such as π and e, ϕ is found in many situations. Many mythical and mystical properties were attributed to ϕ, which may explain the use of the term 'golden'.

How can you find the golden ratio? Comparing the added rectangle with the new rectangle,

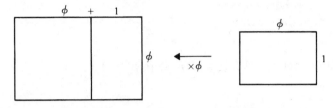

you can see that the ratio of the shorter sides is ϕ. The ratio of the longer sides must also be ϕ and so

$$\phi \times \phi = \phi + 1$$

ϕ therefore satisfies the quadratic equation

$$x^2 = x + 1$$

or, rearranging,

$$x^2 - x - 1 = 0 .$$

This equation can of course be solved using the formula, but in this instance you are going to see how it can be solved numerically.

If you put $x^2 - x - 1$ into the completed square form, $(x - \frac{1}{2})^2 - \frac{5}{4}$, the graph is easy to sketch.

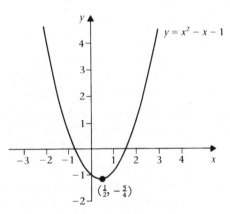

Possible values for ϕ occur at points where the graph cuts the x-axis. There is just one useful solution, between 1 and 2, because the negative solution cannot represent a length.

Now that you know an approximate value of ϕ you can find it more precisely by using the method of **decimal search**.

Begin the decimal search by considering values of x between 1 and 2 in steps of 0.1.

x	$x^2 - x - 1$
1.0	-1
1.1	-0.89
1.2	-0.76
1.3	-0.61
1.4	-0.44
1.5	-0.25
1.6	-0.04 } solution
1.7	0.19 } here
1.8	0.44
1.9	0.71
2.0	1

Since the sign changes between 1.6 and 1.7 the graph must have crossed the *x*-axis as shown in the diagram.

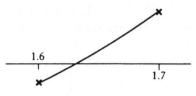

The search continues between 1.6 and 1.7 in steps of 0.01.

x	$x^2 - x - 1$
1.60	−0.04
1.61	−0.0179 } solution
1.62	0.0044 } here
1.63	0.0269
–	–
–	–

After two searches, it can be seen that the solution lies between 1.61 and 1.62, hence the solution is 1.6 (to 1 d.p.). Further searches would increase the accuracy by one decimal place at a time.

When using a numerical technique always investigate to one further place of accuracy than required. An answer to 1 d.p. requires working to the second decimal place.

A similar method, sometimes known as 'interval bisection' works like this. If the sign changes between 1.6 and 1.7 try the point half-way between them, 1.65. If the sign changes between 1.6 and 1.65, try their half-way point, 1.625 – and so on until a sufficiently accurate solution is found.

3D | Can you suggest how to speed up the method of decimal search?

It has been claimed that the golden rectangle

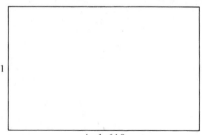

$\phi \approx 1.618$

is *the* most artistically pleasing rectangle.

An attempt to confirm or deny this was made by Gustav Fechner in 1876. His extensive experiments showed that the most aesthetically pleasing shape for a rectangle was something between that of a square and a rectangle with sides in the ratio $1 : 2$.

Architecturally, some very famous and beautiful structures, for example the Parthenon, are said to be based on the golden ratio and golden rectangle.

It would be satisfying if an exact representation of the 'golden' number could be given. For this it is necessary to use the quadratic formula for the solution of $x^2 - x - 1 = 0$.

$$x = \frac{1 \pm \sqrt{1 + 4}}{2}$$

$$= \tfrac{1}{2} + \tfrac{1}{2}\sqrt{5} \quad \text{or} \quad \tfrac{1}{2} - \tfrac{1}{2}\sqrt{5}$$

$\sqrt{5}$ is a number written in **surd** form. This means that the square root sign remains, rather than replacing $\sqrt{5}$ with its decimal value of 2.236 068 (to 7 s.f.), which would be clumsy to write out every time, and which of course is not the exact value.

As seen earlier, the negative value is discarded, so the golden ratio is

$$\phi = \tfrac{1}{2}(1 + \sqrt{5}) \approx 1.618\ 034$$

Exercise F (answers p. 148)

1 In question 2 on p. 18 you sketched appropriate graphs and found integer bounds for all the possible solutions. Now use decimal search to solve each of these correct to two decimal places.

(a) $x^2 - 1 = 5\sqrt{x}$ (b) $x^3 + 3x^2 - 2x - 2 = 0$

(c) $2^x = 5 - x$ (d) $10 - x^2 = 2|x|$

2 Find all possible solutions, to two decimal places, of these.

(a) $0 = x^3 - 2x - 2$ (b) $x^3 - 8x - 9 = 2^{(x-3)}$

G Linear interpolation (answers p. 148)

An alternative method to find an approximate solution to an equation is **linear interpolation**.

Suppose you want to solve $f(x) = 0$ when $f(x) = x^3 - x - 1$ to find the positive root. It is not possible to factorise the polynomial, but $f(1) = -1$ and $f(2) = 5$, so the curve $f(x)$ crosses the x-axis between $x = 1$ and $x = 2$, and therefore there is a root between these two values at X as can be seen in this sketch of $f(x)$.

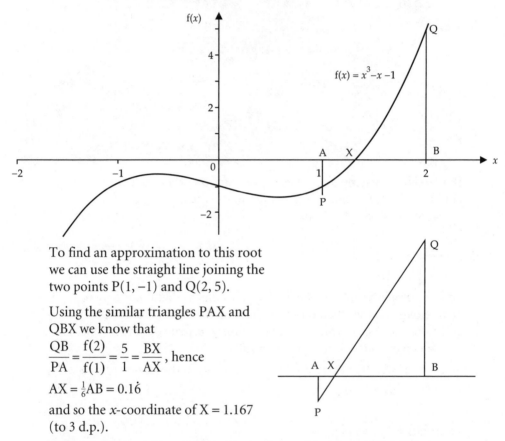

To find an approximation to this root we can use the straight line joining the two points $P(1, -1)$ and $Q(2, 5)$.

Using the similar triangles PAX and QBX we know that

$$\frac{QB}{PA} = \frac{f(2)}{f(1)} = \frac{5}{1} = \frac{BX}{AX}, \text{ hence}$$

$AX = \frac{1}{6}AB = 0.1\dot{6}$

and so the x-coordinate of X = 1.167 (to 3 d.p.).

This may be a good approximation to the positive root of $f(x)$ if the curve is indeed close to a straight line.

This method can also be used to find values from mathematical tables of the kind used before the scientific calculator became available.

Natural sines (sin x°)

x°	0.0	0.1	0.2	0.3	0.4	0.5	0.6	0.7	0.8	0.9
7	0.1219	1236	1253	1271	1288	1305	1323	1340	1357	1374
8	0.1392	1409	1426	1444	1461	1478	1495	1513	1530	1547

The value of sin(7.2) is found by going to the row 7 and across to the 0.2 column where sin(7.2) = 0.1253.

Finding the sine of intermediate values such as 7.68° requires the use of linear interpolation.

Look up sin(7.6°) = 0.1323 and sin(7.7°) = 0.1340.

Assume a straight line joins the points (7.6, 0.1323) and (7.7, 0.1340). 7.68 lies 0.8 of the way along the interval between 7.6 and 7.7, so sin(7.68°) lies 0.8 of the way along the interval between 0.1323 and 0.1340.

Hence

$$\sin(7.68°) = 0.1323 + 0.8 \times (0.1340 - 0.1323)$$
$$= 0.1337$$

Exercise G (answers p. 148)

1 Use linear interpolation for these.

(a) Find the positive root of $y = \dfrac{x^2}{2} - 2x - 1$.

(b) Solve $\dfrac{x}{3} - \dfrac{1}{(2x-1)} = 0$.

2 From the tables of sines above find these.

(a) sin(8.33°) (b) sin(7.28°)

After working through this chapter you should

1 understand the meaning of the term **function**

2 be able to define and describe a function using the correct notation

3 be able to sketch the graphs of functions using:

(a) simple transformations of standard graphs

(b) zeros and the value of the function when $x = 0$

(c) dominance (the behaviour of the graph for large or small values of x, both positive and negative)

(d) the gradient function

(e) second derivatives

4 know how to solve equations approximately by drawing graphs

5 be able to obtain bounds for solutions to $f(x) = 0$ by looking for changes of sign of $f(x)$

6 be able to use a decimal search to find an approximate solution

7 be able to use linear interpolation to find an approximate solution.

2 Sequences and series

A Inductive definition (answers p. 148)

Sequences, or lists of numbers, occur in many contexts. From an early age we learn simple sequences such as the 5-times table:

5, 10, 15, 20, 25, 30, ...

Sequences can also be used to forecast future data. In 1989 the population of Brazil was 160 million and was growing at 2.4 per cent per year. At this rate the population (in millions) over the next five years would be

163.84, 167.77, 171.80, 175.92, 180.14

1D | What would be a sensible forecast for the population in 1995?

To aid the description of a sequence, certain notations are used. If U is the sequence 3, 7, 11, 15, 19, ... then

$u_1 = 3$ is the first term,

$u_2 = 7$ is the second term,

$u_5 = 19$ is the fifth term, and so on.

The subscript indicates the term of the sequence U. So the ith term of sequence U is written as u_i.

2 U is the sequence 2, 8, 14, 20, ...

(a) What are the values of u_1 and u_4?

(b) What value would you expect for u_5?

Give an equation connecting u_5 and u_4.

(c) Give an equation connecting u_{i+1} and u_i.

3 T is the sequence defined by $t_1 = 4$ and $t_{i+1} = t_i + 9$.

(a) What are the values of t_2, t_3, t_4, t_5?

(b) What is the value of t_{20}?

A sequence U may be given by an **inductive definition**. Such a definition requires

(i) a starting value or values, for example u_1, the first term;

(ii) a **recurrence relation**, i.e. a formula which will generate any term from the previous term or terms, for example

$$u_{i+1} = u_i + 6.$$

A sequence can use the subscript value in the recurrence relation. For example if $u_1 = 1$ and $u_{i+1} = u_i + (i+1)$ then $u_2 = 1 + (2) = 3$, $u_3 = 3 + (3) = 6$. The familiar triangle number sequence is the result: $1, 3, 6, 10, 15, ...$

Example 1

Find an inductive definition for the series $1, 2, 6, 24, 120, ...$

Solution

$u_1 = 1$ and the pattern is then

$u_2 = 2 \times u_1$, $u_3 = 3 \times u_2$, $u_4 = 4 \times u_3$, and so on.

So $u_1 = 1$, $u_{i+1} = (i+1)u_i$.

4 For each sequence write out the first five terms and the value of the 20th term.

(a) $u_1 = -5$ and $u_{i+1} = u_i + 2$ (b) $u_1 = 15$ and $u_{i+1} = u_i - 4$

(c) $u_1 = 2$ and $u_{i+1} = 3u_i$ (d) $u_1 = 3$ and $u_{i+1} = \dfrac{1}{u_i}$

We can use graphs to illustrate the behaviour of sequences.

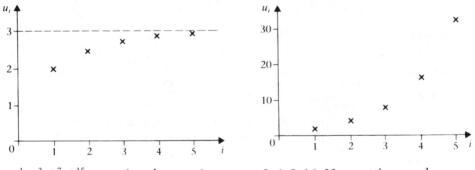

$2, 2\frac{1}{2}, 2\frac{3}{4}, 2\frac{7}{8}, 2\frac{15}{16}, ...$ getting closer to 3. $2, 4, 8, 16, 32, ...$ getting ever larger.

5 For each sequence below, sketch enough points on a graph to show its behaviour. Try using different starting values.

(a) $u_{i+1} = -2u_i$ (b) $u_{i+1} = 2u_i + 4$ (c) $u_{i+1} = u_i^2 + 3$

(d) $u_{i+1} = \sqrt{u_i + 2}$ (e) $u_{i+1} = \dfrac{2}{u_i}$

6E For different starting values, obtain a sufficient number of terms to enable you to describe the behaviour or patterns of each sequence.

(a) $u_{i+2} = u_i + u_{i+1}$ (You will need starting values for u_1 and u_2.)

(b) $u_{i+1} = \dfrac{10}{u_i} - 1.5$ (You will need to generate a considerable number of terms to be sure of the pattern.)

7E Investigate the following sequence, using various positive whole-number starting values.

$$s_{i+1} = \begin{cases} 3s_i + 1, \text{ when } s_i \text{ is odd} \\ \dfrac{s_i}{2}, \text{ when } s_i \text{ is even} \end{cases}$$

You are recommended to begin with starting values of between 1 and 10. What happens with numbers greater than 10?

Sequences can be classified as follows.

Convergent

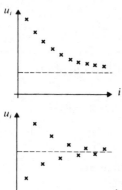

The values get closer and closer to a fixed value.

The values of this convergent sequence **oscillate** back and forth about one value.

Divergent
Any sequence which does not converge to a fixed value is called **divergent**.

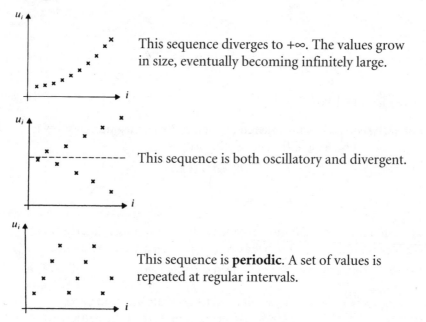

This sequence diverges to $+\infty$. The values grow in size, eventually becoming infinitely large.

This sequence is both oscillatory and divergent.

This sequence is **periodic**. A set of values is repeated at regular intervals.

Exercise A (answers p. 149)

1 Write down the first five terms of the sequence U where $u_{i+1} = 2u_i$ and $u_1 = 4$ and describe the properties of the sequence.

2 Which of the following sequences converge?

(a) $u_{i+1} = \dfrac{2}{3} u_i$, $u_1 = 9$ (b) $u_{i+1} = \dfrac{1}{u_i^2}$, $u_1 = 2$ (c) $u_{i+1} = \dfrac{5}{u_i}$, $u_1 = 1$

3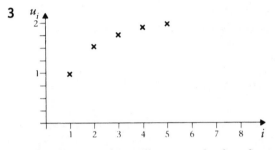

The diagram above illustrates the first five terms of the sequence U where

$$u_{i+1} = u_i + \left(\tfrac{1}{2}\right)^i \qquad \text{and} \qquad u_1 = 1.$$

Describe fully the properties of the sequence.

4 Investigate and describe the sequence T where $t_{i+2} = t_i + t_{i+1}$ and $t_1 = 1$, $t_2 = 2$.

5 Investigate and describe the sequence T where

$$t_{i+1} = \dfrac{27}{(t_i)^2} \qquad \text{and} \qquad t_1 = 2.$$

6 Find inductive definitions for these sequences.

(a) $1, \tfrac{1}{2}, \tfrac{1}{4}, \tfrac{1}{8}, \tfrac{1}{16}, \dots$ (b) $1, -\tfrac{1}{2}, \tfrac{1}{4}, -\tfrac{1}{8}, \tfrac{1}{16}, \dots$

B The general term (answers p. 149)

1 A sequence S has a zero starting value and a term-to-term rule (recurrence relation) $s_{t+1} = s_t + 6$.

(a) What is s_{50}?

(b) What is s_t?

(c) Why is it inappropriate to use an inductive method to calculate s_{50}?

Clearly, there are drawbacks if only inductive definitions are used to generate the terms of a sequence. It can be very useful to have a formula for the general term.

2   Why is $2 \times 3^{n-1}$ the general term of the sequence T where
$$t_{i+1} = 3t_i \qquad \text{and} \qquad t_1 = 2?$$

3   What are the terms of the sequence U where
$$u_i = (-1)^i \frac{1}{i^2}?$$

> A sequence of alternating signs can be achieved by using a factor of $(-1)^i$ or $(-1)^{i+1}$ in the general term.

Example 2

Find an expression for the ith term of the sequence $-1, 3, -5, 7, \dots$

Solution

It is helpful to think of the terms as
$$-1 \times 1, +1 \times 3, -1 \times 5, +1 \times 7, \dots$$
The $-1, +1, -1, +1, \dots$ sequence is generated by $(-1)^i$.
The $1, 3, 5, 7, \dots$ sequence is generated by $2i - 1$.
So $u_i = (-1)^i(2i - 1)$.

Exercise B (answers p. 150)

1   Copy and complete the table below for each of the following patterns of dots.

Position in pattern	1	2	3	4	5	10	20	100	i
No. of dots									

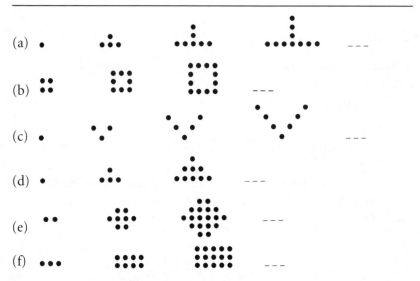

2

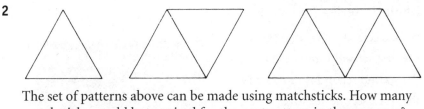

The set of patterns above can be made using matchsticks. How many matchsticks would be required for the next pattern in the sequence? Copy and complete the table.

No. of triangles	1	2	3	4	5	10	20	100	i
No. of matchsticks									

3 Write out the first five terms of the sequences with these ith terms.

(a) $u_i = 3i + 2$ (b) $u_i = 5 \times 2^i$ (c) $u_i = 3i^2$

4 (a) Write out the first five terms of the sequences with these ith terms.

(i) $u_i = (-1)^i$

(ii) $u_i = (-1)^{i+1}$

(iii) $u_i = (-1)^{i+2}$

(iv) $u_i = (-1)^i 2^{i-1}$

(b) Write down the general term of each of these sequences.

(i) $3, -3, 3, -3, 3, \ldots$

(ii) $-3, 3, -3, 3, -3, \ldots$

5 For each of the following sequences complete the table.

Term	1	2	3	4	5	6	9	100	i
A	2	4	6	8					
B	2	5	8	11					
C	2	4	8	16					
D	6	12	24	48					
E	1	-1	1	-1					
F	-1	2	-3	4					
G	1	-2	3	-4					
H	2	-4	6	-8					
I	$\frac{1}{2}$	$\frac{1}{3}$	$\frac{1}{4}$	$\frac{1}{5}$					
J	1	-4	9	-16					

C   **Arithmetic series** (answers p. 150)

A car is accelerating from rest.

In the first second it moves 3 m.

In the second second it moves 5 m.

In the third second it moves 7 m.

In the fourth second it moves 9 m.

If this pattern continues, then the total distance travelled in the first ten seconds will be

$$S = 3 + 5 + 7 + 9 + 11 + 13 + 15 + 17 + 19 + 21$$

A sequence of numbers added together is called a **series**. In this case S will be the sum of the series. To calculate S for the first ten seconds is straightforward, if a little tedious, but if the sum had been for the first thirty seconds, an algebraic technique would have been useful.

1D   As a schoolboy, the German mathematician Carl Friedrich Gauss (1777–1855) spotted a simple fact which helped him to calculate the sum of the series

$$1 + 2 + 3 + 4 + \ldots + 99 + 100$$

Can you find a simple way to sum this series?

Where consecutive terms of a sequence *differ by a constant value*, such a sequence is known as an **arithmetic sequence**, or **arithmetic progression** (**A.P.**).

Gauss's observation makes it straightforward to sum any such series.

$$1 + 2 + 3 + 4 + 5 + 6 + 7 + 8 + 9 + 10$$

This series may be summed by noting how each linked pair of values has the same sum (11).

$$1 + 2 + 3 + 4 + 5 + 6 + 7 + 8 + 9 + 10 = 10 \times \tfrac{11}{2} = 55$$

You can use this method to find the sum of any arithmetic series.

2   (a)   Find the sum of each of these series.

      (i) $1 + 2 + 3 + 4 + \ldots + 20$

      (ii) $1 + 2 + 3 + 4 + \ldots + 9$ (careful!)

      (iii) $1 + 2 + 3 + 4 + \ldots + 29$

   (b)   Describe in your own words how to sum an arithmetic series.

3   Show that the series $5 + 6 + 7 + \ldots + 105$ has 101 terms.

4 For the series below, state the number of terms and sum the series.

   (a) $1 + 2 + 3 + 4 + \ldots + 50$ (b) $10 + 11 + 12 + \ldots + 90$

   (c) $200 + 199 + 198 + \ldots + 100$

For an arithmetic series of n terms, whose first term is a and last term l, the sum of all n terms, S_n, is given by:

$$S_n = n\left(\frac{a + l}{2}\right)$$

---

5 For the series below, state the number of terms and use the results above to sum the series.

   (a) $1 + 3 + 5 + 7 + 9 + 11 + 13 + 15$

   (b) $4 + 7 + 10 + 13 + \ldots + 100$

   (c) $196 + 191 + 186 + \ldots + 71$

For some series, instead of being given the last term, you are given the number of terms. If this is the case you need to find the last term.

6 For each of the series below, find a formula in terms of i for the ith term.

   (a) $3 + 5 + 7 + 9 + \ldots$ (b) $6 + 10 + 14 + 18 + \ldots$

   (c) $12 + 7 + 2 - 3 - \ldots$

7 Consider the series $5 + 9 + 13 + 17 + \ldots$

   (a) (i) Calculate the 15th term.
       (ii) Calculate the sum of the first 15 terms.

   (b) (i) Write down an expression for the ith term.
       (ii) Find a formula for the sum of the first i terms.

You can generalise the method of question 7 to a series having first term a and where each succeeding term is found by adding on d.

d is called the **common difference** for the sequence.

The first few terms are:

   $a, a + d, a + 2d, \ldots$

8 For the sequence $a, a + d, a + 2d, \ldots$, write these down.

   (a) The fifth term   (b) The 50th term

   (c) The nth term   (d) The sum of the first 50 terms.

To obtain a general formula for the sum of n terms of the series, you need:

   ● the first term $= a$ ● the last term $= l = a + (n - 1)d$

9 Show (by substitution into the earlier formula for S_n) that the sum of n terms of the series is

$$S_n = n\frac{[2a+(n-1)d]}{2} = \frac{n}{2}[2a+(n-1)d]$$

You should now know and understand the following results.

> The average term of an arithmetic progression can be found by averaging the first and last terms. The sum of an A.P. is found by multiplying
>
> number of terms × average term
>
> For a series of n terms with first term a and last term l, this can be written as
>
> $$S_n = n\left(\frac{a+l}{2}\right)$$
>
> For an arithmetic series, whose first term is a and whose common difference is d, a useful formula for the sum of the first n terms is
>
> $$S_n = \frac{n}{2}[2a+(n-1)d]$$

Example 3

Sum these series.

(a) $3 + 5 + 7 + \ldots + 99$ (b) $4 + 11 + 18 + \ldots$ as far as the 50th term.

Solution

(a) The first term is 3, the last 99, so the average is $\dfrac{3+99}{2} = 51$.

The difference between the first and last terms is $99 - 3 = 96$. With a common difference of 2, 99 is $\frac{96}{2} = 48$ terms on from 3. Thus the total number of terms is $48 + 1 = 49$ and the sum is $49 \times 51 = 2499$.

(b) The first term $a = 4$, and the common difference $d = 7$, so from the formula, $S_{50} = 25(8 + 49 \times 7) = 8775$.

Exercise C (answers p. 151)

1 Find the sum of these arithmetic series.

(a) $4 + 9 + 14 + 19 + \ldots + 199$

(b) $3 + 9 + 15 + \ldots$ as far as the 50th term

(c) $1 + 1\frac{1}{2} + 2 + 2\frac{1}{2} + \ldots + 100$

(d) $99 + 97 + 95 + \ldots + 25$

2 Complete the following table.

	First term	Common difference	Number of terms	Last term	Sum
(a)	8	2	18		
(b)	6	9		303	
(c)	3		25	195	

3 A small terrace at a football ground comprises a series of 15 steps, which are 50 m long and built of solid concrete. Each step has a rise of $\frac{1}{4}$ m and a tread of $\frac{3}{4}$ m.

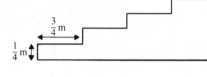

By calculating the area under each step and forming a series, calculate the total volume of concrete required to build the terrace.

4 A child builds a pattern with square building bricks using the sequence of steps as shown.

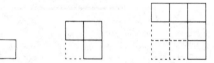

The total number of bricks used is $1 + 3 + 5 + \ldots$

(a) How many bricks does the child use on the nth step?

(b) If the child has 60 bricks, how many steps can be completed?

(c) Use the formula for summing an arithmetic series to show that the total number of bricks used will be n^2.

5E Another child builds a square pattern using bricks that are twice as long as they are wide.

(a) How many bricks does the child use on the nth step?

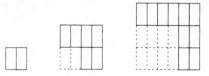

(b) Use the formula for summing an arithmetic series to find the total number of bricks used.

6E   Each year Mrs Smith gives her nephew a birthday present of money (in £) equal to five times his age in years. The money is put into a bank account, but unfortunately does not attract any interest and he is not allowed to withdraw any money until he is 18. She makes the first payment on his first birthday and continues until he is 18.

(a) How much does he have in the account on his 18th birthday?

(b) How old is he when the sum of money in the account first exceeds £500?

7E   220 m of video tape are wound onto a reel of circumference 8.2 cm. Because of the thickness of the tape, each turn is 0.1 cm longer than the previous one.

How many turns are required?

D   Loans and APR (answers p. 151)

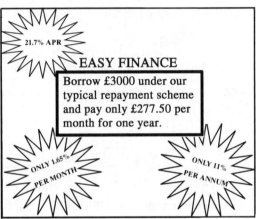

In this diagram, three different ways of describing the interest on the 'Easy finance' loan are shown. Notice that the customer must begin repaying the loan almost immediately. We shall look at how each of these rates is calculated.

11 per cent per annum
The customer repays

$$£277.50 \times 12 = £3330$$

and so has paid £330 in interest charges. Since

$$£3000 \times \tfrac{11}{100} = £330$$

the stated rate of 11 per cent is easy to understand.

The 11 per cent is called a flat rate and, although it is easy to understand, it is nevertheless misleading. The customer certainly pays 11 per cent interest on the £3000 but does *not* have the use of the full £3000 throughout the year!

1   A loan of £800 is repaid by 12 monthly instalments of £100. What is the flat rate of interest?

1.65 per cent per month
This rate in the advertisement above is also easy to understand. The customer pays 1.65 per cent interest on the amount owed during the month.

After one month the customer owes the original £3000 and interest of £3000 × 0.0165 = £49.50: a total of £3049.50 . (A quick way of obtaining this total is to calculate £3000 × 1.0165 .) Since the customer repays £277.50, the amount owing throughout the second month is £2772 .

To find the amount owing after two months, the procedure is repeated. The outstanding debt after two months is $(£2772 \times 1.0165) - £277.50 = £2540.24$.

2 Use a spreadsheet or a calculator to continue the procedure for 12 months.

21.7 per cent APR
The concept of APR or **annual percentage rate** is used to give consumers a simple way of comparing various methods of borrowing. Commercial lenders are currently obliged by law to quote the equivalent APR.

The APR corresponding to the rate of 1.65 per cent per month can be found by calculating the total interest on a year's loan, *assuming the entire repayment is at the end of the year*.

Suppose £100 is borrowed. After one month the amount outstanding is

$$£100 \times 1.0165 = £101.65$$

After two months, the amount has become

$$£101.65 \times 1.0165$$

and so on.

3 By continuing this process and finding the amount to be repaid after 12 months, show that the APR is 21.7 per cent.

Remarkably, the three rates of 21.7 per cent APR, 11 per cent flat rate per annum and 1.65 per cent per month are *all* equivalent! When considering the costs of different loans, the APR enables sensible comparisons to be made.

4 Find the APR corresponding to monthly payments based on these interest rates per month.

(a) 1 per cent   (b) 2 per cent   (c) 5 per cent

5 Describe an algorithm or procedure for converting any monthly interest rate into an APR.

6 Using the method you found in question 5, find the monthly interest rate that corresponds to an APR of 100 per cent.

7 Use a computer or programmable calculator to show the amounts outstanding in successive months for any inputs of the initial loan, a monthly interest rate and monthly repayments.

8E A loan of £800 is repaid by 5 monthly instalments of £200. Use your solution to question 7 and any appropriate method to find the monthly interest rate. Hence find the APR.

Exercise D (answers p. 152)

1

12.4% APR	
CAR PURCHASE FINANCED	
BY A HIRE PURCHASE AGREEMENT	
CASH PRICE (ON THE ROAD)	£7292.86
DEPOSIT (30%)†	£2187.86
BALANCE	£5105.00
36 EQUAL MONTHLY PAYMENTS OF	£127.52*
1 TERMINAL RENTAL	£1786.75
TOTAL PAYABLE	£8565.33

* 36 monthly payments of £127.52 is equivalent to
approx £29.43 per week.   † MINIMUM DEPOSIT 20%

The figures in this car advertisement are the result of certain
calculations. The 'terminal rental' is a final cash payment to clear any
remaining debt.

(a) Explain how the figure of £2187.86 was obtained.

(b) How is the figure of £8565.33 obtained from the other figures?

(c) Show that £29.43 per week and £127.52 per month are equivalent.

(d) Find the monthly interest rate corresponding to an APR of
     12.4 per cent.

E Sigma notation (answers p. 152)

If you invest a sum of £1000 per year into a savings account which
pays 8 per cent interest, then S_k, the sum of money in the account after
k years, and S_{k+1} are related by

$$S_{k+1} = S_k \times 1.08 + 1000$$

This *inductive* definition is useful for programming a spreadsheet, but
is less useful for generating a formula for total savings.

You can think of the savings over the ten-year period as being a set of
ten investments – the first gaining interest for the full ten years, the
second gaining interest for nine years, and so on.

1D

(a) How much is the first investment of £1000 worth after ten
     years?

(b) How much is the second investment of £1000 worth at the end
     of the ten year period?

(c) Explain why the total investment is worth

$$£1000(1.08 + 1.08^2 + 1.08^3 + \ldots + 1.08^{10})$$

after ten years.

Expressions such as $£1000(1.08 + 1.08^2 + 1.08^3 + \ldots + 1.08^{10})$ are cumbersome to handle. However, since each term is of the same form, you can write it more easily using a shorthand notation, known as **sigma notation**. Sigma, written Σ, is a Greek letter, which to mathematicians means 'the sum of'. Using this notation you can write the above series as

$$S = \sum_{i=1}^{10} 1000(1.08^i)$$

Sometimes this is written simply as $\sum_{1}^{10} 1000(1.08^i)$, where it is clear that the summation is taken over the range of values of i.

Stated fully, this reads:

> S is the sum of the series obtained by successively substituting the values of $i = 1$ to $i = 10$ in the general term $1000(1.08^i)$.

Note that the 1000, which multiplies each term, may be taken outside the summation as a common factor, like this:

$$1000 \sum_{i=1}^{10} 1.08^i$$

Example 4

Express the series $3 + 5 + 7 + 9 + \ldots + 99$ using Σ notation.

Solution

The general term of the series is $2i + 3$.

The first term, 3, corresponds to $i = 0$ and the last, 99, corresponds to $i = 48$.

Thus the series is $\displaystyle\sum_{i=0}^{48} (2i + 3)$. It could also be written as $\displaystyle\sum_{i=1}^{49} (2i + 1)$.

Example 5

Sum these arithmetic series.

(a) $\displaystyle\sum_{i=1}^{20} (3i + 4)$ (b) $\displaystyle\sum_{i=1}^{n} (3i + 4)$

Solution

(a) $\displaystyle\sum_{1}^{20} (3i + 4) = 7 + 10 + 13 + \ldots + 64$ (20 terms)

$$= \tfrac{20}{2} (7 + 64)$$

$$= 710$$

(b) $\displaystyle\sum_{1}^{n}(3i+4) = 7 + 10 + \ldots + (3n+4)$ (n terms)

$$= \frac{n}{2}\{7 + (3n+4)\}$$
$$= \frac{n}{2}(3n+11)$$

Exercise E (answers p. 152)

1 Write out the terms of the following series.

(a) $\displaystyle\sum_{i=1}^{5}\frac{1}{i}$ (b) $\displaystyle\sum_{i=3}^{7}i^2$ (c) $\displaystyle\sum_{i=1}^{5}\frac{1}{i(i+1)}$

(d) $\displaystyle\sum_{i=4}^{8}(-1)^i(2i+3)$ (e) $\displaystyle\sum_{i=0}^{5}(i+1)^3$ (f) $\displaystyle\sum_{i=1}^{6}i^3$

2 Rewrite each of these using Σ notation.

(a) $\sqrt{1} + \sqrt{2} + \sqrt{3} + \ldots + \sqrt{50}$

(b) $2^2 + 4^2 + 6^2 + \ldots + 100^2$

(c) $\frac{1}{3} + \frac{1}{5} + \frac{1}{7} + \ldots + \frac{1}{99}$

(d) $1^3 - 2^3 + 3^3 - 4^3 + \ldots + 19^3$

(e) $\frac{1}{2} + \frac{2}{3} + \frac{3}{4} + \frac{4}{5} + \ldots + \frac{99}{100}$

3 Calculate the sum of the following arithmetic series.

(a) $\displaystyle\sum_{i=1}^{20}(2i-1)$ (b) $\displaystyle\sum_{i=5}^{24}(45-2i)$

4 Use sigma notation to express the following.

(a) $20 + 25 + 30 + 35 + \ldots$ (25 terms)

(b) $10\,000 + 1000 + 100 + 10 + \ldots$ (10 terms)

(c) $1 + 1.1 + 1.21 + 1.331 + \ldots$ (15 terms)

(d) $\dfrac{1}{1+2} + \dfrac{1}{2+3} + \dfrac{1}{3+4} + \dfrac{1}{4+5} + \ldots$ (8 terms)

(e) $3 + 2 \times 3^2 + 3 \times 3^3 + 4 \times 3^4 + \ldots$ (20 terms)

5 Write out the following series in full.

(a) $\displaystyle\sum_{1}^{6}i^2(i+1)$ (b) $\displaystyle\sum_{0}^{4}(-1)^i(i+1)$ (c) $\displaystyle\sum_{0}^{5}x^i$

(d) $\displaystyle\sum_{0}^{4}\frac{i}{i+1}$ (e) $\displaystyle\sum_{1}^{6}f(x_i)$

F Geometric series (answers p. 152)

The series on page 36 which represented total savings in the account,

$$£1000(1.08 + 1.08^2 + 1.08^3 + \ldots + 1.08^{10})$$

is an example of a **geometric progression** (**G.P.**), in which each term increases by a constant multiple or **common ratio**, which in this case is 1.08.

You can sum a geometric series but this is not as straightforward as summing an arithmetic series. To simplify matters ignore the 1000 and consider the sum of the series

$$S = 1.08 + 1.08^2 + 1.08^3 + \ldots + 1.08^{10} \tag{1}$$

The trick is to multiply both sides of this statement by the common ratio 1.08,

$$1.08S = 1.08^2 + 1.08^3 + 1.08^4 + \ldots + 1.08^{11} \tag{2}$$

and then subtract the original series S.

$$1.08S = \qquad 1.08^2 + 1.08^3 + \ldots + 1.08^{10} + 1.08^{11}$$
$$S = \quad 1.08 + 1.08^2 + 1.08^3 + \ldots + 1.08^{10}$$

$$(2) - (1)\ 0.08S = -1.08 \qquad\qquad\qquad\qquad\qquad + 1.08^{11}$$

(All of the middle terms cancel out.)

$$\Rightarrow \qquad S = \frac{1.08^{11} - 1.08}{0.08}$$

This method may be generalised for the general geometric series with first term a and common ratio r.

$$S = a + ar + ar^2 + ar^3 + \ldots + ar^{n-1} \qquad \left(\text{or } S = \sum_{i=1}^{n} ar^{i-1} \right)$$

Multiplying by the common ratio r,

$$rS = ar + ar^2 + ar^3 + \ldots + ar^n \qquad \left(\text{or } rS = r\sum_{i=1}^{n} ar^{i-1} = \sum_{i=1}^{n} ar^{i} \right)$$

Subtracting the original series gives

$$rS - S = ar^n - a \qquad \text{(All of the middle terms cancel out.)}$$
$$S(r - 1) = a(r^n - 1)$$
$$\Rightarrow \qquad S = \frac{a(r^n - 1)}{r - 1}$$

In general, for a G.P. with first term a and common ratio r

$$a + ar + ar^2 + \ldots + ar^{n-1}$$

$$\sum_{i=1}^{n} ar^{i-1} = a\left(\frac{r^n - 1}{r - 1} \right)$$

Example 6

Find the sum of these series.

(a) $3 + 6 + 12 + \ldots + 3072$ (b) $\displaystyle\sum_{i=2}^{10} (\tfrac{1}{3})^i$

Solution

(a) The terms are $3, 3 \times 2, 3 \times 2^2, \ldots, 3 \times 2^{10}$.

The series is therefore a G.P. with the first term 3, common ratio 2 and 11 terms. Its sum is

$$3 \times \frac{2^{11} - 1}{2 - 1} = 6141$$

(b) The series is a G.P. with first term $\tfrac{1}{9}$, common ratio $\tfrac{1}{3}$ and 9 terms. Its sum is therefore

$$\frac{1}{9} \times \frac{(\tfrac{1}{3})^9 - 1}{(\tfrac{1}{3}) - 1} \approx 0.1667$$

Exercise F (answers p. 152)

1 Calculate the sum of the series to the number of terms stated.

(a) $2 + 6 + 18 + 54 + \ldots$ (8 terms)

(b) $2 + 10 + 50 + 250 + \ldots$ (12 terms)

(c) $1 + 3 + 9 + 27 + \ldots$ (20 terms)

(d) $8 + 4 + 2 + 1 + \tfrac{1}{2} + \ldots$ (10 terms)

(e) $8 - 4 + 2 - 1 + \tfrac{1}{2} - \ldots$ (10 terms)

2 Calculate the sum of each series.

(a) $\displaystyle\sum_{i=1}^{5} 3^{i-1}$ (b) $\displaystyle\sum_{i=1}^{10} 8^{i-1}$ (c) $\displaystyle\sum_{i=1}^{7} 2^i$

(d) $\displaystyle\sum_{i=3}^{8} (\tfrac{1}{2})^i$ (e) $\displaystyle\sum_{i=1}^{20} (-\tfrac{3}{4})^{i-1}$

3 Legend tells that the Shah of Persia offered a reward to the citizen who introduced him to chess. The citizen asked merely for a number of grains of rice according to the rule:

1 grain for the first square on the chessboard,
2 grains for the second square,
4 grains for the third square,
8 grains for the fourth square, and so on.

(a) How many grains of rice did he request?

(b) If a grain of rice weighs 0.02 g, what weight of rice did he request?

4 The sum of £200 is invested at the beginning of the year at 5 per cent interest per annum. What is the total sum of money in the account at the end of 50 years?

5 Using a typical figure for a school leaver's salary and assuming that it will increase by 5 per cent annually, estimate a person's total earnings during their working life.

6 The sum of £1000 is invested at the beginning of each year at 7.5 per cent interest per annum.

(a) What is the total sum of money at the end of n years?

(b) How long will it take for the total sum of money to be twice the total amount invested?

G Sum to infinity (answers p. 153)

So far, when you have summed series you have taken a finite number of terms. In Section A you noticed that sequences show certain patterns of behaviour (for example convergence and divergence) as you take more and more terms. What happens to the sum as you take more and more terms in a series?

For a series with an infinite number of terms, the sum to infinity is the limit of the sum to n terms as n tends to infinity ($n \rightarrow \infty$) .

For example, the series $1 + \frac{1}{2} + \frac{1}{4} + \frac{1}{8} + \ldots + \left(\frac{1}{2}\right)^{n-1}$ has sum

$$\frac{\left(\frac{1}{2}\right)^n - 1}{\frac{1}{2} - 1} = 2\left(1 - \left(\frac{1}{2}\right)^n\right)$$

As $n \rightarrow \infty$, $\left(\frac{1}{2}\right)^n \rightarrow 0$ and the sum of the series tends to 2.

On page 39 you found that, for a geometric series,

$$\sum_{i=1}^{n} ar^{i-1} = a\left(\frac{r^n - 1}{r - 1}\right)$$

For what values of r will the series have a 'sum to infinity'?

Clearly, if $|r| < 1$, then $r^n \rightarrow 0$, as $n \rightarrow \infty$ and so there is a 'sum to infinity'.

(Recall that $|r| < 1$ means $-1 < r < 1$.)

The sum $\sum_{i=1}^{n} ar^{i-1} = a\left(\frac{r^n - 1}{r - 1}\right)$ can be multiplied by $\frac{(-1)}{(-1)}$ to

give $a\left(\frac{1 - r^n}{1 - r}\right)$.

This can be useful in examples where $|r| < 1$. As $n \rightarrow \infty$, $r^n \rightarrow 0$ if $|r| < 1$ and so there is a 'sum to infinity' of $a\left(\frac{1}{1 - r}\right) = \frac{a}{1 - r}$.

If $|r| \geqslant 1$ then the series will not converge.

An infinite G.P. can be summed provided the common ratio r satisfies $|r| < 1$

$$a + ar + ar^2 + \ldots = \frac{a}{1-r}, \text{ for } |r| < 1$$

Example 7

Find the sum of the infinite series $1 + \frac{2}{3} + \frac{4}{9} + \frac{8}{27} + \ldots$

Solution

First term $a = 1$, common ratio $r = \frac{2}{3}$

$\Rightarrow$ Sum to infinity $S_\infty = \dfrac{1}{1 - \frac{2}{3}} = 3$

Exercise G (answers p. 153)

1 Where possible, calculate the sum of these infinite series.

   (a) $\frac{9}{10} + \frac{9}{100} + \frac{9}{1000} + \ldots$ (b) $4 - 3 + \frac{9}{4} - \frac{27}{16} + \ldots$

   (c) $1 - 2 + 4 - 8 + \ldots$ (d) $5 + \frac{5}{2} + \frac{5}{4} + \frac{5}{8} + \ldots$

2 Calculate the sum of each of these infinite series.

   (a) $\displaystyle\sum_{i=1}^{\infty} \frac{1}{3^{i-1}}$ (b) $\displaystyle\sum_{i=1}^{\infty} (0.25)^{i-1}$ (c) $\displaystyle\sum_{i=1}^{\infty} 2^{-i}$

3 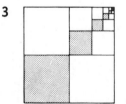 The diagram illustrates the infinite G.P.
   $\frac{1}{4} + \frac{1}{16} + \frac{1}{64} + \frac{1}{256} + \ldots$

   (a) Find the sum of the G.P.

   (b) How could you see this result directly from the diagram?

4 Von Koch's 'snowflake' curve is shown below in its various stages of development. F_0 is an equilateral triangle; F_1 is derived from F_0 by trisecting each side and replacing the centre third of each side of the triangle by two sides of an equilateral triangle; F_2 is obtained in the same way from F_1 and so on.

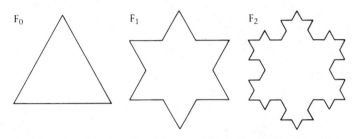

If each side of F_0 is of length 1 and P_n is the perimeter of the nth snowflake curve, write these down.

(a) P_0 (b) P_1 (c) P_2 (d) P_n

What happens to the perimeter of the curve as $n \rightarrow \infty$?

5 How many terms of the series

$$2 + \tfrac{4}{5} + \tfrac{8}{25} + \tfrac{6}{125} + \dots$$

must be taken before its sum to n terms differs from its sum to infinity by less than 0.01?

H Manipulating series using sigma notation (answers p. 153)

When manipulating series, sigma notation can be very powerful. To exploit it to the full you need to become confident in its use.

1 Consider the series $u_1 + u_2 + u_3 + \dots + u_n$.

(a) Write down an expression for the sum of the series in sigma notation.

(b) Write down a simple series and investigate the effect on the sum of the series when each term of the series is multiplied by the same constant.

(c) Show that $\displaystyle\sum_{i=1}^{n} au_i = a\left(\sum_{i=1}^{n} u_i\right)$ for any constant a.

2E (a) Investigate how the sum of a series changes when you add a constant to each term of the series.

(b) Show that $\displaystyle\sum_{i=1}^{n} (u_i + b) = \left(\sum_{i=1}^{n} u_i\right) + nb$

(c) Show that $\displaystyle\sum_{i=1}^{n} (au_i + b) = a\left(\sum_{i=1}^{n} u_i\right) + nb$

For any constants a and b,

$$\sum_{i=1}^{n}(au_i + b) = a\left(\sum_{i=1}^{n} u_i\right) + nb$$

Example 8

Evaluate $\displaystyle\sum_{i=1}^{n}(4i + 2)$.

Solution

$$\sum_{i=1}^{n}(4i + 2) = 4\left(\sum_{i=1}^{n} i\right) + 2n$$

$$\sum_{i=1}^{n} i = \frac{n(n+1)}{2} \text{ using the formula for the sum of an arithmetic series}$$

So $\displaystyle\sum_{i=1}^{n}(4i + 2) = \frac{4n(n+1)}{2} + 2n = 2n^2 + 4n$

3E Find these. (a) $\displaystyle\sum_{i=1}^{n}(2i - 3)$ (b) $\displaystyle\sum_{i=1}^{n}(5i + 1)$

4E Generalise the result of question 2E by showing that

$$\sum_{i=1}^{n}(u_i + v_i) = \left(\sum_{i=1}^{n} u_i\right) + \left(\sum_{i=1}^{n} v_i\right)$$

5E (a) Write down the result of subtracting $1^3 + 2^3 + \dots + n^3$ from $2^3 + 3^3 + \dots + (n+1)^3$.

(b) Hence show that

$$\sum_{i=1}^{n}(i+1)^3 - \sum_{i=1}^{n} i^3 = (n+1)^3 - 1$$

(c) Simplify $(i+1)^3 - i^3$ and show that

$$\sum_{i=1}^{n}(i+1)^3 - \sum_{i=1}^{n} i^3 = 3\sum_{i=1}^{n} i^2 + 3\sum_{i=1}^{n} i + n$$

(d) Hence obtain the formula

$$\sum_{i=1}^{n} i^2 = \frac{n}{6}(n+1)(2n+1)$$

6E Use the result you have obtained in question 5E to find the sum of the first 99 squares.

7E Use the method of question 4E and the result from question 5E to find these.

(a) $\displaystyle\sum_{i=1}^{n} (2i^2 - 6i + 4)$ (b) $1^2 + 3^2 + 5^2 + 7^2 + \ldots + (2n-1)^2$

You should now be familiar with the following results.

$$1 + 2 + 3 + \ldots + n = \sum_{i=1}^{n} i = \frac{n}{2}(n+1)$$

$$1^2 + 2^2 + 3^2 + \ldots + n^2 = \sum_{i=1}^{n} i^2 = \frac{n}{6}(n+1)(2n+1)$$

$$\sum_{i=1}^{n} (au_i + bv_i) = a\sum_{i=1}^{n} u_i + b\sum_{i=1}^{n} v_i$$

After working through this chapter you should

1   know how to recognise, define and describe sequences

2   be able to use $\sum$ notation as a shorthand

3   be able to recognise convergence to a limiting value

4   be able to use the results

   (i)   arithmetic progression:

         sum = number of terms × average of first and last terms,

         $$S_n = n\left(\frac{a+l}{2}\right)$$

         $$S_n = \frac{n}{2}[2a + (n-1)d]$$

   (ii) geometric progression:

         $$\sum_{i=1}^{n} ar^{i-1} = a\left(\frac{1-r^n}{1-r}\right) \qquad \text{or} \qquad a\left(\frac{r^n-1}{r-1}\right)$$

         $$\sum_{i=1}^{\infty} ar^{i-1} = \frac{a}{1-r}, \qquad \text{for } |r| < 1$$

3 Algebra of functions

A Composition of functions (answers p. 154)

Temperatures are often measured in degrees Celsius or degrees Fahrenheit. On the Fahrenheit scale, water freezes at 32 °F and boils at 212 °F. The Celsius scale is such that water freezes at 0 °C and boils at 100 °C.

The function f, given by

$$f(t) = \tfrac{5}{9}(t - 32)$$

converts a temperature of t degrees Fahrenheit to Celsius.

Temperature is a measure of the vibration of molecules and at −273 °C molecules are no longer vibrating, so −273 °C is the lowest temperature that can be obtained. This temperature is called 0 on the Kelvin scale, or 0 K.

In order to convert from Celsius to Kelvin the function g is used.

$$g(t) = t + 273$$

Conversion from a temperature measured on the Fahrenheit scale to one on the Kelvin scale can be achieved by conversion to the Celsius scale first – using f(t) – then to the Kelvin scale – using g(t). It would be helpful to have a function which does this conversion directly.

The rule for converting from °F directly into K can be illustrated by using an arrow graph or a flow diagram.

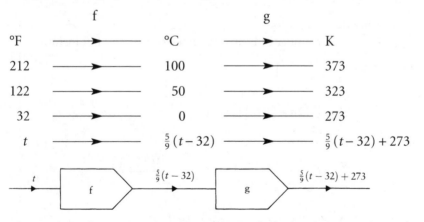

The resulting function is the **composition** of the two functions f and g.

Note that, since f(122) = 50, you can write g(50) as g(f(122)) or, with fewer brackets, as gf(122). So, contrary to what might be expected, the notation for f followed by g is gf.

For fg(x), x is first put through the function g, and the output from g is fed through f.

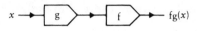

Example 1

If f and g are the functions given by $f(x) = x^2$ and $g(x) = 2x + 3$, then find the functions fg, gf and gg.

Solution

$fg(x) = f(g(x)) = f(2x + 3) = (2x + 3)^2$

$gf(x) = g(f(x)) = g(x^2) = 2x^2 + 3$

$gg(x) = g(g(x)) = g(2x + 3) = 2(2x + 3) + 3$
$$= 4x + 9$$

Further practice on composition of functions is provided in the support material S3.1 (p. 72).

Exercise A (answers p. 154)

1 For each of the functions f and g defined below, evaluate   (i) fg(x),   (ii) gf(x).

(a) $f(x) = 2x + 3$, $g(x) = x^3$

(b) $f(x) = 2x + 1$, $g(x) = \dfrac{1}{x}$

(c) $f(x) = 3x + 2$, $g(x) = 5 - x$

(d) $f(x) = 1 - x^2$, $g(x) = 1 - 2x$

2 On a gas bill, the cost in £ of t therms of gas used by a consumer is given by the function c where

$$c(t) = 9 + 0.4t$$

A gas meter indicates the amount of gas in cubic feet used by a consumer. The number of therms of heat from x cubic feet of gas is given by the function h where

$$h(x) = 1.034x$$

(a) Find the function ch .

(b) What does ch(x) represent?

3 Each of the following is of the form fg(x). Identify possible f(x) and g(x).

(a) $\dfrac{1}{x + 2}$ (b) $\dfrac{1}{x} + 2$ (c) $\dfrac{1}{2x + 3}$ (d) $2\sqrt{x} - 1$

(e) $\dfrac{1}{x^2} + 3$ (f) $(2x + 1)^4$ (g) $x^8 - 4x^4 - 3$

4　ff(x) means the function f applied to x and then applied again to the result.

If each of the expressions below is f(x), write down an expression for ff(x) in each case.

(a) $x+2$　　(b) x^2　　(c) $2x-3$　　(d) x　　(e) $\sin x$　　(f) $\dfrac{1}{x}$

5　If $f(x) = x - 3$ and $g(x) = x^2$, it is possible to combine these functions in many ways.

(a) Explain why $(x-3)^2 - 3 = fgf(x)$.

(b) Express each of the following as combinations of f and g.

　　(i) $x^2 - 3$　　(ii) $(x^2 - 3)^2$　　(iii) $x - 6$
　　(iv) $x^8 - 3$　　(v) $(x-3)^4 - 6$

6　Using $s(x) = \sin x$ and $q(x) = x^2$, distinguish clearly between these.

(a) $\sin^2 x$, i.e. $(\sin x)^2$　　(b) $\sin x^2$, i.e. $\sin(x^2)$

(c) $\sin \sin x$, i.e. $\sin(\sin x)$

7　In each case, find fg(x) and gf(x), and then determine the set of values for which $fg(x) = gf(x)$.

(a) $f(x) = x^2$, $g(x) = x + 3$　　　　　(b) $f(x) = x - 5$, $g(x) = x + 2$

(c) $f(x) = 2x - 1$, $g(x) = 3x + 1$　　　(d) $f(x) = \dfrac{1}{x}$, $g(x) = x^3$

(e) $f(x) = 2x + 1$, $g(x) = \frac{1}{2}(x + 1)$　　(f) $f(x) = \sqrt{x}$, $g(x) = x - 1$

8　Four functions, e, f, g and h, are defined by

$$e(x) = x \qquad f(x) = -x \qquad g(x) = \frac{1}{x} \qquad h(x) = -\frac{1}{x}$$

Then $fg(x) = f\left(\dfrac{1}{x}\right) = -\dfrac{1}{x} \Longrightarrow fg = h$

Complete the following table, where each entry is one of e, f, g or h.

Function applied first

		e	f	g	h
Function	e	e	f		
applied second	f	f	e		
	g				
	h				

The function to be entered here is fg, i.e. h.

B Range, domain and inverse functions (answers p. 155)

You have seen that the function $f(t) = \frac{5}{9}(t - 32)$ converts °F to °C.

The lowest attainable temperature is −273 °C and this places a corresponding restriction on temperatures in °F.

> The set of values for which a function is defined is called the **domain** and the set of values which the function can take is called the **range**.

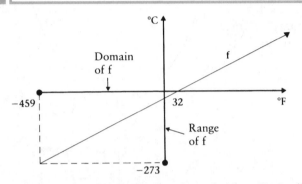

In a Cartesian graph of a function, the **domain** is all or part of the *x*-axis and the **range** is all or part of the *y*-axis.

For example, the function $f(x) = x^2 - 2x$ has domain all real numbers but the range consists only of the real numbers greater than or equal to −1, that is $\{y \in \mathbb{R} : y \geqslant -1\}$.

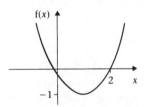

The function $f(x) = \sqrt{x - 4}$ has domain $\{x \in \mathbb{R} : x \geqslant 4\}$ and range $\{y \in \mathbb{R} : y \geqslant 0\}$.

When only the formula for a function is given, it is usual to take as the domain *all* the numbers for which the formula can be worked out; for example, given the function g such that

$$g(x) = \frac{1}{x - 1}$$

you would assume that the domain is all numbers except 1. The range is then all numbers except 0, as can be seen from the graph.

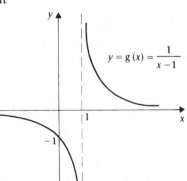

1D

Give the natural domain and find the corresponding range for the function h such that

$$h(x) = \frac{1}{x^2}$$

Sketch the graph of $y = x^2$ and deduce the sketch for $y = \frac{1}{x^2}$.

Two or more values in the domain of a function can correspond to the same value in the range. Such a function is said to be **many-to-one**. For example, the function $y = x^2$ is many-to-one.

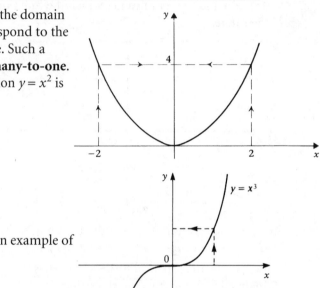

The function $y = x^3$ is an example of a **one-to-one** function.

However, it is a requirement that a value in a function's domain *must correspond to only one value in the range*. Functions, therefore, cannot be one-to-many (although they can be many-to-one). So, for example, $x = y^2$ does not define y as a function of x because, if $x = 9$, $y = \pm 3$ (i.e. there are *two* values in the range).

Inverse functions

To return to the example of temperature, the **inverse** function reverses what was done by f, in other words it converts °C to °F. In building up the function f, two functions were used.

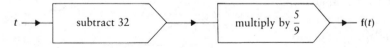

So $f(t) = \frac{5}{9}(t - 32)$

To find the inverse function you need to 'undo' this.

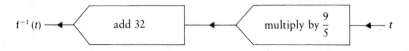

The inverse of f is denoted by f^{-1}. The flow diagram above shows that

$$f^{-1}(t) = \tfrac{9}{5}t + 32$$

As a quick check, note that

$$f(212) = 100 \qquad \text{and} \qquad f^{-1}(100) = 212$$

If $f(x) = x^2$ then both $f(3)$ and $f(-3)$ give $f(x) = 9$ and consequently $f^{-1}(9)$ is ambiguous, since it could mean either -3 or $+3$. A function must be unambiguous: a single input must give rise to a *unique* output.

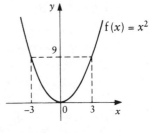

Thus in this case f does not have an inverse function if its domain is unrestricted. The inverse function, $f^{-1}(x)$, does exist if the domain is restricted to non-negative numbers, that is if $f(x) = x^2\{x \geqslant 0\}$, then $f^{-1}(x) = \sqrt{x}$.

In general, a function must be one-to-one in order to have an inverse.

2D | Define a domain for these functions to ensure that they are one-to-one.

(a) $f(x) = x^4 - 3$ (b) $g(x) = \cos x°$ (c) $h(x) = \sin x°$

The square root is a one-to-many mapping from x to $+\sqrt{x}$ or $-\sqrt{x}$.

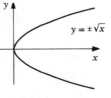

In order to avoid ambiguity, mathematicians take $\sqrt{x}$ to mean the *positive* square root of x, and $\sqrt[4]{x}, \sqrt[6]{x}, \sqrt[8]{x}, ...$, to mean the positive fourth, sixth, eighth, ... roots of x.

The same problem does not arise with $\sqrt[3]{x}$ because $x \rightarrow x^3$ is a one-to-one function.

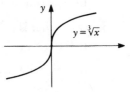

Example 2

Find the inverse of $f(x) = \dfrac{1}{1-x}$ $\{x \neq 1\}$.

Solution

Flow chart for f

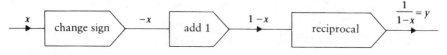

Its reverse for f^{-1}

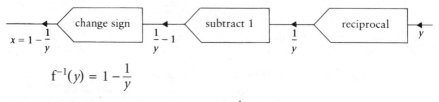

$$f^{-1}(y) = 1 - \frac{1}{y}$$

As a quick check, note that $f(3) = -0.5$, $f^{-1}(-0.5) = 3$.

The letter y can be changed for any other and it is usual to write

$$f^{-1}(x) = 1 - \frac{1}{x}.$$

If a function f is to have an inverse function, the situation must be as follows.

Since f is a function, any vertical line cuts the graph once only.

f^{-1} is a function: any horizontal line from a value in the range of f cuts the graph once only.

The following examples investigate the relationship between the graph of a function f, and the graph of its inverse function f^{-1}.

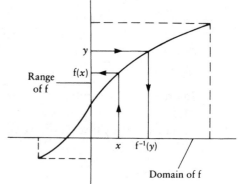

3 (a) What is $f^{-1}(f(x))$?

    (b) Explain why the domain of f is the range of f^{-1}.

    (c) Sketch the graph of a function with no inverse function.

    (d) If both f and f^{-1} are functions, explain why f must be a one-to-one function.

4 For each function given below, choose a suitable domain so that the function has an inverse function and plot on the same axes the graphs of the function, its inverse and $y = x$. (The axes should have the same scales so that $y = x$ is at 45° to both axes.) Define the inverse function in each case.

    (a) $f(x) = 3x + 5$ (b) $g(x) = x^2 - 7$

    (c) $h(x) = (x - 7)^2$ (d) $r(x) = \sqrt{x} + 6$

5 What simple transformation will map the graph of $y = f(x)$ onto the graph of $y = f^{-1}(x)$?

6 The graph of each of these is reflected in the line $y = x$. Find the equation of the image.

(a) $f(x) = (x + 5)^2 - 3$ (b) $f(x) = 3(2x - 1)$

7 (a) Investigate the sequences

(i) $x_{n+1} = \dfrac{1}{x_n}$ (ii) $x_{n+1} = -x_n$

for various values of x_1 in each case.

(b) What is the inverse of these?

(i) $f(x) = \dfrac{1}{x}$, the reciprocal function

(ii) $f(x) = -x$, the 'change sign' or 'multiply by -1' function

Why do you think these functions are called **self-inverse**? sketch the graphs of the two functions and explain how they are related to what you observed in question 5.

8 Find the inverse of each of the functions f defined as follows.

(a) $f(x) = \dfrac{1}{2x + 1}$ $\{x \neq -\frac{1}{2}\}$ (b) $f(x) = 12 - x$ (or $-x + 12$)$\{x \in \mathbb{R}\}$

(c) $f(x) = \dfrac{1}{x} - 1$ $\{x \neq 0\}$ (d) $f(x) = \dfrac{8}{(x + 1)^2}$ $\{x > -1\}$

(e) $f(x) = \sqrt{1 - x^2}$ $\{0 \leqslant x \leqslant 1\}$ (f) $f(x) = 4 - (x - 2)^2$ $\{x \geqslant 2\}$

Which of these functions are self-inverse?

> The graphs of a function and its inverse have reflection symmetry in the line $y = x$.

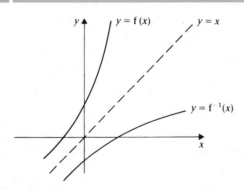

> A function f has an inverse function only if f is one-to-one.

Example 3

If $f(x) = (x-3)^2 + 4$ $\{x \geqslant 3\}$, find $f^{-1}(x)$. Sketch the graphs of $f(x)$ and $f^{-1}(x)$.

Solution

To find the inverse function, represent f by a flow chart showing the simpler functions which compose it.

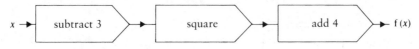

Then reverse the flow chart.

$$f^{-1}(x) = \sqrt{x-4} + 3 \quad \{x \geqslant 4\}$$

Note that x is usually chosen to represent the input variable for the inverse function as well as the original function.

The graphs of the function and the inverse function are sketched below.

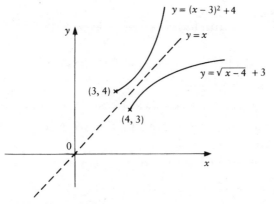

Rearranging formulas

The process of finding an inverse function is identical to that of rearranging a formula. In the temperature example,

$$f(t) = \tfrac{5}{9}(t-32)$$

converts °F to °C, which could be written as

$$C = \tfrac{5}{9}(F - 32)$$

$$f^{-1}(t) = \tfrac{9}{5}t + 32$$

converts °C to °F, which could be written as

$$F = \tfrac{9}{5}C + 32$$

The formula for C in terms of F has been rearranged to give F in terms of C. The process can be seen as applying the same function to both sides of the formula and is often set out in this way.

$$C = \tfrac{5}{9}(F - 32)$$
$$\tfrac{9}{5}C = F - 32 \qquad \text{(multipling both sides by } \tfrac{9}{5})$$
$$\tfrac{9}{5}C + 32 = F \qquad \text{(adding 32 to both sides)}$$

This approach may be used for finding inverse functions and is equivalent to the flow diagram as shown below:

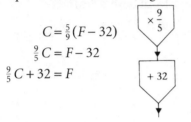

$$C = \tfrac{5}{9}(F - 32)$$
$$\tfrac{9}{5}C = F - 32$$
$$\tfrac{9}{5}C + 32 = F$$

Example 4

Make x the subject of the formula $y = (3x + 1)^2$.

Solution

$$y = (3x + 1)^2$$
$$\pm\sqrt{y} = 3x + 1 \qquad \text{(taking the square root of each side)}$$
$$\pm\sqrt{y} - 1 = 3x \qquad \text{(subtracting 1 from both sides)}$$
$$\frac{\pm\sqrt{y} - 1}{3} = x \qquad \text{(dividing both sides by 3)}$$

The '$\pm$' is appropriate here as we are not defining functions, simply changing the subject of the formula.

There is more practice on rearranging formulas in the support material S3.2 (p. 73).

A particular difficulty arises with the flow chart method when the letter that is to be the subject of the formula appears more than once. A different approach is then required, as illustrated by the next example.

Example 5

Find the inverse of the function

$$f(x) = \frac{x + 1}{x + 2} \quad \{x \ne -2\}$$

Solution

Let $y = f(x)$, then rearrange to find x in terms of y.

$$y = \frac{x+1}{x+2}$$

$y(x+2) = x+1$ (multiplying both sides by $x+2$)

$yx + 2y = x+1$ (multiplying out the brackets)

$yx - x = 1 - 2y$ (collecting x terms together by subtracting $2y$ and then subtracting x from both sides)

$x(y-1) = 1 - 2y$ (factorising the left-hand side)

$$x = \frac{1-2y}{y-1}$$ (dividing both sides by $y-1$)

Thus the inverse of the function which maps x to $\dfrac{x+1}{x+2}$ is

$$f^{-1}(y) = \frac{1-2y}{y-1}$$

x is conventionally chosen as the input variable and so it is usual to write

$$f^{-1}(x) = \frac{1-2x}{x-1} \qquad \{x \in \mathbb{R}, x \neq 1\}$$

When rearranging formulas there may not be a single input variable. The following illustration shows how to work with these cases.

Example 6

Make a the subject of the formula $s = ut + \frac{1}{2}at^2$.

Solution

$s - ut = \frac{1}{2}at^2$ (subtracting ut from both sides)

$2s - 2ut = at^2$ (multiplying both sides by 2)

$\dfrac{2s}{t^2} - \dfrac{2u}{t} = a$ (dividing both sides by t^2)

So $a = \dfrac{2s}{t^2} - \dfrac{2u}{t}$

Exercise B (answers p. 156)

1   Make x the subject of the following formulas.

   (a) $y = \dfrac{5x - 3}{2}$ (b) $y = \dfrac{3}{4}(x - 5)$

   (c) $y = (x - 5)^2 + 4$ (d) $y = \dfrac{1}{x - 3}$

2   Taking the formulas in question 1 as of the form $y = f(x)$, write down
   in each case the formula for $f^{-1}(x)$, stating also the greatest possible
   domain and range of f for which f^{-1} can be defined.

3   A chemical company researching crop yields tries out a new pesticide.
   The results indicate that, per hectare, for a kg of pesticide the extra
   yield y kg of a crop is given by

   $$y = \frac{900a}{2 + a}$$

   (a) What is the formula which gives the amount, a kg, of pesticide
       needed to return an extra yield of y kg?

   (b) Explain why the values of y will lie between 0 and 900.

4   Make x the subject of these formulas.

   (a) $y = \dfrac{x - 1}{x + 1}$ (b) $y = \dfrac{2 - x}{x + 3}$

5   The graph of

   $$y = \frac{x}{2x + 1}$$

   is reflected in the line $y = x$. Find the equation of the image and use a
   graph plotter to check your answer.

   (Hint: how are the graphs of $y = f(x)$ and $y = f^{-1}(x)$ related?)

6   If $f(x) = \dfrac{1 + x^2}{1 - x^2}$ $\{x < -1\}$, find, $f^{-1}(x)$.

7   Make the variable shown in brackets the subject of the formula.

   (a) $P = aW + b$ (W) (b) $C = 2\pi r$ (r) (c) $s = \dfrac{n}{2}(a + l)$ (l)

   (d) $s = \dfrac{a}{1 - r}$ (r) (e) $\dfrac{1}{R} = \dfrac{1}{x} + \dfrac{1}{y}$ (x)

8 The driver of a car travelling at v m.p.h. sees an obstruction ahead of him and immediately applies the brakes. The distance, d feet, that the car travels from the time that the driver sees the obstruction until the car stops is given by

$$d = \frac{(v+10)^2}{20} - 5$$

(a) Find the stopping distance for a car travelling at these speeds.

    (i) 30 m.p.h.   (ii) 50 m.p.h.   (iii) 70 m.p.h.

(b) Rearrange the formula to find v in terms of d.

(c) The driver sees an obstruction 250 feet ahead of him. What is the greatest speed at which he can be driving if he is to pull up before he reaches the obstruction?

9 If a metal rod is heated, the length increases according to the equation

$$l = l_0(1 + \alpha t)$$

where l is the final length, l_0 is the initial length, t is the increase in temperature and α is the coefficient of expansion of the rod.

Find α if a steel rod of length 1 metre expands to a length of 1.004 m when heated through 230 °C.

10 Einstein's famous equation $E = mc^2$ gives the energy equivalent to a mass m, where c is the speed of light. Rearrange this equation to find c in terms of E and m.

11 If a body of mass m moving with velocity u is later observed to be moving with velocity v then the change in kinetic energy of the body is given by

$$E = \tfrac{1}{2}mv^2 - \tfrac{1}{2}mu^2$$

Rearrange this formula to give v in terms of E, m and u.

12 A pendulum consists of a light steel rod with a heavy metal disc attached to the end. The time, T, taken for the pendulum to swing through a complete cycle is given by

$$T = 2\pi \sqrt{\frac{l}{g}}$$

where l is the length of the pendulum and g is a constant.

Complete the following steps to find l in terms of T and g.

$$\_\,\_\,\_\,\_\,\_ = \sqrt{\frac{l}{g}}$$

$$\Rightarrow \_\,\_\,\_\,\_\,\_ = \frac{l}{g} \qquad \text{(squaring both sides)}$$

$$\Rightarrow \_\,\_\,\_\,\_\,\_ = l$$

For a grandfather clock, $T = 2$ and $g = 9.81$ in SI units. The equation then gives a value for l in metres. Find this value.

13 (a) Show that the surface area of a solid cylinder of radius r and height h is
$$S = 2\pi r(r + h)$$

(b) Rearrange the formula $S = 2\pi r(r + h)$ to give h in terms of S and r.

14 In rearranging formulas a student proceeds as follows. Simplify her working in order to arrive at more elegant solutions.

(a) The volume V of a cone of radius r and height h is
$$V = \tfrac{1}{3}\pi r^2 h \implies \frac{V}{\tfrac{1}{3}\pi} = r^2 h$$
$$\implies r = \sqrt{\frac{\left(\dfrac{V}{\tfrac{1}{3}\pi}\right)}{h}}$$

(b) The total interest £I on £P invested at r% for n years is given by
$$I = \frac{Prn}{100} \implies I \times 100 = Prn$$
$$\implies r = \frac{\left(\dfrac{I \times 100}{P}\right)}{n}$$

15 Locate and correct the errors in the following.

(a) The current I flowing in a circuit consisting of a resistance R and n batteries of voltage E each and internal resistance r each is given by
$$I = \frac{nE}{R + nr} \implies IR = \frac{nE}{nr} \implies R = \frac{E}{Ir}$$

(b) The kinetic energy E of a body of mass m moving with speed v is
$$E = \tfrac{1}{2}mv^2$$
$$\implies v = \frac{\sqrt{\tfrac{1}{2}m}}{E}$$

C Functions and transformations of graphs (answers p. 157)

You have seen that the graph of the inverse of a function is obtained by reflecting the graph of that function in the line $y = x$. You can now look at other transformations of graphs and find how the equations of the resulting graphs relate to those of the original graphs.

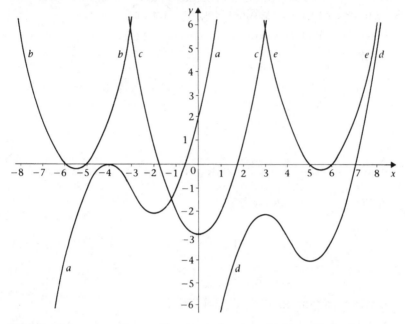

1 Which of these graphs can be mapped onto other graphs in the diagram?

2 What transformations would map these?
   (a) Graph b onto graph c
   (b) Graph a onto graph d
   (c) Graph b onto graph e

3 Is there more than one possible answer to any of parts (a) to (c) of question 2?

In Chapter 1 you saw that the image of the graph of $y = x^2$ under the translation $\begin{bmatrix} -3 \\ -4 \end{bmatrix}$ is the graph of $y = (x+3)^2 - 4$. Using function notation, you can say the image of $y = f(x)$ under a translation $\begin{bmatrix} -3 \\ -4 \end{bmatrix}$ is

$$y = f(x+3) - 4$$

In general:

> The image of $y = f(x)$ under a translation $\begin{bmatrix} -p \\ q \end{bmatrix}$ is $y = f(x + p) + q$.

4 The function f is defined by $f(w) = w^4$.

(a) Write down the expressions $f(x)$, $f(x) + 2$ and $f(x + 3)$, then plot the graphs of $y = f(x)$, $y = f(x) + 2$ and $y = f(x + 3)$ on the same screen of a graph plotter.

(b) What translation would transform the graph of $y = f(x)$ onto these graphs?

(i) $y = f(x) + 2$ (ii) $y = f(x + 3)$

5 The function g is defined by $g(u) = \dfrac{1}{u}$.

(a) Write down the expressions $g(x)$, $g(x + 4)$ and $g(x + 4) + 3$, then plot the graphs of $y = g(x)$, $y = g(x + 4)$ and $y = g(x + 4) + 3$ on the same screen of a graph plotter.

(b) What translation transforms the graph of $y = g(x)$ onto these graphs?

(i) $y = g(x + 4)$ (ii) $y = g(x + 4) + 3$

6

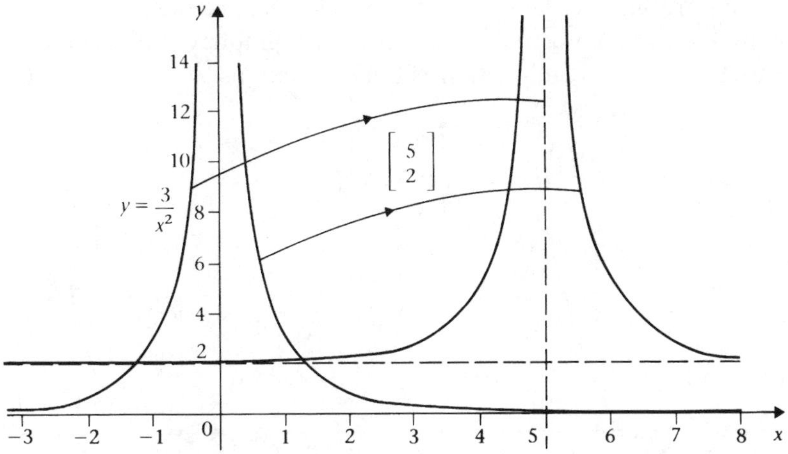

The graph of $y = \dfrac{3}{x^2}$ is translated through $\begin{bmatrix} 5 \\ 2 \end{bmatrix}$ as shown above. Suggest an equation for the new curve. Check your answer by plotting the graph of your equation.

7 By completing the square, rewrite $y = x^2 + 4x + 3$ in the form $y = (x + p)^2 + q$.

What translation will map the graph of $y = x^2$ onto the graph of $y = x^2 + 4x + 3$? Check your answer by plotting both graphs on the same screen.

Example 7

Find the image of the graph of $y = 5\sqrt{x}$ under a translation $\begin{bmatrix} 4 \\ 3 \end{bmatrix}$.

Solution

Taking

$$f(x) = 5\sqrt{x} \qquad \text{and} \qquad p = -4, q = 3$$

then

$$f(x + p) + q = f(x - 4) + 3 = 5\sqrt{x - 4} + 3$$

so the image of

$$y = 5\sqrt{x}$$

is

$$y = 5\sqrt{x - 4} + 3$$

Combining transformations of graphs

On p. 3 you saw how translations of graphs changed their equations. Here, we shall consider other transformations and combinations of transformations of graphs, together with their effect on the general equation $y = f(x)$.

Graphs b, c and e can be mapped onto each other by translations, reflections or rotations. Graphs a and d can be mapped onto each other by a reflection or a half-turn. Some of the graphs can be mapped onto each other by a combination of transformations.

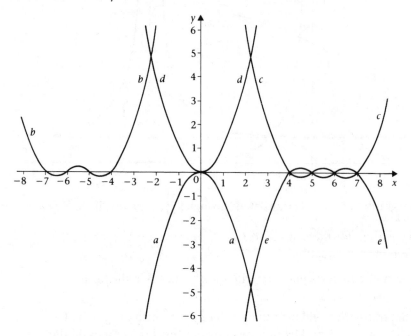

Graph b maps to c by a translation through $\begin{bmatrix} 11 \\ 0 \end{bmatrix}$ or a reflection in the y-axis.

Graph a maps to d by a reflection in the x-axis or a half-turn about the origin.

Graph c maps to e by a half-turn about the point $(5\frac{1}{2}, 0)$ or a reflection in the x-axis.

Graph b maps to e by a half-turn about the origin or reflections in the x-axis and in the y-axis.

These ideas are explored below.

8 (a) If $f(w) = w^2 - w$, write down expressions for $f(x)$, $f(-x)$ and $-f(x)$ and draw their graphs.

(b) (i) What transformation will map $y = f(x)$ onto $y = f(-x)$?

(ii) What transformation will map $y = f(x)$ onto $y = -f(x)$?

(c) For any function f, will the transformations found in (b) always be the same? Give reasons for your answer.

9 (a) $f(x) = x^4 - 2x^3$. The graph of $y = f(x)$ is reflected in the x-axis. Use the ideas of question 8 to find the equation of the new graph. Plot both graphs to check your answer.

(b) The original graph is now reflected in the y-axis. Write down the equation of the new graph. Plot the graph of your equation to check your answer.

10 (a) If $f(x) = 3x^2 - x^4$, write down $f(-x)$. Plot the graphs of $f(x)$ and $f(-x)$. Explain what occurs.

(b) If $f(x) = x^3 - 5x$, write down $f(-x)$ and $-f(x)$. Plot the graphs of $f(x)$, $f(-x)$ and $-f(x)$. Explain what occurs.

> If $f(-x) = f(x)$, then f is called an **even** function and its graph has line or reflection symmetry in the y-axis.
>
> If $f(-x) = -f(x)$, then f is called an **odd** function and its graph has rotational (half-turn) symmetry about the origin.

11 Classify the following functions f as odd, even or neither.

(a) $f(x) = \dfrac{3}{x^2}$ (b) $f(x) = 2x^5 - 3x^3$ (c) $f(x) = x^3 + 2$

12 Classify the following functions f as odd, even or neither.

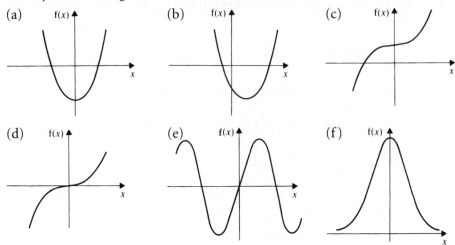

(a)

(b)

(c)

(d)

(e)

(f)

Example 8

Find the image of $y = \dfrac{x^3}{4}$ after a translation of $\begin{bmatrix} -2 \\ -7 \end{bmatrix}$ followed by a reflection in the x-axis.

Solution

Under a translation of $\begin{bmatrix} -2 \\ -7 \end{bmatrix}$, the image of $y = f(x)$ is $y = f(x + 2) - 7$. So the image of $y = \dfrac{x^3}{4}$ is

$$y = \dfrac{(x + 2)^3}{4} - 7$$

Under a reflection in the x-axis, the image of $y = f(x)$ is

$$y = -f(x)$$

So the image of $y = \dfrac{(x + 2)^3}{4} - 7$ is

$$y = -\left\{ \dfrac{(x + 2)^3}{4} - 7 \right\}$$

i.e.

$$y = 7 - \dfrac{(x + 2)^3}{4}$$

13 $f(x) = x^2 + 3x - 2$. The graph of $y = f(x)$ is first reflected in the x-axis and then the new curve is reflected in the y-axis.

   (a) Find the equations of these two new curves and plot the three graphs to check your answers.

   (b) How could you have transformed the first curve onto the third using a single transformation?

14 $f(x) = 2x^2 - \dfrac{1}{x}$. The graph of $y = f(x)$ is first reflected in the y-axis and then translated through $\begin{bmatrix} 4 \\ 3 \end{bmatrix}$. Find the equation of the final curve.

Check your answer by using the graph plotter.

You have now seen the effects of translations and reflections in the axes. The general rules for these transformations are summarised below.

Translations

The graph of $y = f(x + p) + q$ is the image of the graph of $y = f(x)$ after translation through $\begin{bmatrix} -p \\ q \end{bmatrix}$.

Reflections in the axes

The graph of $y = f(-x)$ is the image of the graph of $y = f(x)$ after it has been reflected in the y-axis. The graph of $y = -f(x)$ is the image of the graph of $y = f(x)$ after it has been reflected in the x-axis.

Exercise C (answers p. 158)

1 *Without* using a calculator, use translations of simple graphs to sketch the graphs of the following. In each case give the equation of the basic graph and the translation used.

   (a) $y = x^2 + 9$ (b) $y = x^3 - 2$

   (c) $y = (x - 1)^2$ (d) $y = 5(x - 3)^2 + 6$

   (e) $y = \dfrac{3}{x + \frac{1}{2}}$ (f) $y = x^2 + 2x$

2   For each of the following pairs of graphs, the equation of one graph is given. Find the equation of the other.

Use the graph plotter to check your answers.

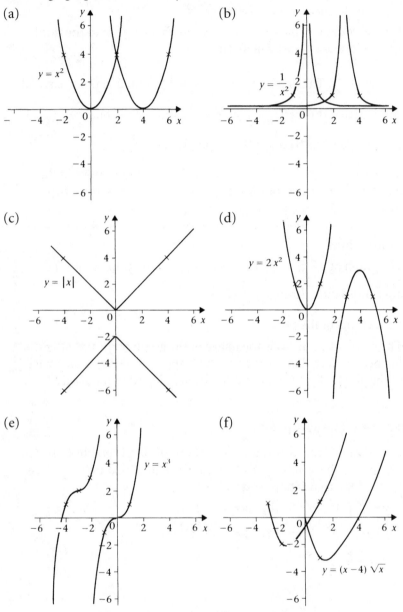

(a)

$y = x^2$

(b)

$y = \dfrac{1}{x^2}$

(c)

$y = |x|$

(d)

$y = 2x^2$

(e)

$y = x^3$

(f)

$y = (x - 4)\sqrt{x}$

3 Find the images of the graphs of the following functions under the transformations given.

(a) $y = \dfrac{1}{x}$

reflection in the x-axis followed by a translation through $\begin{bmatrix} -6 \\ -7 \end{bmatrix}$

(b) $y = 3x - 7$

reflection in the y-axis followed by a reflection in the x-axis

(c) $y = \dfrac{1}{x^2}$

translation through $\begin{bmatrix} 2 \\ -3 \end{bmatrix}$ followed by a reflection in the x-axis

D   The modulus function: using graphs (answers p. 159)

You have already met $|x|$, known as the modulus of x or the absolute value of x. It means the positive numerical value of x. For example, if $x = 7.2, |x| = 7.2$ and if $x = -5.6, |x| = 5.6$.

1 Given that $f(x) = |x - 5|$, evaluate these.

    (a) f(7)   (b) f(2)   (c) f(5)   (d) f(−7)   (e) f(4.5)

To transform the graph of $y = x$ to the graph of $y = |x|$ we need do nothing to the part where y is positive.

But where y is negative we need to change the sign by reflecting that part of the graph in x-axis.

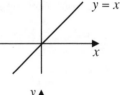

2D Sketch the following graphs.

    (a) $y = |2x|$ (b) $y = \left|\dfrac{x}{2}\right|$ (c) $y = |-x|$ (d) $y = -|x|$

3 (a) Sketch the graph of $y = x + 1$, marking the values at which the graph cuts the axes.

    (b) On a fresh pair of axes, sketch the graph of $y = |x + 1|$, using your first sketch for guidance.

4 Use the approach in question 3 to sketch the following graphs, marking the values at which each graph meets the axis.

(a) $y = |2x - 2|$ (b) $y = \left|\dfrac{x}{2} + 3\right|$ (c) $y = |4 - x|$

More complicated graphs involving the modulus function can be sketched by considering the graphs of the functions from which they are composed.

Example 9

Sketch the graph of $y = 1 - |3x + 1|$.

Solution

$y = 3x + 1$ is sketched and key points marked.

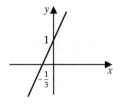

The negative part of $y = 3x + 1$ is reflected in the x-axis to get the graph of $y = |3x + 1|$.

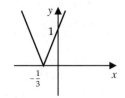

The whole graph is reflected in the x-axis to get the graph of $y = -|3x + 1|$.

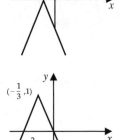

This is raised by one unit to give the graph of $y = -|3x + 1| + 1$, which is the same as $y = 1 - |3x + 1|$.

5 Sketch these graphs.

(a) $y = |x| + 1$ (b) $y = |x - 3| - 1$

(c) $y = -|2 - x|$ (d) $y = |2x + 4| + 2$

Equations and inequalities

Sketches of graphs play a key part in solving equations and inequalities that involve the modulus function.

Example 10

Solve the equation $|x| = 4 - \left|\dfrac{x+1}{2}\right|$.

Solution

The equation is solved where the graphs of $y = |x|$ and $y = 4 - \left|\dfrac{x+1}{2}\right|$ intersect.

We see from sketch graphs drawn on the same axes that there are two points of intersection.

The lines that intersect at point A can be shown to have these equations.

$$y = -x \qquad (1)$$
$$y = 0.5x + 4.5 \qquad (2)$$

Substituting (1) into (2),

$$-x = 0.5x + 4.5$$
$$-1.5x = 4.5$$
$$x = -3$$

Substituting in (1), $y = 3$, so point A is $(-3, 3)$.

The lines that intersect at point B can be shown to have these equations.

$$y = x \qquad (3)$$
$$y = -0.5x + 3.5 \qquad (4)$$

Substituting (3) into (4),

$$x = -0.5x + 3.5$$
$$1.5x = 3.5$$
$$x = \frac{7}{3}$$

Substituting in (3), $y = \frac{7}{3}$, so point B is $(\frac{7}{3}, \frac{7}{3})$.

Hence the equation $|x| = 4 - \left|\dfrac{x+1}{2}\right|$ has the solution $x = -3$ or $\frac{7}{3}$.

Example 11

Find the values of x for which $|x| < 4 - \left| \dfrac{x+1}{2} \right|$.

Solution

The two sides of the inequality correspond with the functions sketched for Example 10.

The sketch shows that $|x| < 4 - \left| \dfrac{x+1}{2} \right|$ between the points of intersection A and B.

So the solution of the inequality is $-3 < x < \dfrac{7}{3}$.

6 (a) Solve the equation $3 - |x| = 4 - |2x - 4|$.

   (b) Find the values of x for which $3 - |x| < 4 - |2x - 4|$.

The modulus function graphs you have met so far have been based on linear graphs. The approach to dealing with curved graphs is just the same.

7D (a) Sketch the graph of $y = (x-1)(x-3)$ marking values where it meets the axes.

   (b) On a fresh pair of axes sketch the graph of $y = |(x-1)(x-3)|$.

Essentially, the graph of the function within the modulus symbols has to be considered and those parts of it that are below the x-axis have to be reflected upwards in the x-axis. Again, as in Example 10, graphs of more complicated functions can then be worked out.

8 Match each function to a graph.

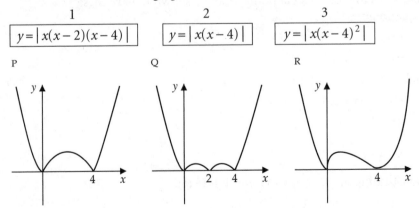

      1   2   3

$y = |x(x-2)(x-4)|$ $y = |x(x-4)|$ $y = |x(x-4)^2|$

9 Sketch these graphs.

   (a) $y = |x^3|$ (b) $y = |x^2 - 2| + 3$ (c) $y = |x^3 - 1|$

Exercise D (answers p. 160)

1   Evaluate f(−4) for each of these functions.

   (a) $f(x) = |x^2|$ (b) $f(x) = |x - 5|$ (c) $f(x) = |x + 5|$

   (d) $f(x) = |x|^3$ (e) $f(x) = 3 - |2x|$ (f) $f(x) = 7 - |x - 7|$

2   Sketch a graph for each of these, marking values at which each graph meets the axis.

   (a) $y = |3x|$ (b) $y = |2x + 1|$ (c) $y = -|x|$

   (d) $y = |x + 2| - 2$ (e) $y = |(x + 2)(x + 5)|$ (f) $y = -|x^2 - 1|$

3   (a) Solve the equation $|x| = |3x - 6|$.

    (b) Use your result to solve the inequality $|x| < |3x - 6|$.

4E   Solve the equation $x + 3 = |(x - 3)(x + 1)|$.

After working through this chapter you should

1   understand the terms domain, range, one-to-one, even, odd, as applied to functions

2   be able to combine functions

3   be able to find the inverse of a function

4   be able to rearrange formulas

5   be able to find the images of graphs after

   (a) translation

   (b) reflections in the axes

   (c) reflection in the line $y = x$

6   be able to use your knowledge of transformations to help you sketch graphs

7   be able to solve problems involving the modulus function by sketching graphs.

S3.1 **Composition of functions** (see p. 47, answers p. 160)

1 The functions f and g given by $f(x) = x^2$ and $g(x) = 3x + 1$ can be described by the following flow charts.

$x \longrightarrow$ [square $\rangle \longrightarrow x^2 = f(x)$

$x \longrightarrow$ [multiply by 3 $\rangle \longrightarrow 3x \longrightarrow$ [add 1 $\rangle \longrightarrow 3x + 1 = g(x)$

(a) (i) What is f(4)?   (ii) What is g(16)?

(b) If the output from $f(x)$ is used as input to $g(x)$, you can write $g(f(x))$. What is $g(f(4))$?

(c) Write down these.
(i) $g(f(2))$ (ii) $g(f(-3))$ (iii) $f(g(-2))$

(d) Draw a flow chart to describe the composite function $gf(x)$ and hence find a formula for $gf(x)$.

(e) Check whether your formula is correct by substituting a few numbers in $gf(x)$ and in your formula.

(f) Now find a formula for $fg(x)$.

2 (a) Use the ideas above to find $gf(x)$ and $fg(x)$ for these.

(i) $f(x) = \dfrac{1}{x}, g(x) = x - 3$ (ii) $f(x) = 2x, g(x) = \sqrt{x}$

(iii) $f(x) = x + 5, g(x) = x - 9$ (iv) $f(x) = 10 - x, g(x) = 10 - x$

(v) $f(x) = \dfrac{1}{x}, g(x) = \dfrac{1}{x}$

(b) Comment on the cases where $fg(x) = gf(x)$.

3 Each of the expressions below is of the form $fg(x)$ where $f(x) = 1 - x^2$. What is $g(x)$ in each case?

(a) $1 - (x + 2)^2$ (b) $1 - x^4$ (c) $1 - \dfrac{1}{x^2}$ (d) $1 - x$

4 Each of the expressions below is of the form $fg(x)$ where $g(x) = x^3$. What is $f(x)$ in each case?

(a) $x^3 + 8$ (b) x^6 (c) $3x^3 + 1$ (d) $\dfrac{12}{x^3}$ (e) x (f) $4x^3 - x^6$

S3.2 Rearranging formulas (see p. 55, answers p. 160)

1 Complete the steps to make x the subject of the formula $y = 5(x-7)^2$.

$$y = 5(x-7)^2$$

$$\underline{} = (x-7)^2 \qquad \text{(dividing both sides by 5)}$$

$$\underline{} = (x-7) \qquad \text{(finding the square root of each side)}$$

$$\underline{} = x \qquad \text{(adding 7 to both sides)}$$

2 Make x the subject of these formulas.

(a) $y = 3x^2 - 7$ 　　(b) $y = \dfrac{(2x+1)^2}{9}$ 　　(c) $y = 3\sqrt{x} - 1$

3 Complete the steps to find x in terms . of y if $y = \dfrac{3}{x} - 4$.

$$y = \frac{3}{x} - 4$$

$$\underline{} = 3 - 4x \qquad \text{(multiplying both sides by } x)$$

$$\underline{} = 3 \qquad \text{(adding } 4x \text{ to both sides to collect terms in } x \text{ together)}$$

$$(\underline{})x = 3 \qquad \text{(factorising the left-hand side)}$$

$$x = \frac{3}{\underline{}}$$

4 Make x the subject of these formulas.

(a) $y = 2 - \dfrac{1}{x}$ 　　(b) $y = \dfrac{3}{x^2}$ 　　(c) $y = 5 + \dfrac{1}{2\sqrt{x}}$

(d) $y = \dfrac{2}{x+1}$ 　　(e) $y = \dfrac{4}{2x+1}$ 　　(f) $y = \dfrac{7}{1-2x}$

(g) $y = (1+x)^2$ 　　(h) $y = (1-2x)^2$ 　　(i) $y = 1 - \left(\dfrac{x}{2}\right)^2$

4 Circular functions

A Graphs of the sine and cosine functions (answers p. 161)

The mathematics of the sine and cosine functions describes the behaviour of many physical systems. Illustrated below are a few examples; others include the motion of the tides and the current flow in an electric circuit.

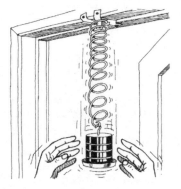

Although some of these movements are obviously circular (the rotation of the big wheel, for example), others are not (for example, tidal movements).

Our study begins with definitions of the functions themselves. Initially, we shall concentrate on the sine and cosine functions.

Introductory work on the sine and cosine of angles greater than 90° is provided in the support material S4.1 (p. 94.)

Consider a point P rotating around a unit circle (a circle of radius 1 unit) as shown.

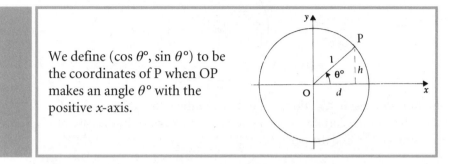

We define $(\cos \theta°, \sin \theta°)$ to be the coordinates of P when OP makes an angle $\theta°$ with the positive x-axis.

So $h = \sin \theta°$ and $d = \cos \theta°$, where $\theta°$ is the angle through which the point has turned from the horizontal position.

These values for d and h are consistent with those obtained from the elementary ratios in a right-angled triangle.

In a right-angled triangle for which the hypotenuse is of length 1,

$$\sin \theta° = \frac{h}{1} \quad \text{and} \quad \cos \theta° = \frac{d}{1}$$

that is, $\sin \theta° = h$ and $\cos \theta° = d$.

The definitions of the sine and cosine in terms of the coordinates of a point rotating around the unit circle apply for *all* values of the angle $\theta°$. If the point P moves in an anticlockwise direction then the angle generated is taken to be positive. In a clockwise direction the angle is negative.

By considering the height h of the point P above the horizontal as θ varies, the sine curve can be obtained. The cosine curve is obtained by considering the horizontal distance, d, from the origin O.

A few values are calculated below.

$h = \sin 30° = 0.5$
$d = \cos 30° = 0.866$

$h = \sin 120° = 0.866$
$d = \cos 120° = -0.5$

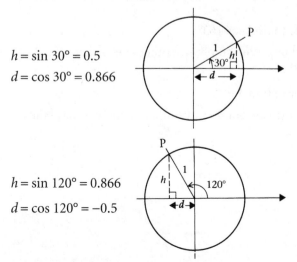

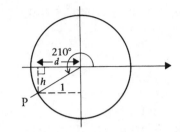

$h = \sin 210° = -0.5$

$d = \cos 210° = -0.866$

The sine and cosine functions are both **periodic** – that is, they repeat themselves after a certain interval known as the **period**. In the case of both sine and cosine the period is 360°.

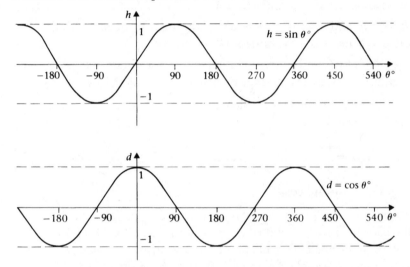

Observe that sin ('anything') is *always* a number between +1 and −1 inclusive (the range of the function); similarly, for cos ('anything').

1 (a) Use your calculator to give the value of sin 50°.

  (b) Write down, from the sine graph, four other angles that have the same sine as 50°.

2 (a) Use your calculator to find cos 163°.

  (b) Write down, from the cosine graph, five other angles that have the same cosine as 163°.

3 (a) Use your calculator to find 339°.

  (b) Write down, from the sine graph, three other angles that have the same sine as 339°.

Transformations

Now we consider the effect of various transformations on the graphs of the sine and cosine functions. This will help when you sketch graphs of related functions, such as $\cos(2x + 60)°$, for example. Consider first the sine and cosine functions themselves.

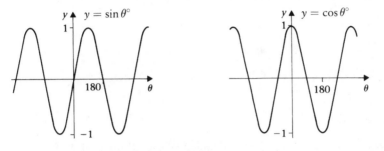

The function $\sin\theta°$ is an **odd function**, as the graph has rotational symmetry about the origin.

$$\sin(-\theta°) = -\sin\theta°$$

so that $\sin(-50°) = -\sin 50° = -0.766$

The function $\cos\theta°$ is an **even function**, as the graph has reflection symmetry in the y-axis.

$$\cos(-\theta°) = \cos\theta°$$

so that $\cos(-50°) = \cos 50° = 0.643$

The graph of $\cos\theta°$ may be obtained by a translation of $\begin{bmatrix} -90° \\ 0° \end{bmatrix}$ of the $\sin\theta°$ graph.

$$\sin(\theta + 90)° = \cos\theta°$$

so, for example, $\sin 120° = \cos 30° = 0.866$

4 Use a graph plotter, working in degrees, to plot the graph of

$$y = \sin\theta°$$

Investigate the graph of $y = a\sin\theta°$ for various values of a, including negative values, and describe the transformations involved. a is called the **amplitude** of the function.

5 (a) Investigate $y = \sin b\theta°$ for various values of b and comment on the significance of the factor b.

(b) What is the period of $\sin b\theta°$ in terms of b?

6 Investigate $y = \sin(\theta + c)° + d$ for various values of c and d and describe the transformations involved.

7 Investigate these for various values of b and c and describe carefully the transformations involved.

(a) $y = \cos b\theta°$ (b) $y = \cos(b\theta + c)°$

8

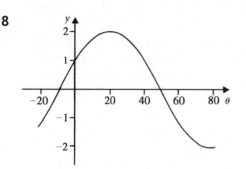

The diagram shows a part of the graph of

$y = a \sin(b\theta + c)^\circ$.

Find a, b and c.

9 Describe fully a sequence of transformations to map the graph of

$$y = \cos \theta^\circ$$

onto the graph of

$$y = a \cos(b\theta + c)^\circ + d$$

where a, b, c and d may take any values. Illustrate your conclusions with appropriate diagrams.

You should have noted the following results.

Starting with $y = \sin x^\circ$,

$y = \sin(x + c)^\circ + d$ is obtained by a translation of $\begin{bmatrix} -c \\ d \end{bmatrix}$.

$y = a \sin x^\circ$ is obtained by a one-way stretch parallel to the y-axis which changes the **amplitude** of the function from 1 to a.

$y = \sin bx^\circ$ is obtained by a one-way stretch parallel to the x-axis which changes the **period** of the function from 360° to $\left(\dfrac{360}{b}\right)^\circ$.

$y = \sin(bx + c)^\circ$ can be obtained by a stretch of $\dfrac{1}{b}$ followed by a horizontal translation of $\dfrac{-c}{b}$, called a phase shift of $\dfrac{-c}{b}$.

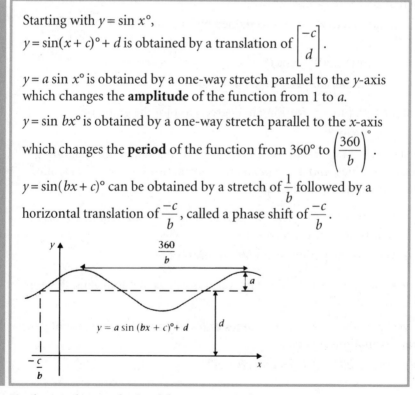

Similar results are obtained for $y = \cos x^\circ$.

Example 1

(a) For $y = 3\cos(6\theta + 180)°$, what are the amplitude, period and phase shift? Sketch the graph.

(b) Describe a sequence of transformations which maps the graph of $y = \cos\theta°$ onto that of $y = 3\cos(6\theta + 180)°$.

Solution

(a)

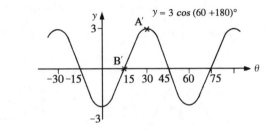

Amplitude 3.
Period 60.
Phase shift $-30°$.

(b) The transformations are:

- a one-way stretch, parallel to the x-axis, of scale factor $\frac{1}{6}$, followed by

- a one-way stretch, parallel to the y-axis, of scale factor 3, followed by

- a translation $\begin{bmatrix} -30 \\ 0 \end{bmatrix}$.

It is informative to track some of the points from the graph of $y = \cos\theta°$ to $y = 3\cos(6\theta + 180)°$.

For example, point A $(360°, 1)$

$$(360°, 1) \rightarrow (60°, 1) \rightarrow (60°, 3) \rightarrow (30°, 3) = A'$$

point B $(270°, 0)$

$$(270°, 0) \rightarrow (45°, 0) \rightarrow (45°, 0) \rightarrow (15°, 0) = B'$$

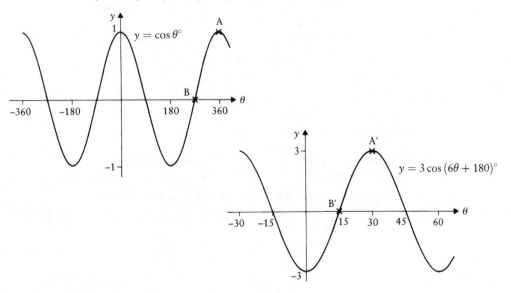

Exercise A (answers p. 162)

1 Suggest suitable equations for the following graphs. Check your
answers using a graph plotter.

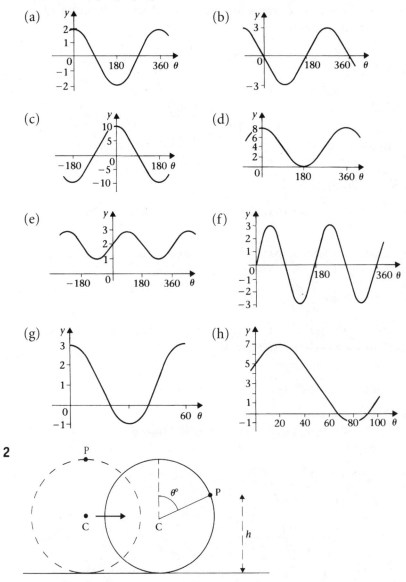

(a)

(b)

(c)

(d)

(e)

(f)

(g)

(h)

2

A wheel of radius 0.2 metres rolls along a straight horizontal line.
Initially, a spot P on the rim is directly over the centre C. After turning
through $\theta°$, the height of the spot P is h metres. Find an equation for h
in terms of θ and sketch the graph of h against θ.

3 (a) Describe a sequence of transformations that maps the graph of
$y = \sin x°$ to $y = 2 \sin(3x + 60)°$.

(b) Find the image point of (i) $(180°, 0)$ (ii) $(90°, 1)$
under the transformations in (a).

B Modelling periodic behaviour (answers p. 162)

A big wheel has a radius of 4.8 m and a seat in
the lowest position is 0.8 m above ground
level. One complete revolution takes
60 seconds.

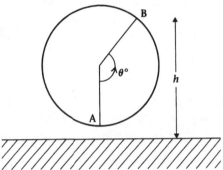

1 (a) If a seat starts from the bottom in position A, and if after t seconds
it has turned through an angle $\theta°$, express θ in terms of t.

(b) Draw a rough sketch to show how the height in metres, h, will
vary with (i) θ (ii) t.
(There is no need to perform any detailed calculations.) In each
case, suggest a possible formula for h.

(c) Plot a graph of the first part of the motion by completing the
following table of values of h for various values of θ.

θ	0	30	60	90	120	150	180
h							

(d) Repeat part (c), but this time using t as the variable.

t	0	5	10	15	20	25	30
h							

You may have noticed that a subtle change has occurred in this
example. Until now sine and cosine have been used exclusively with
angles as input. In part (d), however, the input to the function was t.
There is no reason why, having drawn the basic graphs of the circular
functions, you should not use *any variable* you choose as input.

Example 2

When a particular tuning fork is struck, each prong vibrates at a frequency of 256 Hz (hertz, or cycles per second) with a maximum displacement at the tip of 0.3 mm.

(a) Sketch a graph to show the displacement of the tip of a prong with time.

(b) Assuming that this a sine graph, express d, the displacement in millimetres, as a function of t, the time in seconds from the start of the motion.

Solution

(a) Assume the initial displacement is 0.3 mm.

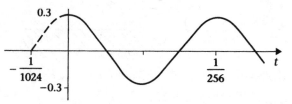

(b) $d = a \sin(bt + c)°$

Amplitude: $a = 0.3$

Period: $\dfrac{360}{b} = \dfrac{1}{256} \Rightarrow b = 92\,160$

Phase shift: $\dfrac{-c}{b} = -\dfrac{1}{1024} \Rightarrow c = 90$

So $d = 0.3 \sin(92\,160t + 90)°$

Example 3

(a)

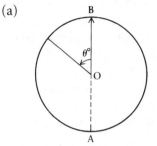

A wave machine in a swimming pool comprises a cylinder of radius 2 m which rotates at 1 revolution every 10 seconds. The cylinder starts with the bar, B, uppermost and has rotated through an angle $\theta°$ after t seconds. A is a fixed point just beneath the cylinder. Express θ in terms of t.

(b) Hence write down the height, after t seconds, of the bar above

    (i) O   (ii) A.

Solution

(a) There is a rotation of 36° in 1 second
    So $\theta = 36t$

(b) (i) Height $= 2 \cos(36t)°$ (ii) Height $= 2 + 2 \cos(36t)°$

Exercise B (answers p. 162)

1 As the Moon circles the Earth, its gravitational force causes tides. The height of the tide can be modelled by a sine or cosine function.

  (a) Assume an interval of 12 hours between successive high tides.

    (i)   Sketch the graph of the height if it is 5.7 metres at low tide and 7.3 metres at high tide.

    (ii) Use the graph to help express the height of the tide, h metres, as a function of the time t hours after high tide.

  (b) Express h as a function of t if h is 3.6 at low tide and 4.9 at high tide.

2 The times for sunset at four-weekly intervals over a year are as follows.

Jan. 2	16:03	July 16	21:10
Jan. 30	16:45	Aug. 13	20:27
Feb. 27	17:36	Sep. 10	19:26
Mar. 26	18:24	Oct. 8	18:22
Apr. 23	20:11	Nov. 5	16:26
May 21	20:55	Dec. 3	15:54
June 18	21:21		

Plot these data on a graph and, making any necessary adjustments, find a suitable function to model the data approximately.

3

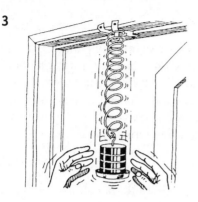

A mass oscillates up and down at the end of a spring. The unstretched length of the spring is 12 cm, and it is extended to 14.5 cm and released. One complete oscillation takes one second. Sketch a graph to show the length of the spring as a function of time. Assuming that this is a cosine graph, express l, the length in centimetres, as a function of t, the time in seconds from the start of the motion.

C Inverses and equations (answers p. 163)

In studying periodic behaviour it is often useful to be able to solve equations of the form $\sin x° = a$.

1D
(a) Use your calculator to find a solution to the equation $\sin x° = 0.6$.

(b) How many more solutions can you find to this equation?

(c) Why is the inverse of f, where $f(x) = \sin x°(x \in \mathbb{R})$, **not** a function?

If $\sin a° = b$, then $a° = \sin^{-1} b$, where $\sin^{-1} b$ means 'the angle whose sine is b'.

In order to ensure that $\sin^{-1}$ is a function, you need to restrict the domain to those values given by a calculator. These values are known as the **principal values**.

For $\sin^{-1} x$ the principal values used by most calculators lie in the range $-90° \leqslant \sin^{-1} x \leqslant 90°$.

2D Use your calculator to find its range of principal values for $\cos^{-1} x$.

The graphs of $\sin^{-1} x$ and $\cos^{-1} x$ are shown below.

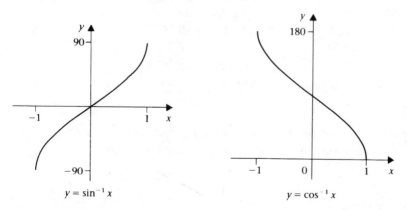

$y = \sin^{-1} x$ $y = \cos^{-1} x$

Example 4

(a) Find the value of $\cos^{-1}(-0.25)$.

(b) Solve $\cos x° = -0.25$ for $-360 \leqslant x \leqslant 360$.

Solution

(a) A calculator gives $\cos^{-1}(-0.25)$ as 104.5°, which is the principal value.

(b) A graph shows there are four solutions. Angles having the same cosine are found using the symmetry of the graph. They are:

A $-360° + 104.5° = -255.5°$

B $-104.5°$

C $104.5°$

D $360° - 104.5° = 255.5°$

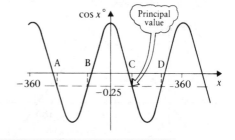

The functions $\sin^{-1}$ and $\cos^{-1}$ both have domain $\{x \in \mathbb{R} : -1 \leqslant x \leqslant 1\}$.

Their ranges are restricted to the sets of principal values

$$-90° \leqslant \sin^{-1} x \leqslant 90° \quad \text{and} \quad 0° \leqslant \cos^{-1} x \leqslant 180°$$

---

3 To solve the equation $4 \cos x° = 3$ follow these steps.

(a) Write down the value of $\cos x°$.

(b) Use your calculator to give one solution for x.

(c) Sketch the graph of $y = \cos x°$.

(d) (i)   Mark on the graph the solution from the calculator.

(ii) Mark on the graph the other solution between 0 and 360.

(iii) Write down the value of this other solution.

4 Find all the solutions between 0 and 360 for the following equations, illustrating your answers with sketch graphs.

(a) $\cos x° = 0.56$ (b) $\sin x° = -0.23$ (c) $\cos x° = -0.5$

5 Copy and complete the solution of $5 \sin(3t + 40)° = 4$.

$$5 \sin(3t + 40)° = 4 \Longrightarrow \sin(3t + 40)° = \dots$$

This is equivalent to $\sin x° = \dots$, where $x = 3t + 40$

From a calculator, $x = \dots$

So (using a sketch of the graph of $\sin x°$) six possible solutions are

$$x = \dots, \quad \dots, \quad \dots, \quad \dots, \quad \dots, \quad \dots$$
$$\Longrightarrow 3t + 40 = \dots, \quad \dots, \quad \dots, \quad \dots, \quad \dots, \quad \dots$$
$$\Longrightarrow \qquad t = \dots, \quad \dots, \quad \dots, \quad \dots, \quad \dots, \quad \dots$$

6E

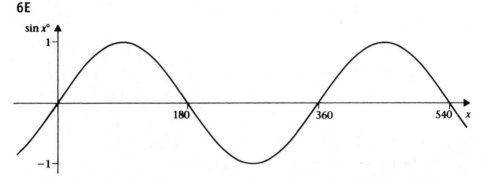

(a) Use your calculator to find a solution of $\sin x° = 0.4$.

(b) Use the graph above to find three more solutions in the range $0 \leqslant x \leqslant 540$.

(c) Write down two solutions in the $3600 \leqslant x \leqslant 3960$.

(d) Write down two solutions in the range $360n \leqslant x \leqslant 360(n + 1)$.

(e) Does your formula apply if n is negative?

Your solution to question 6E(d) is known as the **general solution** of the equation. It is possible to write the general solution in a rather more elegant form, as question 7E demonstrates.

7E (a) Find a solution, p, of $\sin x° = 0.5$ in the range $0 \leqslant x \leqslant 90$.

(b) Two more solutions are $180 - p$ and $360 + p$. Write down the next two in the same form.

(c) Write down the 20th and 21st terms of the sequence starting $p, 180 - p, 360 + p$.

(d) Write down the nth term. (Hint: $(-1)^n$ equals $+1$ if n is even, -1 if n is odd.)

8E Find the general solutions of these equations.

(a) $\sin x° = 0.7$ (b) $\sin x° = -0.7$ (c) $\cos x° = 0.7$

Exercise C (answers p. 164)

1 Give the (principal) values of the following.
   (a) $\sin^{-1} 0.2$ (b) $\cos^{-1} 0.9$ (c) $\sin^{-1}(-0.36)$
   (d) $\cos^{-1}(-0.74)$ (e) $\sin^{-1}(1)$ (f) $\cos^{-1}(-1)$

2 Solve the following equations, giving solutions in the range
   $-360 \leqslant x \leqslant 720$.
   (a) $\sin x° = 0.3$ (b) $\cos x° = 0.8$ (c) $\cos x° = -0.3$
   (d) $\sin x° = -0.5$ (b) $\cos x° = -1$ (f) $3 \sin x° = 1$

3 Find all the solutions between -180 and 180 for these equations,
   illustrating your answers with sketch graphs.
   (a) $\sin x° = 0.65$ (b) $\cos x° = -0.38$ (c) $\sin x° = -0.47$

4 Find all the solutions between 0 and 360 for the following equations.
   (a) $3 \sin x° = 2$ (b) $5 \cos x° + 2 = 0$ (c) $2 \cos x° + 5 = 0$

5 Solve these equations for values of t between 0 and 360.
   (a) $\sin 2t° = 0.7$ (b) $2 \cos 3t° = 1$ (c) $3 \cos(0.5t + 20)° = 2$

6 Find the values of t in the range $0 \leqslant t \leqslant 60$ which satisfy the following
   equations.
   (a) $8 \sin 10t° = 5$ (b) $4 - 7 \cos(t + 35)° = 0$
   (c) $3 + 4 \sin(8t - 21)° = 0$ (d) $10 \cos \frac{1}{2} t° = 9$

7E Find the general solutions to the equations
   (a) $3 \sin x° = 0.6$ (b) $\cos x° = -0.8$

8E Find the smallest (positive or negative) angle for which each of the
   following pairs of conditions is true.
   (a) $\sin \theta° = -0.4$ and $\cos \theta°$ is positive
   (b) $\cos \theta° = -0.8$ and $\tan \theta°$ is negative
   (c) $\tan \theta° = 20$ and $\sin \theta°$ is negative
   (d) $\cos \theta° = 0.9$ and $\sin \theta°$ is positive
   (e) $\tan \theta° = -0.3$ and $\cos \theta°$ is negative
   (f) $\sin \theta° = 0.2$ and $\tan \theta°$ is negative

D Solving problems with sine and cosine (answers p. 165)

1 Suppose that the height of the tide, h metres, at a harbour entrance is modelled by the function

$$h = 2.5 \sin 30t° + 5$$

where t is the number of hours after midnight.

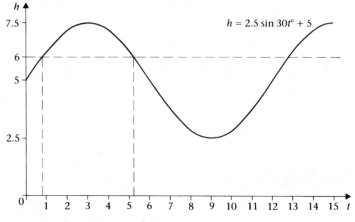

(a) When is the height of the tide 6 m?

(b) If a boat can only enter and leave the harbour when the depth of water exceeds 6 m, for how long each day is this possible?

Example 5

A girl is sitting on a big wheel which rotates once every 30 seconds. When the wheel begins to rotate for the ride, she is sitting in the position marked A on the diagram. The diameter of the wheel is 16 m.

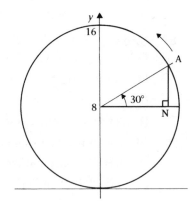

(a) Show that her height y metres above the lowest point of the wheel t seconds later is given by

$$y = 8 + 8 \sin(12t + 30)°.$$

(b) At what times is she

    (i)   15 metres above the ground,

    (ii) at the highest point?

Solution

(a) $AN = 8 \sin(12t + 30)°$

So height of A $= y = 8 + 8 \sin(12t + 30)°$

(b) (i) When $y = 15$, you need to solve the equation

$$8 + 8 \sin(12t + 30)° = 15$$

$\Longrightarrow \qquad 8 \sin(12t + 30)° = 7$

$\Longrightarrow \qquad \sin(12t + 30)° = 0.875$

Now solve $\sin x° = 0.875$, where $x = 12t + 30$.

The calculator gives $x = 61.0$ so the possible solutions are

$$x = 61.0, \quad 180 - 61.0, \quad 360 + 61.0, \ ...$$

$\Longrightarrow \quad 12t + 30 = 61.0, \quad 119.0, \quad 421.0, \quad 479.0, \ ...$

$\Longrightarrow \qquad \qquad t = 2.6, \quad 7.4, \quad 32.6, \quad 37.4, \ ...$

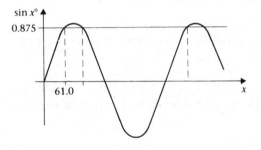

(ii) At the highest point, $y = 16$, so you have to solve the equation

$$8 + 8 \sin(12t + 30)° = 16$$

$\Longrightarrow \qquad 8 \sin(12t + 30)° = 8$

$\Longrightarrow \qquad \sin(12t + 30)° = 1$

Now solve $\sin x° = 1$, where $x = 12t + 30$.

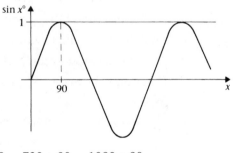

This time there is only a single solution for each cycle and you do not need a calculator to tell you that the basic solution is $x = 90$. So the possible solutions are

$$x = 90, \quad 360 + 90, \quad 720 + 90, \quad 1080 + 90, \ ...$$

$\Longrightarrow \quad 12t + 30 = 90, \quad 450, \quad 810, \quad 1170, \ ...$

$\Longrightarrow \qquad \qquad t = 5, \quad 35, \quad 65, \quad 95, \ ...$

> The function $\sin(12t + 30)°$ has a period of $\dfrac{360}{12} = 30$, so if $t = a$ is a solution then so is $t = 30n + a$, where n is any integer.

Exercise D (answers p. 165)

1   The height above ground of a chair in a big wheel is given by

$$h = 5.6 - 4.8 \cos 6t°$$

where t is the time measured in seconds from the instant when the chair is at the lowest point. For how many seconds during one complete revolution is the chair more than 9 metres above ground level?

2   If the height of the tide is h metres at time t hours, where

$$h = 5 + 2.5 \sin 30t°$$

find all the times in the first 24 hours when these heights occur.

(a) 6.7 metres   (b) 4.5 metres

3   A cowboy ties a handkerchief to a lasso which he then spins so that the height in metres of his handkerchief above the ground after t seconds is given by

$$h = 2 + 1.5 \sin 500t°$$

Find at what times the height of the handkerchief above the ground has these values.

(a) 2.75 metres   (b) 2 metres   (c) 3.5 metres

4   A mass is suspended from the ceiling on the end of a spring. It is pulled down then released, and oscillates up and down. The length of the spring, L centimetres, is given by $L = 56 + 10 \sin 130t°$.

(a) Find the length of the spring after 3 seconds.

(b) Find the minimum length of the spring.

(c) Find the maximum length of the spring.

(d) Determine the first two times when the spring has a length of 62 cm.

(e) How long does a complete oscillation take?

E The tangent function (answers p. 165)

1D   A tennis umpire, U, is watching a rally between two players. The ball, B, is hit straight down the court from P to Q over the centre of the net, C.

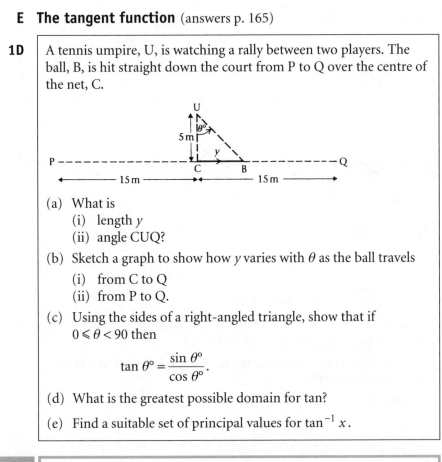

(a) What is
   (i) length y
   (ii) angle CUQ?

(b) Sketch a graph to show how y varies with θ as the ball travels
   (i) from C to Q
   (ii) from P to Q.

(c) Using the sides of a right-angled triangle, show that if $0 \leqslant \theta < 90$ then
$$\tan \theta° = \frac{\sin \theta°}{\cos \theta°}.$$

(d) What is the greatest possible domain for tan?

(e) Find a suitable set of principal values for $\tan^{-1} x$.

$$\tan x° = \frac{\sin x°}{\cos x°} \quad \{\cos x° \neq 0\}$$

$\tan x°$ is an odd function: $\tan(-x)° = -\tan x°$

$\tan^{-1}(x)$ has domain $\{x \in \mathbb{R}\}$, range $-90° < \tan^{-1} x < 90°$.

Although these results were illustrated for $0 \leqslant x < 90$, they are true for values of x outside this range.

The graph of the tangent function is shown.

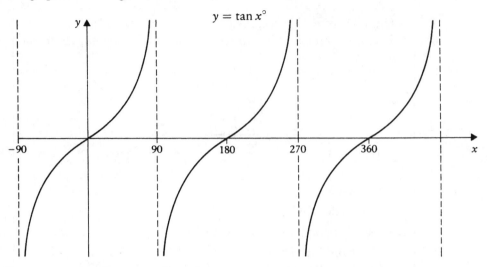

$y = \tan x^{\circ}$

Features to note about $\tan x^{\circ}$ are these.

- The graph of $\tan x^{\circ}$ has asymptotes at $x = -90$, $x = 90$, $x = 270$, ...
- The value of $\tan 90^{\circ}$ is undefined.
- $\tan x^{\circ}$ is an odd function (its graph has rotational symmetry about the origin): $\tan(-x^{\circ}) = -\tan x^{\circ}$
- The period of $\tan x^{\circ}$ is 180°, not 360°.
- It makes no sense to talk of the amplitude of a tangent function.

2 Given that $\tan 45^{\circ} = 1$, and using the sketch of $\tan x^{\circ}$ write down these values.

(a) $\tan(-45^{\circ})$ (b) $\tan(135^{\circ})$ (c) $\tan(225^{\circ})$ (d) $\tan(315^{\circ})$

The inverse tangent function has the following graph.

$$y = \tan^{-1}(x)$$

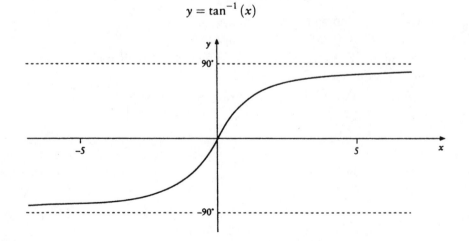

Example 6

State the general solution to the equation $\tan x° = 0.8$.

Solution

The calculator gives $x = 38.66$. However, it is clear from the graph above that there is an infinite number of solutions. The solutions occur every $180°$, so the general solution to the equation is

$$x = 38.66 \pm 180n \qquad (n = 0, 1, 2, \dots)$$

The graph of $y = \tan x°$ can be transformed into the graph of $y = a \tan(bx + c)° + d$ in the same way as the graph of $y = \sin x°$ is transformed into the graph of $y = a \sin (bx + c)° + d$.

Exercise E (answers p. 166)

1 Find these values.

(a) $\tan^{-1} 1$ (b) $\tan^{-1}(-6)$ (c) $\tan^{-1} 0$

2 Sketch these graphs.

(a) $y = \tan 2x°$ (b) $y = \tan(x + 45)°$

3 Solve the equations for values of x in the ranges $0 \leqslant x \leqslant 360$.

(a) $\tan x° = 3$ (b) $5 \tan(2x + 30)° = 4$
(c) $\tan^2 x° = 1$ (d) $4 \sin x° = 3 \cos x°$

4 For each of these functions, find
 (i) the period
 (ii) the phase shift.

(a) $f(\theta) = 6 \tan(3\theta - 40)°$ (b) $g(x) = 3 \tan(\tfrac{1}{6} x + 48)°$
(c) $h(t) = 2 \tan(\tfrac{2}{3} t + 30)°$

After working through this chapter you should be able to

1 define sin, cos, tan and their inverses

2 sketch the graph of a circular function such as

$$y = a \sin(bx + c)°$$

3 obtain solutions to equations of the form

$$a \cos(bx + c)° = d$$

in a specified range

4 apply circular functions in modelling periodic behaviour

5 obtain general solutions to trigonometric equations.

S4.1 **Sine and cosine of angles greater than 90°** (see p. 74, answers p. 166)

A cowboy is sitting on the top raid of a fence spinning a lasso, to which is tied a handkerchief. The handkerchief is moving anticlockwise in a circle of radius 1 metre and its height above the top rail is changing continuously.

Draw two pairs of axes like this on graph paper and use them to answer the following questions.

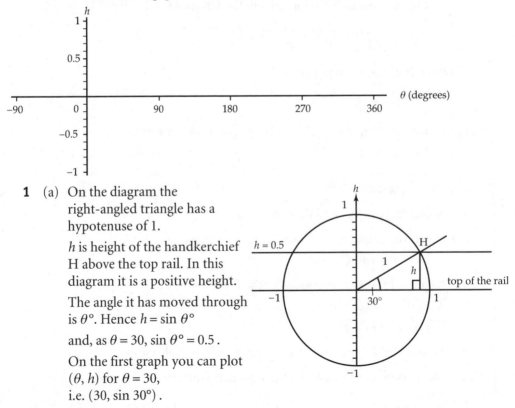

1 (a) On the diagram the right-angled triangle has a hypotenuse of 1.

h is height of the handkerchief H above the top rail. In this diagram it is a positive height.

The angle it has moved through is $\theta°$. Hence $h = \sin \theta°$

and, as $\theta = 30$, $\sin \theta° = 0.5$.

On the first graph you can plot (θ, h) for $\theta = 30$, i.e. $(30, \sin 30°)$.

(b) Find and plot the point (θ, h) on graph 1 for the following values of θ. (Work to 2 significant figures.)

(i) $\theta = 45$	(ii) $\theta = 60$	(iii) $\theta = 0$
$h =$	$h =$	$h =$
$(\theta, h) = (45, \ )$	$(\theta, h) = (60, \ )$	$(\theta, h) = (0, \ )$
(iv) $\theta = 90$	(v) $\theta = 20$	(vi) $\theta = 70$
$h =$	$h =$	$h =$
$(\theta, h) = (90, \ )$	$(\theta, h) = (20, \ )$	$(\theta, h) = (70, \ )$

2 (a) In this diagram the height of the handkerchief above the top rail is again positive and $h = \sin 150°$.

By symmetry you can see that $\sin 150° = \sin 30° = 0.5$.

Check this with your calculator.

Plot the point (θ, h) on graph 1.

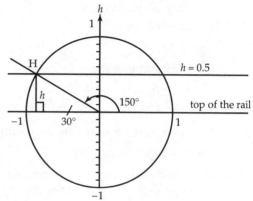

(b) Find and plot the point (θ, h) on graph 1 for these values of θ.

(i) $\theta = 135$ (ii) $\theta = 120$ (iii) $\theta = 180$

(iv) $\theta = 170$ (v) $\theta = 110$

3 (a) In this diagram the handkerchief is below the θ-axis and so $h = \sin 210°$ is negative.

By symmetry you can see that

$\sin 210° = -\sin 30° = -0.5$

Check this with your calculator.

Plot the point (θ, h) on graph 1.

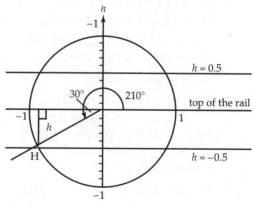

(b) Find and plot the point (θ, h) on graph 1 for these values of θ.

(i) $\theta = 225$ (ii) $\theta = 240$ (iii) $\theta = 270$

(iv) $\theta = 200$ (v) $\theta = 260$

4 (a) In this diagram the handkerchief is below the θ-axis and so $h = \sin 330°$ is negative.

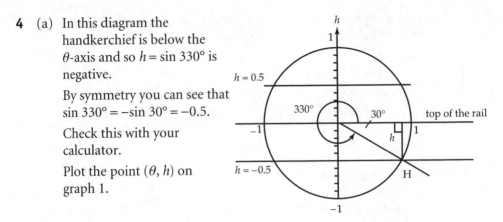

By symmetry you can see that $\sin 330° = -\sin 30° = -0.5$.

Check this with your calculator.

Plot the point (θ, h) on graph 1.

(b) Find and plot the point (θ, h) on graph 1 for these values of θ.

    (i) $\theta = 315$ (ii) $\theta = 300$ (iii) $\theta = 360$

    (iv) $\theta = 350$ (v) $\theta = 280$

Now join all the points with a smooth curve to complete the graph of the sine function.

5 The cowboy's lasso does not stop, so the handkerchief will keep on going around. Work out h for the following values of θ.

390, 405, 420, 450, 480, 495, 510, 540.

6 The distance from the origin to D represents the distance that the handkerchief H is from the vertical line through the origin.

In the right-angled triangle ODH the length of OD is $1 \times \cos 30°$

$\cos 30° = 0.87$ (to 2 d.p.)

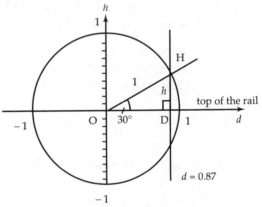

On your second pair of axes label the vertical axis d, representing the distance OD, and then plot (30, 0.87) to start a plot of the cosine function.

Find the distance OD for the angles in question 1(b).

7   As before, you can increase the angle beyond 90° to see the corresponding angles to 30° in the other three quadrants: 150°, 210°, and 330°.

The diagrams demonstrating these cosine values are shown.

$\cos 150° = -\cos 30° = -0.87$

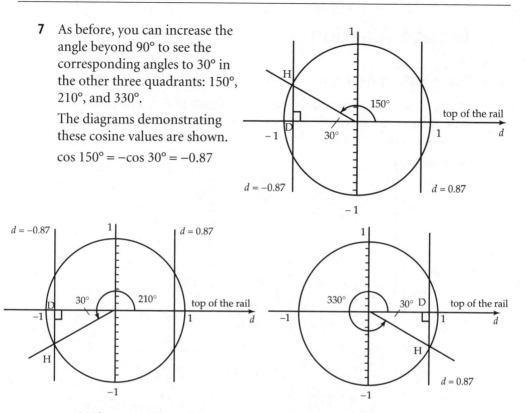

$\cos 210° = -\cos 30° = -0.87$ $\cos 330° = \cos 30° = 0.87$

Plot the points on your second graph.

8   Find the cosine values for all the angles given in questions 2(b), 3(b) and 4(b), plot the points onto your graph and join the points with a smooth curve to complete the cosine function graph.

5 Growth functions

A Exponential growth (answers p. 167)

Under favourable circumstances some organisms exhibit a particular
type of unrestricted growth. The graph shows the growth of a number
of bacteria starting with roughly 3000 at time $t = 0$ (hours).

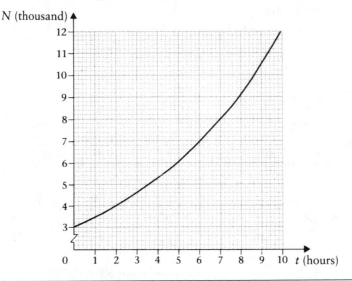

1D

Estimate, using the graph, the times when the numbers of bacteria
were these.
(a) 4000, 8000   (b) 5000, 10 000

Estimate when the numbers of bacteria were these.
(c) 24 000   (d) 1500

Describe the feature of the graph that enabled you to make these
estimates.

Growth is called **exponential** when there is a constant, called the
growth factor, such that during each unit time interval the
amount present is multiplied by this factor.

Example 1

The graph shows the growth of world
population from 1650 to 1950. Is the
growth exponential?

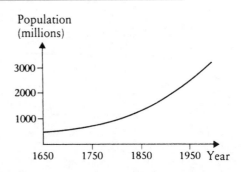

Solution

The populations in 1650, 1750, 1850 and 1950 were approximately 500 million, 700 million, 1300 million and 2500 million.

The growth factors over successive hundred-year intervals are:

Time interval	Growth factor
1650–1750	$\frac{700}{500} = 1.4$
1750–1850	$\frac{1300}{700} = 1.857$
1850–1950	$\frac{2500}{1300} = 1.923$

The growth factors for successive equal time intervals are not constant, so the growth is not exponential.

Exponential decay occurs when the growth factor is less than 1.

Example 2

A scientist was analysing the decay of a radioactive form of lead, lead-214.

The mass of lead-214 remaining in a particular sample of lead was as shown below.

Time (minutes)	0	1	2	3	4	5	6	7	8
Mass (kg)	3.127	3.047	2.969	2.894	2.820	2.748	2.678	2.609	2.542

Was the radioactive lead decaying exponentially?

Solution

In the first minute, the growth factor was $\frac{3.047}{3.127} = 0.974$.

As you can verify, the growth factors in succeeding minutes were all 0.974.

The lead decayed exponentially (the constant growth factor was less than 1).

Exercise A (answers p. 167)

1 A construction company publishes its pre-tax profit figures for the last ten years.

Profit before tax
(millions of pounds)

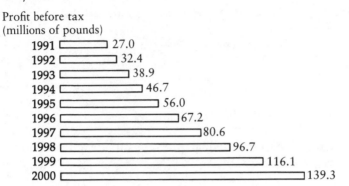

1991	27.0
1992	32.4
1993	38.9
1994	46.7
1995	56.0
1996	67.2
1997	80.6
1998	96.7
1999	116.1
2000	139.3

Was the growth of profits exponential?

2 £5000 is deposited in a fixed interest building society account. The amount in the account increases as shown below.

End of year	1	2	3	4	5
Amount	£5450	£5940.50	£6475.15	£7057.91	£7693.12

What is the interest rate? Is the growth exponential?

3 A girl's annual pocket money is £50 plus £10 for each year of her age. Does her pocket money increase exponentially with age?

4 The following table shows the population of Latin America over a period of 24 years.

Year	1950	1954	1962	1966	1974
Population (millions)	164	183	227	254	315

Is this exponential growth? Justify your answer.

5 A capacitor is an electrical component that can store charge.

(a) A capacitor is initially charged to 9 volts. It is discharged across a particular circuit, the voltage dropping by one volt each second.

(b) In another circuit, the voltage would have dropped by one quarter of its value each second.

Is either of the above an example of exponential decay? Find the growth factors, if appropriate.

B   Growth factors (answers p. 168)

In many fields of study it can be useful to find equations which closely model given data. For example, the population figures for England and Wales from 1841 to 1901 are as follows.

Year	1841	1851	1861	1871	1881	1891	1901
Population, P millions	15.9	17.9	20.1	22.7	26.0	29.0	32.5

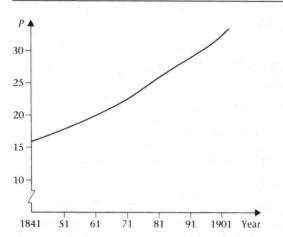

If you could fit an equation to such data, then you could make reasonable estimates for populations in years when a census was not taken, and you could project the figures beyond the years for which data are available. However, great care must be taken in relying on such projections because changes in conditions dramatically alter population trends.

The table gives the data in 10-yearly intervals. To find out whether it is suitable for modelling using a growth function, you can check to see if the 10-yearly growth factor is approximately constant.

Year	Population	Growth factor
1841	15.9	
1851	17.9	1.13
1861	20.1	1.12
1871	22.7	1.13
1881	26.0	1.15
1891	29.0	1.12
1901	32.5	1.12

The 10-yearly growth factor is roughly constant, so the data can be modelled using a growth function. To do this, it is necessary to find an estimate for the yearly growth factor.

In the sixty years from 1841 to 1901 the population grows by a factor

of $\dfrac{32.5}{15.9} = 2.044$. If the yearly growth factor is a, this means that

$$a^{60} = 2.044 \implies a = 2.044^{\frac{1}{60}} = 1.0120$$

Some properties of equations and graphs of growth functions are investigated in the following questions.

You have seen that $y = a^x$ may be used as a model for exponential growth. Here you will see how, by changing the function to Ka^x, you can model *any* exponential data.

1 (a) Investigate the graph of $K \times 2^x$ for various values of K. What is the significance of the factor K?

   (b) What is the significance of K if $y = K \times a^x$?

2 (a) If $y = a^t$, what is the **initial** value of y, i.e. The value of y when $t = 0$?

   (b) If $y = K \times a^t$ what is the initial value of y?

3 Investigate the graph of $K \times \left(\frac{1}{2}\right)^x$ for various values of K. What is the significance of the factor K?

4 Use the ideas developed in questions 1–3 to sketch these graphs.

   (a) $y = 5 \times 3^t$ (b) $y = 2 \times \left(\frac{1}{3}\right)^t$ (c) $y = \frac{1}{2} \times 5^t$ (d) $y = 2 \times \left(\frac{1}{5}\right)^t$

   Check your answers using a graph plotter.

5 The population P of Great Britain has been estimated at 1.5 million in 1066 and 6.1 million in 1700. Assume that an exponential growth model is appropriate and that, t years after 1066, $P = Ka^t$.

   (a) Write down the value of K.

   (b) Use the data for the population in 1700 to explain why

$$a = \left(\frac{6.1}{1.5}\right)^{\frac{1}{634}}$$

   Evaluate this to 5 decimal places.

   (c) Use this model to estimate the population of the UK in 1990.

   (d) Comment on the model.

> The general growth function has an equation of the form $y = Ka^x$, where K and a are constants. K is the value of y when x is zero and a is the growth factor.

Example 3

Model the population data for England and Wales given on page 101 with an equation for P in terms of t, the number of years after 1841.

Solution

Assuming the growth is exponential, $P = K \times a^t$. $K = 15.9$, the initial value and, since $32.5 = 15.9 \times a^{60}$, the annual growth factor can be estimated by

$$\left(\frac{32.5}{15.9}\right)^{\frac{1}{60}} \approx 1.012$$

The equation is then

$$P = 15.9 \times 1.012^t$$

A check on the suitability of this model can be made by comparing tabulated values of the original data and populations predicted by the equation.

t	0	10	20	30	40	50	60
P	15.9	17.9	20.1	22.7	26.0	29.0	32.5
15.9×1.012^t	15.9	17.9	20.2	22.7	25.6	28.9	32.5

Although there is some variation, this model gives results close to the true values.

The model predicts that the population in 1990 would be 15.9×1.012^{149}, that is, 94.0 million. This figure is much higher than the true value of about 49 million. Many factors help explain this, including the world wars, contraception and a different social structure (women working outside the home, and so on).

Exercise B (answers p. 168)

1   A colony of bacteria has a growth factor of 6 per hour. Initially there are 400 bacteria.

(a) After how many hours will there be 14 400 bacteria?

(b) When will there be 1 000 000 bacteria?

(c) Write down an expression for the number of bacteria t hours after the start.

2   The compound interest on a savings account is 8% per annum.

(a) What is the growth factor?

(b) Explain why the number, n, of years before an initial investment of £4000 grows to £5000 is given by $1.08^n = 1.25$.

(c) Find an approximate value for n.

3 A radioactive element, bismuth-210, was observed every few days, and the mass remaining was measured.

The following figures were obtained.

No. of days from start of experiment	0	2	3	6	7	10
Mass (kg)	10	7.57	6.57	4.34	3.77	2.48

(a) Estimate the growth factor.

(b) Write down an equation for M, the mass of bismuth remaining, in terms of t, the number of days from the start of the experiment.

(c) Check how well your equation models the data.

(d) How much will remain after 3 weeks?

(e) What is the half-life of bismuth-210 (i.e. after how many days does only half of the original amount remain), to the nearest whole day?

4 In an electric circuit, the voltage V across a capacitor drops from 15 volts to 6 volts in 12 seconds. Assuming that the process is one of exponential decay, find a formula for V in terms of t, the time in seconds from the start.

C **Logarithms** (answers p. 169)

The graph shows the growth of aquatic plants starting with an initial surface coverage of 1 m^2.

The times taken to reach 2 m^2 and 4 m^2 are 1 and 2 weeks respectively.

The growth factor is 2 per week.

$$\text{Area } (A) = 2^t$$

A is the surface area covered after t weeks.

The exponential equation expresses A as a function of t. Often though, you require the *inverse function*, t in terms of A. This inverse function is called the **logarithm of A to base 2**, written as $\log_2 A$.

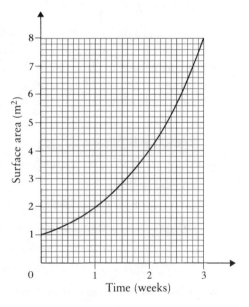

From the graph, the area is 8 m^2 after 3 weeks, because $8 = 2^3$.
Conversely, it takes 3 weeks before the area is 8 m^2, so $3 = \log_2 8$.

The function 2^x is a one-to-one mapping with domain $\{x \in \mathbb{R}\}$ and range $\{f(x) \in \mathbb{R} : f(x) > 0\}$.

Since $\log_2 x$ is the inverse function of 2^x, the graph of $\log_2 x$ is the reflection of the graph of 2^x in the line $y = x$. Since $\log_2 1 = 0$, the graph cuts the x-axis at $x = 1$.

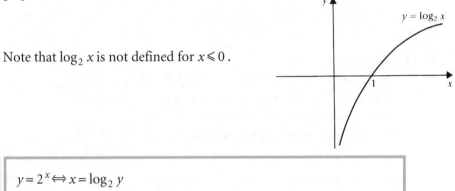

Note that $\log_2 x$ is not defined for $x \leqslant 0$.

$$y = 2^x \Longleftrightarrow x = \log_2 y$$

Example 4

Write down the value of $\log_2 32$.

Solution

Since $32 = 2^5$, 5 is the logarithm of 32 to base 2, i.e. $\log_2 32 = 5$.

1 Find these.

(a) $\log_2 64$ (b) $\log_2 \frac{1}{8}$ (c) $\log_2 2$ (d) $\log_2 \sqrt{2}$

Just as you can find the logarithm of a number to base 2, you can find logarithms to any positive base. The power to which a must be raised to equal y is called $\log_a y$. So,

$$y = a^x \Longleftrightarrow x = \log_a y$$

Example 5

Write down these values.

(a) $\log_5 25$ (b) $\log_{10} 1000$ (c) $\log_3 27$

Solution

(a) Since $5^2 = 25$, $\log_5 25 = 2$.

(b) $10^3 = 1000 \Longrightarrow \log_{10} 1000 = 3$

(c) $3^3 = 27 \Longrightarrow \log_3 27 = 3$

2   Find these values.

(a) $\log_3 9$ (b) $\log_5 125$ (c) $\log_5 \frac{1}{25}$ (d) $\log_7 1$ (e) $\log_6 \frac{1}{216}$
(f) $\log_3 {}^4\sqrt{3}$ (g) $\log_4 2$ (h) $\log_{11} 11$ (i) $\log_3 (-3)$

3   Find these.   (a) $\log_a 1$ (b) $\log_a a$ (c) $\log_a \frac{1}{a}$ (d) $\log_a a^2$

4   Use your calculator to find these values.

(a) $\log_{10} 10^{3.7}$ (b) $10^{\log_{10} 3.7}$

5   (a)   Write these down.
   (i) $\log_2 8$ (ii) $\log_2 16$ (iii) $\log_2 128$

(b) Since $8 \times 16 = 128$, you can write this as $2^a \times 2^b = 2^c$. What are a, b and c? How is c related to a and b?

(c) Use this to explain why $\log_2 8 + \log_2 16 = \log_2(8 \times 16)$.

6 $3^2 \times 3^3 = 3^5$

Explain how this verifies that $\log_3 9 + \log_3 27 = \log_3(9 \times 27)$.

7   (a)   Use your calculator to verify that $3 \approx 10^{0.4771}$, $5 \approx 10^{0.6990}$.

(b) What are these?   (i) $\log_{10} 3$ (ii) $\log_{10} 5$

(c) Use these results to find $\log_{10} 15$.

8   Use your calculator to verify that $\log_{10} 9 + \log_{10} 8 = \log_{10} 72$.

Questions 5–8 suggest that logs are related by the law

$$\log_a m + \log_a n = \log_a mn$$

If fact, it is possible to prove that this result is true for any positive base a by using the result

$$a^{\log_a x} = x$$

The proof is as follows.

$$a^{\log_a m + \log_a n} = a^{\log_a m} \times a^{\log_a n} \text{ (law of indices)}$$
$$= m \times n$$
$$= a^{\log_a (mn)}$$
$$\Rightarrow \log_a m + \log_a n = \log_a(mn)$$

Question 9 extends this result to logs of quotients.

9   In the law above, replace n by $\dfrac{1}{m}$. Hence show that

$$\log_a l - \log_a m = \log_a \frac{l}{m}$$

Verify that this holds by choosing two arbitrary numbers for l and m.

10 $\log_{10} 2 = 0.3010$ $\log_{10} 3 = 0.4771$

Use the properties of logs and the result that $\log_{10} 10 = 1$ to find these (in any order).

$\log_{10} \frac{1}{2}$, $\log_{10} \log_{10} 2.5$, $\log_{10} 4$, $\log_{10} 5$, $\log_{10} 6$, $\log_{10} 8$, $\log_{10} 9$

You have obtained the following results.

> The power to which a must be raised to equal y is called $\log_a y$, i.e.
>
> $$y = a^x \Longleftrightarrow x = \log_a y$$
>
> Logarithms have the following properties for any positive base a.
>
> $\log_a a = 1$
>
> $\log_a 1 = 0$
>
> $\log_a \left(\dfrac{1}{a}\right) = -1$
>
> $\log_a mn = \log_a m + \log_a n$
>
> $\log_a \left(\dfrac{m}{n}\right) = \log_a m - \log_a n$
>
> $\log_a a^x = x;\ a^{\log_a x} = x$

In pre-calculator days, tables of logarithms were used to help perform various calculations. Part of a table of logarithms to base 10 is given below. From the table, $\log_{10} 1.351 = 0.1306$ and so on.

	0	1	2	3	4	5	6	7	8	9	1	2	3	4	5	6	7	8	9
1.0	.0000	0043	0086	0128	0170	0212	0253	0294	0334	0374	4	8	12	17	21	25	29	33	37
1.1	.0414	0453	0492	0531	0569	0607	0645	0682	0719	0755	4	8	11	15	19	23	27	30	34
1.2	.0792	0828	0864	0899	0934	0969	1004	1038	1072	1106	3	7	10	14	17	21	24	28	31
1.3	.1139	1173	1206	1239	1271	1303	1335	1367	1399	1430	3	6	10	13	16	19	23	26	29
1.4	.1461	1492	1523	1553	1584	1614	1644	1673	1703	1732	3	6	9	12	15	18	21	24	27
1.5	.1761	1790	1818	1847	1875	1903	1931	1959		2014	3	6	8	11	14	17	20	22	25
1.6	.2041	2068	2095	2122	2148	2175	2201				3	5	8	11			18	21	24

11D How can you use the table of logarithms shown above to calculate $1.17 \div 1.091$?

In 1615, the Scottish mathematician John Napier discussed the idea of using logarithms with the Oxford professor Henry Briggs. Two years later, Briggs published his first table of logarithms (to 14 decimal places!) and after much further work published his *Arithmetica Logarithmica* in 1624.

Nowadays logarithms can be found using a calculator but originally their calculation involved considerable hard work and ingenuity. 'Log' is usually taken to mean $\log_{10}$, and you will find that the $\boxed{\log}$ key on calculators evaluates logarithms to the base 10.

Exercise C (answers p. 169)

1 You have seen that
$$2^3 = 8 \Rightarrow \log_2 8 = 3 \,.$$
From these equations with indices, form equations using logarithms.

(a) $3^2 = 9$ (b) $4^{-3} = \frac{1}{64}$ (c) $(0.5)^{-2} = 4$

(d) $(\frac{1}{8})^{-\frac{1}{3}} = 2$ (e) $27^{\frac{2}{3}} = 9$

2 Write down the values of these.

(a) $\log_2(\frac{1}{4})$ (b) $\log_5 125$ (c) $\log_7(\frac{1}{7})$ (d) $\log_8(\frac{1}{4})$

3 Simplify these.

(a) $\log_3 9 + \log_3 27 - \log_3 81$ (b) $\log_5 15 - \log_5 3$ (c) $2\log_7 \sqrt{7}$

4 Sketch, on the same axes, $y = \log_{10} x$, $y = \log_{10} 2x$ and $y = \log_{10} 3x$.
How are the graphs related? Use the laws of logs to explain this
relationship.

5 (a) Use the log tables given earlier to calculate 1.05×1.267.

(b) Use the properties of logs to write down $\log_{10} 10.5$ and $\log_{10} 1267$.
Hence use log tables to find 10.5×1267.

6 The notation 4! means $4 \times 3 \times 2 \times 1$ and is read as '4 factorial'. Given
that $\log_5 4! = 1.9746$, write down $\log_5 5!$.

7 A colony of bacteria doubles every hour. Explain why the time t hours
for the colony to increase in size 1000-fold is given by $2^t = 1000$.
Express t as a logarithm to base 2 and explain why $9 < t < 10$. Use a
numerical method to find t to two decimal places.

D **Equations of the form $a^x = b$** (answers p. 170)

In answering the problem in Exercise C about a colony of bacteria you
used a numerical method to solve the equation
$$2^t = 1000 \,.$$
Problems concerning growth often lead to such equations, in which
the unknown occurs as an index.

Example 6

Suppose that a radioactive isotope decays by 10% each year.

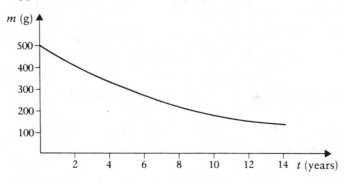

(a) Initially there is 500 g of the isotope. Find an expression for the amount t years later.

(b) The half-life of the isotope is the time taken for the amount present to decrease by 50%. Use the graph to estimate this half-life.

(c) What equation must be solved to find the half-life more precisely?

(d) Use a decimal search to solve the equation in (c).

Solution

(a) If 10% of the isotope decays each year then 90% will remain, so the growth factor must be 0.9. After t years, 500×0.9^t g will remain.

(b) The half-life will be the time taken for the amount to drop to 250 grams. From the graph, this is approximately 6.3 years.

(c) To find the half-life more precisely, the equation

$$500 \times 0.9^t = 250$$

must be solved. This simplifies to

$$0.9^t = 0.5$$

(d)

t	6	7	6.5	6.6	6.58
0.9^t	0.531	0.478	0.504	0.499	0.499 94

Equations of the form

$$a^x = b$$

can be solved by a numerical method. There is, however, a more direct way of solving such equations, which is explored in the following questions.

1 (a) Use your calculator to find the relationship between these.

   (i) $\log_{10} 49$ and $\log_{10} 7$ (ii) $\log_{10} 64$ and $\log_{10} 2$

   (iii) $\log_{10} 125$ and $\log_{10} 5$

   (b) What is the relationship between $\log_{10} m^p$ and $\log_{10} m$?

2 (a) Use the result $\log_a mn = \log_a m + \log_a n$ to explain why $\log_a m^2 = 2 \log_a m$.

   (b) Generalise this method to explain the law that you found in question 1(b).

3D (a) What is the relationship between $\log 2^x$ and $\log 2$?

   (b) Solve the equation

   $$2^x = 7$$

   by first taking logs to base 10 of both sides and then using the relationship you stated for (a).

4 £1000 is invested in an account which earns 1% interest per month, all interest being reinvested.

   (a) Explain why the number m of months taken for the total investment to reach £2000 is given by the equation

   $$1.01^m = 2.$$

   (b) Use logs to find m.

5 The half-life, t days, of bismuth-210 is given approximately by the equation

   $$10 \times (0.87)^t = 5.$$

   Use logs to find its half-life in days, correct to 2 significant figures.

   If $a > 0$,

   $$\log a^p = p \log a$$

Example 7

Find the half-life of the radioactive isotope considered in Example 6.

Solution

$$500 \times 0.9^t = 250$$

$\Rightarrow \qquad 0.9^t = 0.5 \qquad$ (dividing both sides by 500)

$\Rightarrow \quad \log 0.9^t = \log 0.5 \qquad$ (taking logs of both sides)

$\Rightarrow \quad t \log 0.9 = \log 0.5 \qquad$ (using the property of logs above)

$\Rightarrow \qquad\qquad t = \dfrac{\log 0.5}{\log 0.9} \approx 6.58$

The half-life is approximately 6.58 years.

Exercise D (answers p. 171)

1 Solve these equations for x.

  (a) $2^x = 32$ (b) $9^x = 243$ (c) $8^x = 256$

  (d) $3^x = 10.05$ (e) $5^x = 9.2$ (f) $2.073^x = 7.218$

2 Explain how you could have obtained the answers to 1(a), 1(b) and 1(c) without using a calculator.

3 A colony of bacteria has a growth factor of 3.7 per hour and initially there are 250 bacteria.

  (a) Write down an expression for the number of bacteria after t hours.

  (b) Find the time (to the nearest minute) after which there are 10 000 bacteria.

4 A capacitor is discharging with a growth factor of 0.9 per second. After how long will there be $\frac{1}{5}$ of the original charge? (Give your answer in seconds to 2 d.p.)

5 The number, n, of years needed for an investment of £4000 to grow to £5000 at 8% per annum compound interest is given by $1.08^n = 1.25$. Find n using logarithms.

6 In 1980, the population of Africa was 470 million and growing at a rate of 2.9% per annum. In what year will its population reach one thousand million according to this model?

7 In 1980, the population of China was 995 million and growing at a rate of 1.4% per annum. After how many years will the population of China equal that of Africa?

8E Solve these equations for x.

  (a) $3^{x-1} = 5$ (b) $7^{2x+1} = 5$

  (c) $5(3^x) + 1 = 3$ (d) $2^{2x} + 3(2^x) - 10 = 0$

E Using logarithms in experimental work (answers p. 171)

An important practical use of logarithms is in experimental work, and you may have the opportunity in your other studies to employ the following procedure.

Suppose that you obtained the following results while investigating the relationship between the time of swing of a pendulum and its length.

Length of pendulum, l(m)	0.6	1.0	1.4	1.8	2.2
Average time of swing, t(s)	1.54	2.03	2.39	2.67	2.97

It would be natural to plot the graph of t against l.

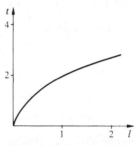

The shape of the graph does not make it easy to predict what the relationship is, although it clearly indicates a definite relationship which it would be convenient to represent algebraically.

If either the shape of the graph or other considerations lead you to suspect that the relationship is that t is proportional to some power of l, then you can test this with the help of logarithms.

$$t = kl^n$$
$$\log t = \log(kl^n)$$
$$\log t = n \log l + \log k$$

Comparing this with the equation of the straight line, $y = mx + c$, indicates that, if the power relationship is correct, then the graph of **log t** (the 'y' variable) against **log l** (the 'x' variable), should be a straight line having gradient n and intercept of $\log k$ on the log t-axis.

You can now take logs and tabulate the values (here we have used logs to base 10).

$\log_{10} l$	−0.222	0.000	0.146	0.255	0.342
$\log_{10} t$	0.187	0.307	0.378	0.426	0.473

The graph is plotted here. You can read off the values for n and log k.

$$\log_{10} k \approx 0.30$$
$$\Rightarrow \quad k = 10^{0.30} = 2.0 \text{ (to 2 s.f.)}$$
$$n = 0.50$$

Hence the relationship is

$$t = 2.0 l^{0.5}$$
$$\text{or} \quad t = 2\sqrt{l}$$

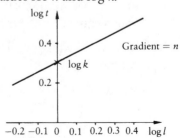

A very similar method is employed if the relationship is thought to be a power function. If

$$y = kb^x$$

then taking logs of both sides of this equation gives

$$\log y = \log(kb^x)$$
$$= \log(b^x) + \log k$$
$$\log y = x \log b + \log k$$

A graph of log y against x would be a straight line of gradient log b and intercept log k.

Exercise E (answers p. 171)

1 In an experiment to determine how the sag of a beam varies with the distance between its supports the following results were obtained

d (cm)	500	540	580	620	660	700
z (cm)	1.1	1.3	1.7	2.0	2.4	2.8

where d is the distance between the supports and z is the sag.

By drawing the graph of log z against log d, determine the power of d to which z is proportional.

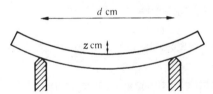

2 The charge on a capacitor, t milliseconds after a switch is closed, is believed to decay exponentially. The results of a set of measurements are as follows.

Time, t	2	3	4	5	6
Charge, Q	7.6	2.8	1.0	0.4	0.1

Find the relationship between Q and t, assuming it is of the form $Q = kb^t$, by taking logs and plotting an appropriate straight line graph.

3 The period of oscillation, P seconds, for bars of uniform material is thought to be proportional to some power of their length, L metres $(P = kL^n)$. One set of measurements is given in the table below.

L	2	3	4	5	6
P	4.5	5.5	6.4	7.2	8.7

However, one result has been incorrectly copied. Plot an appropriate straight line graph. Give the corresponding formula connecting P and L and state what you think the incorrect result might have been.

4 The rate of decay of a radioactive substance is usually measured in terms of its half-life, the time taken for its mass to halve.

Suppose that the formula for its mass at time t is $m = m_0 e^{-kt}$ where m_0 is the initial mass, e = 2.718 and k is a constant with a value particular to these circumstances.

If $m = 0.9m_0$ when $t = 2$, show that $k = 0.0527$; hence find the value of t when $m = 0.5m_0$.

F Differentiating growth functions (answers p. 171)

You have seen how functions given by equations of the form $y = Ka^x$ can be used to model growth. In this section we shall look in detail at *rates* of growth for these functions and see how all functions of this kind are very closely related.

In the following questions you will investigate the gradient function for $y = a^x$.

You will need a graph plotter which can plot the gradient graph of a function, so that you can check your results.

1 (a) Sketch the graphs of $y = 2^x$ and $\dfrac{dy}{dx}$, the gradient function.

(b) Suggest an equation for the function $\dfrac{dy}{dx}$, and check your answer using a graph plotter.

2 Repeat question 1 for each of the following functions.

(a) $y = 3^x$ (b) $y = 1.5^x$ (c) $y = 10^x$

3 Given that $y = a^x$ suggest a value for a for which $\dfrac{dy}{dx} = a^x$. Check your answer by sketching appropriate graphs.

4 Suggest an appropriate gradient function for ke^x, where e is the value for a that you suggested in question 3.

The gradient function for $y = 2^x$ can be found by 'zooming-in' at any point $P(x, y)$ on the graph of $y = 2^x$ until the curve looks straight.

The gradient of the graph at P is approximately equal to the gradient of PQ, where Q is a nearby point on the graph.

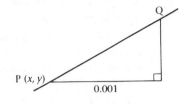

5 (a) Explain why the y-coordinate of Q is $2^{0.001} 2^x$.

(b) Explain why the gradient PQ is $\dfrac{2^{0.001} 2^x - 2^x}{0.001}$.

(c) Show how the expression in (b) can be simplified to 0.693×2^x.

(d) You have seen that $y = 2^x \Rightarrow \dfrac{dy}{dx} \approx 0.693 \times 2^x$. How could you increase the accuracy of this result?

6 Adapt the method of question 5 to find $\dfrac{dy}{dx}$ when $y = 5^x$.

The gradient of an exponential function at any point is proportional to its value at that point.

$$y = 2^x \Rightarrow \frac{dy}{dx} = 0.69 \times 2^x$$

$$y = 3^x \Rightarrow \frac{dy}{dx} = 1.10 \times 3^x$$

$$y = 10^x \Rightarrow \frac{dy}{dx} = 2.30 \times 10^x$$

Generally, $y = a^x \Rightarrow \dfrac{dy}{dx} = k \times a^x$, where k is a constant.

The value of a for which $k = 1$ is denoted by the letter e. This gives the important results

$$y = e^x \Rightarrow \frac{dy}{dx} = e^x$$

$$\int e^x \, dx = e^x + c$$

$e = 2.718\ 281\ 828\ 4$ to ten decimal places.

Like π, e is an irrational number. The Swiss mathematician Leonhard Euler (1707–1783) first used the letter e to represent this number. Euler introduced several other mathematical notations, including that for functions, f(x). He was also the first to use the summation sign Σ, the letter π for the ratio of circumference to diameter of a circle and i for $\sqrt{-1}$ (both i and j are in common use today). He continued to work after becoming totally blind in 1768.

The shapes of the graphs of $y = e^x$ and $y = e^{-x}$ are typical of exponential growth and decay respectively. Some calculators and textbooks express e^x as exp x. This notation is also used in some computer programs.

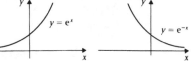

Notice that $\dfrac{dy}{dx} > 0$ for all x for the exponential function $y = e^x$. Such a function is called an **increasing function** of x.

If $f'(x) > 0$ for all x, then $f(x)$ is an increasing function of x.

$f'(x) < 0$ for all $x \Longrightarrow f(x)$ is a decreasing function of x.

Clearly e^x is an increasing function of x, while e^{-x} is a decreasing function.

Exercise F (answers p. 172)

1 Use your calculator to find these.

(a) e^3 (b) exp(5.1)   (c) e^{-2} (d) $\dfrac{5}{e^3}$ (e) exp(0.5)

2 Make tables of values for $-4 \leqslant x \leqslant 4$ and draw the graphs of these functions.

(a) $y = e^{2x}$ (b) $y = e^{-x}$

3 Draw the graph of

$$y = 5(1 - e^{-x})$$

for $0 \leqslant x \leqslant 5$. Check the shape using a graph plotter.

4 (a) When certain drugs are injected into the body, the amount remaining in the bloodstream decays exponentially. The amount of a particular drug in the bloodstream is modelled by the equation

$$y = 5e^{-0.2t}$$

where t is the time in hours after the dose is administered, and y is the amount remaining, in milligrams.

   (i) What is the initial value of y?

   (ii) What is the value of y when $t = 10$?

   (iii) Sketch the graph of y against t.

 (b) The amount of a second drug is modelled by the equation $y = 5e^{-0.5t}$. Does it decay more or less rapidly than the first drug?

5 The growth of a colony of bacteria is modelled by the equation $y = 4e^t$, where t is measured in hours and y is the population.

By differentiating, show that $\dfrac{dy}{dt} = y$. What does this tell you about the rate of growth of the bacterial colony?

How rapidly is the colony growing at a time when it contains 500 bacteria?

G Differentiating e^{ax} (answers p. 173)

One of the great benefits of introducing e as a base for the growth function is that it can replace all the other bases. This simplifies subsequent work, particularly in calculus.

Example 8

(a) Find alternative expressions of the form 2^{at} for these.
   (i) 8^t (ii) 5^t

(b) Is it *always* possible to express b^t in the form 2^{at}?

Solution

(a) (i) $8^t = (2^3)^t = 2^{3t}$

   (ii) $5^t = 2^{at} \Longrightarrow 5 = 2^a$, i.e. $a = \dfrac{\log 5}{\log 2} = 2.32$. Therefore $5^t = 2^{2.32t}$.

(b) When $b > 0$, it is clear that you can always write b^t in the form 2^{at}, since you can always solve the equation $b = 2^a$. As has been noted already, when $b < 0$ the meaning of b^t is not defined for some values of t (for example, $t = \frac{1}{2}$).

This idea of changing the base of an exponential function is explored below.

1 (a) Use a graph plotter to verify that the graphs of 9^x and 3^{2x} coincide.

   (b) Find the value of a so that the following pairs of graphs coincide.

   (i) 5^x and 3^{ax} (ii) 7^x and 3^{ax} (iii) 2^x and 3^{ax}

It appears that, for any positive value of b, you could replace b^x by 3^{ax}. In other words, only one base is needed for all exponential functions. The base used in practice is not 3 but e.

2 (a) Use a graph plotter to sketch the family of curves $y = e^{ax}$

   (i)   for a few positive values of a, of your own choice

   (ii) for a few negative values of a.

   What shape is the graph if $a = 0$?

   (b) If $a > b > 0$, describe the relationship of the graph of e^{ax} to that of e^{bx}. For what values of x is $e^{ax} > e^{bx}$?

3 Using the same method as in question 1, find the value of a so that the following pairs of graphs coincide.

   (a) 5^x and e^{ax} (b) 8^x and e^{ax} (c) 2^x and e^{ax}

4 (a) You know from Section F that, if $y = 2^x$, $\dfrac{dy}{dx} \approx 0.69 \times 2^x$ and, from question 3, that $2^x \approx e^{0.69x}$. Explain how these results can be combined to show that

$$\frac{d}{dx}(e^{0.69x}) = 0.69e^{0.69x} \text{ (the derivative of } e^{0.69x} = 0.69e^{0.69x})$$

   (b) Suggest a possible derivative for e^{5x}.

The previous question suggests that $\dfrac{d}{dx}(e^{ax}) = ae^{ax}$. In the next question you investigate how this result arises.

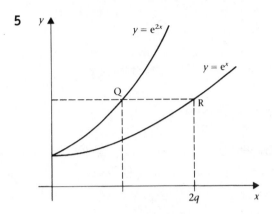

5

(a) In the diagram, Q and R have the same y-coordinate. What is it?

(b) What is the x-coordinate of Q?

(c) The graph of $y = e^{2x}$ can be obtained from the graph of $y = e^x$ by squashing by a factor of 2 in the x-direction. What effect does this have on the gradient of the graph?

(d) If the gradient at R is g, what is the gradient at Q?

(e) Write down, in terms of q, the gradient of $y = e^x$ at the point R. Hence write down the gradient of $y = e^{2x}$ at the point Q.

(f) Complete this.

$$\frac{d}{dx}(e^{2x}) = \cdots \times e^{2x}$$

You have seen that, if $b > 0$, you can express b^x in the form e^{ax} and that

$$\frac{d}{dx}(e^{ax}) = ae^{ax}$$

6D | What is $\displaystyle\int e^{ax}\,dx$?

Example 9

If $y = 5\left(\dfrac{e^{2x} + 1}{e^{2x}}\right)$, show that y is a decreasing function of x.

Solution

$$y = 5\left(\frac{e^{2x} + 1}{e^{2x}}\right) = 5 + 5e^{-2x}$$

$$\frac{dy}{dx} = 5(-2)e^{-2x} = -10e^{-2x}$$

Since $e^{-2x} > 0$ for all x, $\dfrac{dy}{dx} = -10e^{-2x} < 0$ for all x, so y is a decreasing function of x.

Exercise G (answers p. 173)

1 Differentiate these.

(a) e^{4x}　　(b) e^{-2x}　　(c) $(e^x)^5$　　(d) $\dfrac{1}{e^{3x}}$

(e) $5e^{4x}$　　(f) $e^x + \dfrac{1}{e^x}$　　(g) $\sqrt{e^x}$　　(h) $\dfrac{5}{e^{9x}}$

2 Integrate the functions of x in question 1.

3 Sketch these graphs.

(a) $y = e^{-4x}$　　(b) $y = 3(1 - e^{-2x})$　　(c) $y = e^x + \dfrac{1}{e^x}$

4 When a drug such as penicillin is prescribed, it is usual to take it 3 or 4 times a day. One or two days may elapse before the drug starts to take effect. A simple model of this process is known as the 'Rustogi' drug model.

Suppose that for a certain drug, the amount in milligrams in the bloodstream t hours after taking a dose of size A mg is given by

$$x = Ae^{-\frac{1}{8}t}$$

and that a dose of 10 mg is administered at 8-hourly intervals. On graph paper, using a scale of 1 cm to 2 hours on the t-axis and 1 cm to 2 mg on the x-axis, plot the drug level in the body over the first 32 hours as follows.

(a) For the first 8 hours calculate the drug level for $t = 0, 2, 4, 6, 8$ and plot these values.

(b) Add the next dose of 10 mg and plot this point, also at $t = 8$.

(c) This gives the 'effective dose' at this time, i.e. the new value for A. Recalculate the drug level for the next 8-hour period, again taking $t = 0, 2, 4, 6, 8$.

(d) Repeat steps (b) and (c) to show how the drug level varies in the body for the remainder of the period.

What value does the maximum drug level in the body approach?

5 In hospitals, when it is necessary for a patient to respond rapidly to treatment, a doctor will often give a 'booster' dose, equivalent to 1.6 times the standard dose. Repeat question 4, but with an initial dose of 16 mg and subsequent doses of 10 mg. (It should only be necessary to consider the first 8 hours.)

Note: this method is not used for drugs available on prescription to the general public; if subsequent doses of 16 mg were taken in error the drug level would rise to $1.6 \times 16 = 25.6$ mg, with potentially dangerous consequences.

H Natural logarithms (answers p. 174)

You saw in Section C that the power of 2 that was equal to y was called $\log_2 y$, i.e.

$$\text{if } 2^x = y, \text{ then } x = \log_2 y.$$

You also saw how this idea can be extended to other bases, so that, for example, if $10^x = y$ then $x = \log_{10} y$.

Since e was chosen as the base for exponential functions in order to simplify results in calculus, it is useful to consider e as a base for logarithms. Logarithms to base e are called **natural logarithms** and $\log_e x$ may be written as $\ln x$ (n for 'natural'). Some older texts simply use $\log x$ for $\ln x$.

As with any other base, $\ln x$ is defined so that, if $y = \ln x$, then $x = e^y$. $\ln x$ and e^x are therefore inverse functions.

Since $\ln x$ and e^x are inverse functions, the application of one followed by the other restores the original value.

At this stage you may find it useful to recall the laws of logarithms, as applied to logarithms with base e.

$$\ln e = 1 \qquad \ln 1 = 0$$

$$\ln(ab) = \ln a + \ln b \qquad \ln\left(\frac{a}{b}\right) = \ln a - \ln b$$

$$\ln(a^n) = n \ln a$$

Example 10

Express these in terms of $\ln x$.   (a) $\ln 4x^5$ (b) $\ln\left(\frac{1}{\sqrt{x}}\right)$

Solution

(a) $\ln 4x^5 = \ln 4 + \ln x^5 = \ln 4 + 5 \ln x$

(b) $\ln\left(\frac{1}{\sqrt{x}}\right) = \ln 1 - \ln\sqrt{x} = 0 - \ln x^{\frac{1}{2}} = -\frac{1}{2}\ln x$

    or

$\ln\left(\frac{1}{\sqrt{x}}\right) = \ln(x^{-\frac{1}{2}}) = -\frac{1}{2}\ln x$

Natural logarithms are sometimes called Napierian logarithms, after John Napier. However, this is a misnomer as they were not developed by Napier.

1 (a) $\ln y \,(= \log_e y)$ is the power of e that equals y, that is $y = e^x \Leftrightarrow x = \ln y$. Use this result to find these.

   (i) $\ln 1$ (ii) $\ln e$ (iii) $\ln e^2$

   (iv) $\ln \dfrac{1}{e}$ (v) $\ln \dfrac{1}{e^5}$ (vi) $\ln(-1)$

   (b) Use your results to sketch the graph of $\ln x$.

Derivative of ln x

The graphs of e^x and of $\ln x$ are sketched below. Since they are inverse functions, the graph of $\ln x$ is a reflection of that of e^x in the line $y = x$. You can use this idea to find the derivative of $\ln x$.

Q is the reflection of $P(a, b)$ in the line $y = x$.

The relationship between the two graphs can be used to find the gradient of $y = \ln x$ at Q.

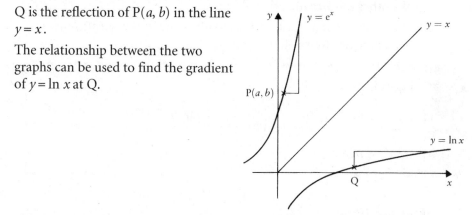

2D (a) For the graph above, express b in terms of a.

   (b) Write down the coordinates of Q.

   (c) Use the fact that the triangle at Q is a reflection of the triangle at P to explain why the gradient of the curve at Q is

$$\frac{1}{\text{gradient of } y = e^x \text{ at P}}.$$

   (d) Since P lies on the curve $y = e^x$, you know that the gradient at $P(a, b)$ is e^a. What is the gradient of $y = \ln x$ at Q?

   (e) Explain why $\dfrac{d}{dx} (\ln x) = \dfrac{1}{x}$.

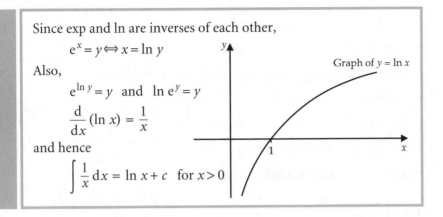

Since exp and ln are inverses of each other,

$$e^x = y \Leftrightarrow x = \ln y$$

Also,

$$e^{\ln y} = y \quad \text{and} \quad \ln e^y = y$$

$$\frac{d}{dx}(\ln x) = \frac{1}{x}$$

and hence

$$\int \frac{1}{x}\, dx = \ln x + c \quad \text{for } x > 0$$

Graph of $y = \ln x$

Exercise H (answers p. 174)

1 Use your calculator to evaluate these.

(a) $\ln 3.5$ (b) $\ln 0.35$ (c) $\ln 7$

2 Use the laws of logarithms to prove these.

(a) $\ln 3 + \ln 4 = \ln 12$ (b) $\ln 10 - \ln 2 = \ln 5$

(c) $3 \ln 5 = \ln 125$

3 Use the laws of logarithms to express the following in terms of $\ln x$.

(a) $\ln x^3$ (b) $\ln 4x$ (c) $\ln \frac{1}{3} x$

4 Find these.   (a) $\dfrac{d}{dx}(4 \ln x)$ (b) $\dfrac{d}{dx}(\ln x^3)$ (c) $\dfrac{d}{dx}(\ln 4x)$

5 A cup of coffee, initially at boiling point, cools according to Newton's law of cooling, so that after t minutes its temperature, $T\,°C$, is given by

$$T = 15 + 85e^{-t/8}$$

Sketch the graph of T against t. How long does the cup take to cool to $40\,°C$?

6 In the process of carbon dating, the level of the isotope carbon-14 (^{14}C) is measured. When a plant or animal is alive the amount of ^{14}C in the body remains at a constant level, but when it dies the amount decays at a constant rate according to the law $m = m_0 e^{-Kt}$, where m_0 is the initial mass and m the mass after t years.

(a) If the half-life of ^{14}C is 5570 years, find the decay constant K.

(b) A piece of oak from an old building contains $\frac{9}{10}$ of the level of ^{14}C that is contained in living oak. How old is the building?

After working through this chapter you should

1 recognise data which exhibits exponential growth

2 understand the relationship between logarithms and indices

3 be able to draw the graph of a logarithmic function

4 be able to use the laws of indices and logarithms

5 be able to model data using the equation $y = Ka^x$

6 be able to solve equations of the form $a^x = b$

7 be able to use the logarithmic function when investigating experimental data

8 understand the reason for the choice of e as base for exponential and logarithmic functions

9 be able to sketch graphs of exponential growth and decay and of logarithmic functions

10 be able to differentiate e^{ax} and $\ln ax$, and to integrate e^{ax} and $\dfrac{1}{x}$

11 appreciate that exp and ln are inverse functions

12 be able to solve problems involving e^x and $\ln x$ by using appropriate algebraic manipulation

13 be able to show whether a function is increasing or decreasing by considering its derivative.

6 Radians and trigonometry

A Rates of change and radians (answers p. 175)

The function graphed here was used in Chapter 4 to model the height of the tide, h metres, at a harbour entrance t hours after midnight.

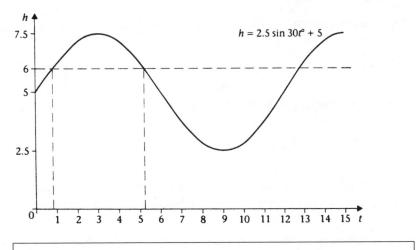

$h = 2.5 \sin 30t° + 5$

1D
(a) At what times does the tide rise most rapidly?

(b) At what times does the tide fall most rapidly?

(c) When is the rate of change zero?

Consider the graph of $y = \sin \theta°$.

The graph of its gradient, $\dfrac{dy}{d\theta}$, is like this.

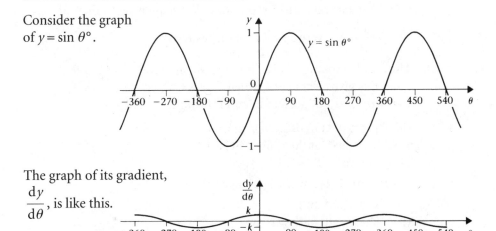

$y = \sin \theta°$

You should be able to sketch this graph from the graph of $\sin \theta°$ by noting the points on $\sin \theta°$ where the gradient is zero ($-270°$, $-90°$, $90°$, ...), where it is at its greatest value (at $-360°$, $0°$, $360°$, ...) and at its least value ($-180°$, $180°$, ...). The value of k is the gradient of the graph $y = \sin \theta°$ at the origin.

Zooming in to the origin of the graph of $y = \sin \theta°$
and using the principle of local straightness, the
gradient of $y = \sin \theta°$ at the origin is

$$\frac{dy}{d\theta} \approx \frac{\sin \theta°}{\theta}$$

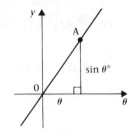

Observe that

- the gradient appears to be a cosine curve, with amplitude k. It has
  equation
  $$\frac{dy}{d\theta} = k \cos \theta°$$

- k is the gradient of $y = \sin \theta°$ at 0. Thus, from the diagram and
  argument above
  $$k \approx \frac{\sin \theta°}{\theta} \text{ for small } \theta$$

- you can obtain a sequence of values which approaches k by taking
  smaller and smaller values of θ. This is explored further below.

For these questions you will need a graph plotter which can plot the
gradient graph of a function.

2 (a) (i) Calculate the values of $\dfrac{\sin \theta°}{\theta}$ for $\theta = 10, 5, 2, 1$ and 0.1 .

   (ii) To what value (to 5 d.p.) does your sequence of values of
         $\dfrac{\sin \theta°}{\theta}$ converge, as θ approaches zero?

   (b) Use a graph plotter to obtain the gradient graph of $y = \sin \theta°$.
        Does this give a value of k which agrees with your solution to
        part (a)? You will need to be careful with the vertical scale.

3 Consider a sector AOB of a circle of unit
   radius with angle $\theta°$ at the centre. BC is the
   perpendicular from B to OA.

   (a) For $\theta = 10, 5, 2, 1$ and 0.1 calculate these.
        (i)   The length of BC
        (ii) The length of the arc BA
   (b) What do you notice about the results?

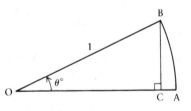

4 Express the length BC and the length of arc BA as functions of θ.

From the previous question it is evident that these two lengths are approximately equal for small values of θ. Use this fact to explain why

$$\frac{\sin \theta°}{\theta} \approx \frac{\pi}{180}$$

5 Calculate the value of $\dfrac{\pi}{180}$ and compare it with the answer to question 2(a)(ii).

6 What is the gradient of $y = \sin \theta°$ at the origin?

7 Suggest a suitable expression for $\dfrac{dy}{d\theta}$, if $y = \sin \theta°$.

The questions above demonstrate the result

$$\frac{d}{d\theta}(\sin \theta°) = \frac{\pi}{180} \cos \theta°$$

At $(0, 0)$, gradient $= \dfrac{\pi}{180}$

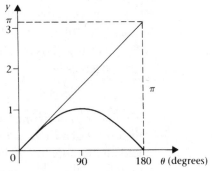

If angles were measured in units other than degrees, with π of these new units equivalent to 180°, then the diagram above would look like this:

At $(0, 0)$, gradient $= \dfrac{\pi}{\pi} = 1$

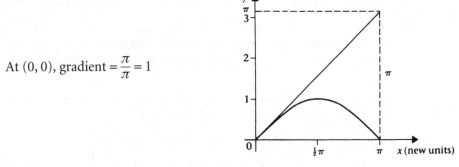

The new units would then give the simple result

$$y = \sin x \implies \frac{dy}{dx} = \cos x$$

Scientific calculators provide the option of using these new units, which are called **radians** and are defined by the relationship

$$\pi \text{ radians} = 180°$$

8D (a) Sketch the gradient graph for $y = \cos x°$.

(b) What do you think is the derivative of these?

(i) $\cos x$ (x in radians)   (ii) $\cos x°$

Radian measure

9D Consider a circle of radius r and arc AB of length r.

(a) How many arcs AB of length r can be placed around the circumference of the circle?

(b) What will be the size, in degrees, of the angle θ?

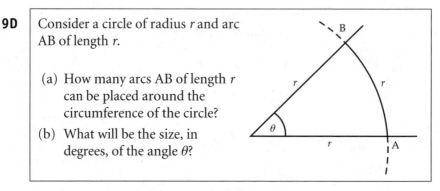

A radian can be defined as the angle subtended by an arc of length r at the centre of a circle radius r. It is the angle θ in the diagram above. Radian measure for angles can be directly related to circles and is therefore called circular measure. The symbol used to indicate a radian is ^{c} (the 'c' suggests **circular measure**).

$$1^c \text{ or } 1 \text{ radian} = \frac{180°}{\pi} \approx 57.3° \quad \text{and} \quad \pi^c \text{ or } \pi \text{ radians} = 180°$$

When an angle is given in degrees the '°' symbol is shown. When an angle is in radians the 'c' is usually omitted, thus sin 2 means the sine of 2 radians.

Calculators will accept either degrees or radians as input for circular functions, depending on the 'mode' to which they are set.

10 Use your calculator in appropriate mode to find these.

(a) $\sin 1^c$ (b) $\sin 1°$ (c) $\cos -5°$ (d) $\cos -5^c$

(e) $\tan \frac{1}{4}\pi^c$ (f) $\tan \frac{1}{4}\pi°$

It is often very convenient to express angles in radians as multiples of π.

For example, $\sin 270°$ can be written as $\sin \dfrac{3\pi}{2}$.

11 (a) Find these. (i) $\sin 30°$ (ii) $\sin \frac{1}{6}\pi^c$
What do you notice?

(b) You know π radians are equal to 180°. This can be used to establish a number of other reference points between the two scales. Copy and complete the following table.

Radians	$\frac{1}{2}\pi$			$\frac{1}{6}\pi$	$\frac{3}{2}\pi$	
Degrees	180	60	45			360

(c) What formula will convert $\theta°$ to radians?

(d) What formula will convert θ^c to degrees?

12 It is very easy to leave your calculator in the wrong mode! Suppose you are asked to find $\sin \frac{1}{3}\pi$ and you have your machine in degree mode.

(a) What is $\frac{1}{3}\pi$ to 3 decimal places?

(b) What is $\sin \frac{1}{3}\pi$ (taking $\frac{1}{3}\pi$ in radians)?

(c) What answer does your calculator give if left in degree mode?

13 Suppose you try to evaluate $\sin 60°$, but leave your calculator in radian mode. What should you get in degree mode? What in fact do you get?

14 Working in radians, plot on graph paper the graph of $y = \sin x$ for values of x from 0 to 7, increasing in steps of 0.5. In addition, mark on the x-axis the numbers $\frac{1}{4}\pi$, $\frac{1}{2}\pi$, $\frac{3}{4}\pi$, π, $\frac{3}{2}\pi$, 2π.

Exercise A (answers p. 176)

1 Express these angles, measured in degrees, in radians.

(a) 90° (b) 360° (c) 45° (d) 120°

(c) 60° (f) 720° (g) −30° (h) 135°

2 Express these angles, measured in radians, in degrees.

(a) $\frac{1}{4}\pi$ (b) 3π (c) $-\pi$ (d) $\frac{3}{2}\pi$

(e) -2π (f) $\dfrac{\pi}{6}$ (g) $\dfrac{5\pi}{6}$ (h) $-\dfrac{3\pi}{4}$

B   Area and arc length (answers p. 176)

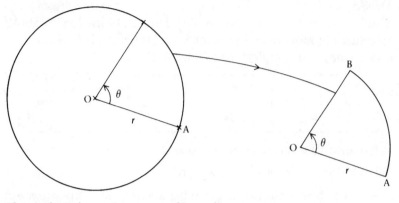

The angle θ shown is measured in radians.

Since the circumference of a full circle of radius r is $2\pi r$ units and the

arc AB is $\dfrac{\theta}{2\pi}$ of the full circle, the length of arc AB is $\dfrac{\theta}{2\pi} \times 2\pi r = r\theta$.

This gives rise to the alternative definition of a radian as that angle which is subtended at the centre by an arc of length 1 in a circle of radius 1.

The area of the sector OAB is $\dfrac{\theta}{2\pi}$ of the area of the full circle. For a

circle of radius r, then, the sector of angle θ radians has area

$$\frac{\theta}{2\pi} \times \pi r^2 = \tfrac{1}{2}r^2\theta$$

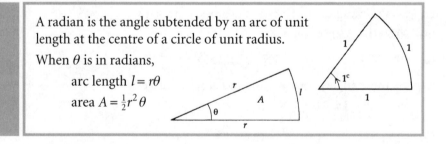

A radian is the angle subtended by an arc of unit length at the centre of a circle of unit radius.

When θ is in radians,

> arc length $l = r\theta$
>
> area $A = \tfrac{1}{2}r^2\theta$

Exercise B (answers p. 176)

1   The sector OAB is cut from a circle of radius 2 cm.

   (a) What is the area of the sector?

   (b) What is the length of arc AB?

   (c) What is the perimeter of the sector?

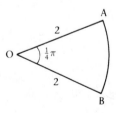

2 If the perimeter of sector CDE is numerically equal to the area of sector CDE, find r.

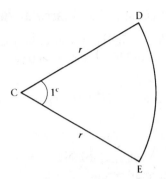

3 An area is to be fenced off for a crowd at a pop concert.
   (a) Calculate the length required to fence off the perimeter.
   (b) Calculate the maximum crowd if the police decide that the crowd density should not exceed 1 person per 2 square metres.

400 m

2^c

400 m

4 OAB is a sector of a circle of radius r. Find these in terms of r and θ.
   (a) The length BC
   (b) The area of triangle OAB
   (c) The area of the sector OAB
   (d) The area of the shaded segment

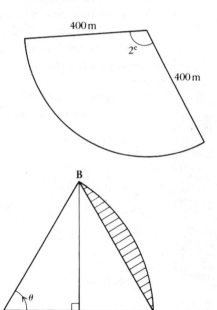

5 A circular cake of diameter 20 cm is cut along AB, half-way from the centre to the rim. Show that the angle θ is 120°. Calculate the areas of the sector OAB, the triangle OAB, and hence the area of cake cut off.

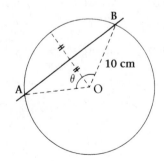

C Pythagoras and circular functions (answers p. 176)

Some values of the circular functions can be found using Pythagoras's rule and ideas of symmetry.

Using $h^2 = a^2 + b^2$, the hypotenuse must be $\sqrt{2}$.

You will find this triangle useful for remembering these values of the circular functions.

$$\sin 45° = \frac{1}{\sqrt{2}} \qquad \cos 45° = \frac{1}{\sqrt{2}} \qquad \tan 45° = 1$$

1D If an equilateral triangle is divided along a line of symmetry, two right-angled triangles are formed. Using half of an equilateral triangle of side 2 units, find, without using a calculator, the values of sin 30°, cos 30°, tan 30° and sin 60°, cos 60°, tan 60°. Leave your answers in surd form.

It is very useful to know the following trigonometric ratios.

$$\sin \frac{\pi}{4} = \sin 45° = \frac{1}{\sqrt{2}}$$

$$\cos \frac{\pi}{4} = \cos 45° = \frac{1}{\sqrt{2}}$$

$$\tan \frac{\pi}{4} = \tan 45° = 1$$

$$\sin \frac{\pi}{6} = \sin 30° = \frac{1}{2}$$

$$\cos \frac{\pi}{6} = \cos 30° = \frac{\sqrt{3}}{2}$$

$$\tan \frac{\pi}{6} = \tan 30° = \frac{1}{\sqrt{3}}$$

$$\sin \frac{\pi}{3} = \sin 60° = \frac{\sqrt{3}}{2}$$

$$\cos \frac{\pi}{3} = \cos 60° = \frac{1}{2}$$

$$\tan \frac{\pi}{3} = \tan 60° = \sqrt{3}$$

2 Copy this table and complete it, giving exact values for the trigonometric ratios. All angles are between 0 and 2π.

Radians	Degrees	$\sin\theta$	$\cos\theta$	$\tan\theta$
$\dfrac{\pi}{6}$		0.5		$\dfrac{1}{\sqrt{3}}$
$\dfrac{2\pi}{3}$				
	135			
$\dfrac{5\pi}{6}$				
$\dfrac{5\pi}{4}$				
	240			
		-1	0	
		$\dfrac{-\sqrt{3}}{2}$	$\dfrac{-1}{2}$	
		$\dfrac{-1}{\sqrt{2}}$		-1
	330			

3 Copy this table and complete it, giving exact values for the trigonometric ratios.

Radians	Degrees	$\sin\theta$	$\cos\theta$	$\tan\theta$
	390			
$-\dfrac{2\pi}{3}$				
	450			
$\dfrac{-5\pi}{6}$				
$\dfrac{15\pi}{4}$				
	420			
	-330			

Trigonometric identities

Points on a circle of unit radius, centre the origin, have coordinates given by $(\cos\theta, \sin\theta)$ where θ is the angle measured anticlockwise from the x-axis.

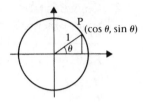

The diagram can be used to illustrate two useful results.

By Pythagoras's theorem

$$x^2 + y^2 = 1, \quad \text{where } (x, y) \text{ are the coordinates of P on the circle.}$$

Since $x = \cos\theta$ and $y = \sin\theta$, then $\cos^2\theta + \sin^2\theta = 1$.

Also, as $\tan\theta = \dfrac{y}{x}$, then $\tan\theta = \dfrac{\sin\theta}{\cos\theta}$.

Both of these results are true for any value of θ. They are trigonometric identities.

The symbol $\equiv$ is sometimes used to mean 'identically equals'. So we can write

$$\cos^2\theta + \sin^2\theta \equiv 1$$

to emphasise that the result is true for all values of θ.

Example 1

In the triangle shown above, if $\sin\theta = \frac{1}{3}$, find these.

(a) $\cos\theta$ (b) $\tan\theta$

Solution

(a) Since $\cos^2\theta = 1 - \sin^2\theta$, $\cos\theta = \sqrt{1 - \dfrac{1}{9}} = \dfrac{2\sqrt{2}}{3}$

(b) Using $\tan\theta = \dfrac{\sin\theta}{\cos\theta}$, $\tan\theta = \dfrac{1}{3} \div \dfrac{2\sqrt{2}}{3} = \dfrac{1}{2\sqrt{2}}$

$$\tan\theta = \frac{\sin\theta}{\cos\theta}; \qquad \sin^2\theta + \cos^2\theta = 1$$

These results are true for angles in either radians or degrees.

You can make use of the identities above to solve some trigonometric equations.

Example 2

Solve the equation $2\sin^2 x = 3\cos x$ for $0 \leqslant x \leqslant 2\pi$.

Solution

(The given range indicates that we should give the solutions in radians.)

$$2 \sin^2 x = 3 \cos x$$

$\Longrightarrow \qquad 2(1 - \cos^2 x) = 3 \cos x$ (replacing $\sin^2 x$ with $1 - \cos^2 x$)

$\Longrightarrow \qquad 2 - 2 \cos^2 x = 3 \cos x$

$\Longrightarrow 2 \cos^2 x + 3 \cos x - 2 = 0$ (rearranging and noting that this is a quadratic equation of the form $2c^2 + 3c - 2 = 0$ with $c = \cos x$)

$\Longrightarrow (2 \cos x - 1)(\cos x + 2) = 0$ (factorising)

$\Longrightarrow \cos x = \frac{1}{2} \qquad$ or $\qquad \cos x = -2$ ($\cos x = -2$ has no solutions)

$\Longrightarrow x = \dfrac{\pi}{3}$ or $\dfrac{5\pi}{3}$ in the range $0 \leqslant x \leqslant 2\pi$

The solutions can be illustrated by sketch graphs.

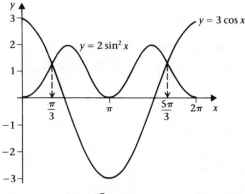

Hence $x = \dfrac{\pi}{3}$ and $\dfrac{5\pi}{3}$ are solutions to the equation $2 \sin^2 x = 3 \cos x$.

Example 3

Solve the equation $3 \sin \theta = 4 \cos \theta$ for $0° \leqslant \theta \leqslant 360°$.

Solution

As $\cos \theta = 0$ is not a possible solution, you can divide through by $\cos \theta$.

$\dfrac{3 \sin \theta}{\cos \theta} = 4$ (dividing both sides by $\cos \theta$)

$\Longrightarrow 3 \tan \theta = 4$ $\left(\text{using } \dfrac{\sin \theta}{\cos \theta} = \tan \theta\right)$

$\Longrightarrow \quad \tan \theta = \frac{4}{3} = 1.33$

$\Longrightarrow \qquad \theta = 53.1° \qquad$ or $\qquad 233.1°$

Exercise C (answers p. 177)

1 (a) By replacing $\sin^2 x$ by $1 - \cos^2 x$, show that the equation
$1 + \cos x = 3 \sin^2 x$ is equivalent to $3 \cos^2 x + \cos x - 2 = 0$.

(b) By writing $c = \cos x$, factorise the left-hand side of this equation.

(c) Solve the equation to find all values of x between $0°$ and $360°$.

2 Solve the following equations for $0° \leqslant \theta \leqslant 360°$.

(a) $3 \sin \theta = 2 \cos \theta$ (b) $0.5 \sin \theta = 0.8 \cos \theta$

(c) $5 \sin 2\theta = 7 \cos 2\theta$

3 Solve the following equations for $0 \leqslant \theta \leqslant 2\pi$.

(a) $2 \cos^2 \theta = \cos \theta + 1$ (b) $\sin \theta - \sqrt{3} \cos \theta = 0$

(c) $8 \sin^2 \theta = 7 - 2 \cos \theta$

4 Solve the following equations for $0 \leqslant x \leqslant 2\pi$.

(a) $\sin^2 x = 0.25$ (b) $\cos^2 x - \sin^2 x = 1$

(c) $\cos^2 x - 4 \sin^2 x = 0$ (d) $\cos^2 x = 2 + 2 \sin x$

5E A cyclist, C, cycles around a circular track, centre O and of radius 100 m. A photographer is at P, 30 m from the edge of the track.

(a) If angle $COP = \theta$ show that

$$PC^2 = (100 \sin \theta)^2 + (130 - 100 \cos \theta)^2$$

(b) Hence show that $PC = \sqrt{26\,900 - 26\,000 \cos \theta}$.

(c) If the photographer has a lens which can focus on objects at between 30 m and 70 m, for what range of values of θ is he able to take photographs of the cyclist?

6E Find the relationship between y and x, given that

$x = 3 \cos \theta,$ $y = 2 \sin \theta$.

7E Prove the following identity.

$$\frac{\sin \theta}{1 + \cos \theta} \equiv \frac{1 - \cos \theta}{\sin \theta}$$

(Hint: start by multiplying both the numerator and the denominator of the left-hand side by $(1 - \cos \theta)$.)

8E Prove this identity.

$$(1 + \sin \theta + \cos \theta)^2 \equiv 2(1 + \sin \theta)(1 + \cos \theta)$$

D Solution of non-right-angled triangles: the cosine rule
(answers p. 177)

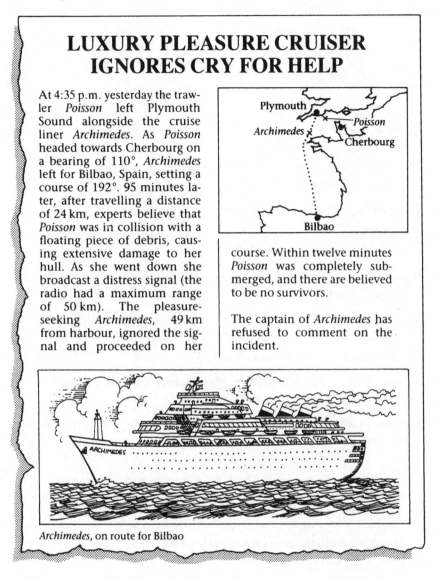

LUXURY PLEASURE CRUISER IGNORES CRY FOR HELP

At 4:35 p.m. yesterday the trawler *Poisson* left Plymouth Sound alongside the cruise liner *Archimedes*. As *Poisson* headed towards Cherbourg on a bearing of 110°, *Archimedes* left for Bilbao, Spain, setting a course of 192°. 95 minutes later, after travelling a distance of 24 km, experts believe that *Poisson* was in collision with a floating piece of debris, causing extensive damage to her hull. As she went down she broadcast a distress signal (the radio had a maximum range of 50 km). The pleasure-seeking *Archimedes*, 49 km from harbour, ignored the signal and proceeded on her

course. Within twelve minutes *Poisson* was completely submerged, and there are believed to be no survivors.

The captain of *Archimedes* has refused to comment on the incident.

Archimedes, on route for Bilbao

1D Was the journalist right to say that the liner *Archimedes* ignored the signal or is it possible that they were unable to hear it? Use an accurate scale drawing to decide.

Instead of using scale drawing for a problem of this type we can calculate lengths (and angles) using trigonometry, even though the triangle is not right-angled.

The process of 'solving a triangle' means finding all its angles and lengths of its sides.

First we need to develop formulas for doing this.

A triangle with sides a, b, c and angles A, B, C can be divided into two right-angled triangles.

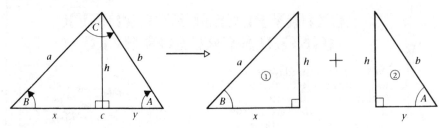

From triangle ①, Pythagoras's theorem gives

$$a^2 = h^2 + x^2$$

2   From triangle ②, express both h and y in terms of b and angle A.

3   Explain why $x = c - y$. Using this and the previous result, express x in terms of b, c and angle A.

4   Replace h and x in $a^2 = h^2 + x^2$ by the expressions found for h and x in terms of b, c and A.

5   Simplify the expression for a^2 found in question 4 by multiplying out the brackets and using the fact that $\cos^2 A + \sin^2 A = 1$.

The result is known as the **cosine rule** for triangles.

6   How does the cosine rule relate to Pythagoras's theorem for right-angled triangles?

7   By treating side b as the base of the triangle and using properties of symmetry, find similar expressions for these.

(a) c^2 (b) b^2

8D   So far, you have only considered acute-angled triangles. Modify the diagram and extend the proof to obtuse-angled triangles.

Notice that we use the convention that the length of the side opposite angle A is labelled a, and so on.

The cosine rule for a triangle with side a, b, c and angles A, B, C:

$$a^2 = b^2 + c^2 - 2bc \cos A$$
$$b^2 = a^2 + c^2 - 2ac \cos B$$
$$c^2 = a^2 + b^2 - 2ab \cos C$$

The cosine rule applies to both acute- and obtuse-angled triangles.

9   Use the cosine rule to get an accurate answer to question 1D.

Example 4

The hands of a clock are 10 cm and 7 cm long. Calculate the distance between their tips at 2 o'clock.

Solution

The angle between the hands is 60°. Using the cosine rule with the triangle labelled as shown:

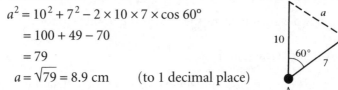

$$a^2 = 10^2 + 7^2 - 2 \times 10 \times 7 \times \cos 60°$$
$$= 100 + 49 - 70$$
$$= 79$$
$$a = \sqrt{79} = 8.9 \text{ cm} \qquad \text{(to 1 decimal place)}$$

Exercise D (answers p. 178)

1 Triangle ABC is such that AB = 4 cm, AC = 8 cm and angle $A = 43°$. Calculate the length of BC.

2 (a) For triangle ABC, with sides BC = a, AC = b, AB = c, express cos A in terms of a, b, c.

   (b) A triangle has sides 4 cm, 5 cm, 7 cm. Calculate its angles.

3 The hands of a clock have lengths 10 cm and 7 cm. Calculate the distance between the tips of the hands at these times.

   (a) 4:30   (b) 8:00   (c) 6:00

4 ABC is a triangle in which BC = 8, CA = 6, AB = 7, and M is the midpoint of BC. Suppose that angle AMC = θ. Write down by the cosine rule expressions for AB^2 and AC^2 in terms of cos θ and add the results. Hence calculate the length of AM.

5 A is 2.1 km due north of B; C is 3.7 km from B on a bearing 136°. Find the distance from C to A.

E Solution of non-right-angled triangles: the sine rule
(answers p. 178)

The area of a triangle can be found using area $= \frac{1}{2} \times$ base $\times$ height.

1 Complete the following.

In the triangle with sides a, b, c and angles A, B, C as shown, the height h_1 can be expressed as

$$h_1 = \_\sin A$$

Thus the area of the triangle is

$$\tfrac{1}{2}bh_1 = \text{\_\_\_\_}$$

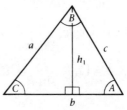

This new formula gives the area of a triangle in terms of the lengths of two sides and the angle between them, i.e.

$$\text{Area} = \tfrac{1}{2}bc \sin A$$
$$= \tfrac{1}{2} \times \text{product of two sides} \times \text{sine of included angle}$$

2 Treating a as the base, the height h_2 of the triangle can be expressed as

$$h_2 = b \sin\_\_$$

Thus the area of the triangle is $\tfrac{1}{2}ah_2 = \_\_\_$

3 Use these two expressions for the area of the triangle to form an equation.

Simplify it and write it in the form $\dfrac{a}{\sin A} = \_\_\_$

4 Treating side c as the base, find an expression for the height of the triangle in terms of a and B, and hence find an expression for the area of the triangle.

5 Use the expression obtained in question 4 with each of the previous expressions to obtain two more equations simplified to the form

$$\frac{b}{\sin B} = \_\_\_ \qquad \frac{c}{\sin C} = \_\_\_$$

6 Find the area of triangle ABC such that $AC = 7$ cm, $BC = 4$ cm and angle $C = 30°$.

The sine rule for a triangle with sides a, b, c and angles A, B, C:

$$\frac{a}{\sin A} = \frac{b}{\sin B} = \frac{c}{\sin C}$$

The area of the triangle is $\tfrac{1}{2}ab \sin C$.

Example 5

In a triangle with sides $a = 7$, $b = 12$ and angle $A = 23°$, angle A is opposite side a and angle B is opposite side b. Find angle B.

Solution

The first step in solving this triangle is to calculate the value of

$$\frac{a}{\sin A} = \frac{7}{\sin 23°} = 17.915$$

Using the sine rule, $\dfrac{b}{\sin B} = 17.915$

and since $b = 12$, $\dfrac{12}{\sin B} = 17.915$

Rearranging this equation gives

$$\sin B = \frac{12}{17.915} = 0.670$$

$B = 42.1°$ (to 1 decimal place) is a possible solution, but we know that more than one angle can have a particular sine.

Indeed, a sketch of the triangle shows **two** possible position for B, corresponding to two solutions.

This is sometimes called the 'ambiguous case' of the sine rule.

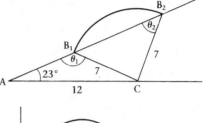

There are many angles which have sine equal to 0.670. Two of these angles are in the range $0° < \theta < 180°$.

From the graph, θ could be either $42.1°$ or $180° - 42.1 = 137.9°$.

When solving triangles

- always sketch a diagram as a rough check on possible solutions and to record the letters you have used for unknown lengths and angles

- remember that to 'solve a triangle' means to find *all* the unknown sides and angles,

- remember that there are simpler methods of solving *right-angled* triangles – there is no need to use the sine or cosine rule!

Exercise E (answers p. 178)

1 Use the sine rule to solve these triangles.

(a)　　　　　　　　　　　　　　(b)

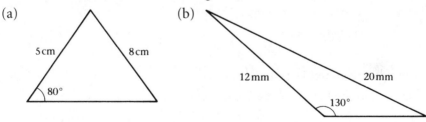

2 Use the cosine rule and then the sine rule to solve these triangles.

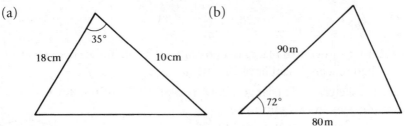

(a)

35°

18 cm   10 cm

(b)

90 m

72°

80 m

3 Find the areas of two triangles in question 2.

4 Solve these triangles.

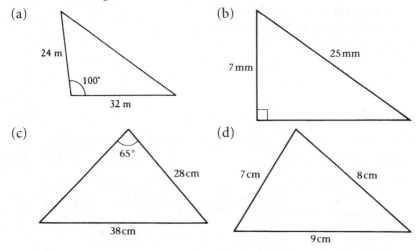

(a)

24 m

100°

32 m

(b)

7 mm   25 mm

(c)

65°

28 cm

38 cm

(d)

7 cm   8 cm

9 cm

5 A plane flies north-east with an airspeed of 400 km h^{-1}. If the wind is blowing at a steady speed of 50 km h^{-1} from the west, calculate the distance covered over the ground in one hour, and the direction in which the plane has travelled.

After working through this chapter you should

1 be able to understand and use radian measure

2 know that for a sector of angle θ radius r

$$\text{arc length} = r\theta$$
$$\text{area} = \tfrac{1}{2}r^2\theta$$

3 be able to differentiate $\sin\theta$ and $\cos\theta$

4 know and be able to use the identities

$$\tan\theta = \frac{\sin\theta}{\cos\theta}$$
$$\sin^2\theta + \cos^2\theta = 1$$

5 know and be able to use the cosine rule and sine rule to solve triangles

6 know that the area of a triangle is $\tfrac{1}{2}ab\sin C$.

Answers

1 Functions and graphs

A Function notation (p. 1)

1D The notation $L = \dfrac{20}{2^c}$ shows very simply the relationship between two variables where one variable is dependent upon the other. $f(c) = \dfrac{20}{2^c}$ emphasises that the quantity $\dfrac{20}{2^c}$ is dependent upon c, and provides a convenient notation for referring to particular values: $f(0)$, $f(1)$, etc.

Exercise A (p. 2)

1 (a) 3 (b) 4 (c) 5 (d) 4

2 (a) $\frac{5}{9}$ (b) $\frac{5}{3}$ (c) 5 (d) 15 (e) $\dfrac{5}{3^x}$

3 (a) (i) 6 (ii) 0 (iii) 2 (iv) 0
    (v) $n^2 + 3n + 2$

   (b) (i) 6 (ii) 0 (iii) 2 (iv) 0
    (v) $n^2 + 3n + 2$

   (c) No, except that a different symbol is used for the variable.

4 (a) (i) $(x-2)^2$ (ii) $a^2 + 4a + 5$

   (b) $x = 0$ (c) $x = 3$

5 (a) $\dfrac{x^2 + 2x + 1}{x + 1} = \dfrac{(x+1)^2}{x+1} = x + 1$

   (b) (i) $4x^2 + 4x + 1$ (ii) x^2

B Relationships between functions (p. 3)

1 (b) $f(x-2) + 5 = (x-2)^2 + 5$
$$= x^2 - 4x + 4 + 5$$
$$= x^2 - 4x + 9$$

(a) and (c)

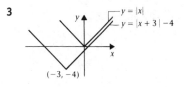

$f(x) = x^2$

$f(x) = x^2 - 4x + 9$

$(2, 5)$

The graph of $f(x-2) + 5$ is obtained from the graph of $f(x)$ by a translation of $\begin{bmatrix} 2 \\ 5 \end{bmatrix}$.

2 (a) (ii) $g(x-2) + 5 = (x-2)^3 + 5$
$$= x^3 - 6x^2 + 12x - 3$$

   (b) (ii) $g(x-2) + 5 = 2^{x-2} + 5$

   (c) (ii) $g(x-2) + 5 = \sqrt{x-2} + 5$

   (a)–(c)
    (iii) In each case, a translation of $\begin{bmatrix} 2 \\ 5 \end{bmatrix}$ will superimpose $g(x)$ onto $g(x-2) + 5$.

3

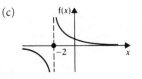

$y = |x|$

$y = |x + 3| - 4$

$(-3, -4)$

4 The graph of $f(x)$ is translated onto the graph of $f(x+a) + b$ by a translation of $\begin{bmatrix} -a \\ b \end{bmatrix}$, for any function f.

5E The effect of a is to translate the graph through $-a$ parallel to the x-axis.

The effect of b is to translate the graph through b parallel to the y-axis.

The graph of $\sin(x+a) + b$ will be identical to the graph of $\sin x$ if $b = 0$ and a is any multiple of 2π.

6E The effect of a is a stretch, parallel to the y-axis.

The effect of b is a stretch, parallel to the x-axis.

The effect of c is a translation, parallel to the x-axis.

The effect of d is a translation, parallel to the y-axis.

Exercise B (p. 6)

1 (a) (i) $\dfrac{1}{2}$ (ii) 1 (iii) $\dfrac{1}{a+2}$ (iv) $\dfrac{1}{a}$
    (v) $f(-2)$ is undefined.

   (b) All values of x, except $x = -2$

   (c)

$f(x)$

-2

x

2 (a) (i) $\sqrt{2}$ (ii) 3 (iii) $\sqrt[4]{2}$ (iv) $\sqrt{\pi}$
(v) π

(b) $x \geqslant 0$

(c)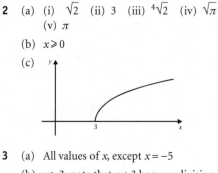

3 (a) All values of x, except $x = -5$

(b) $x > 3$; note that $x \neq 3$ because division by zero is undefined.

(c) All values of x

(d) All values of x, except $x = -2$

4 (a) (i) 5 (ii) 7 (iii) $\sqrt{2}$ (iv) π
(v) 0

(b) $x \in \mathbb{R}$

(c) (i) 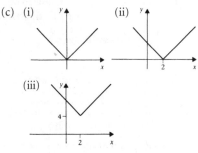 (ii)

(iii)

C Graph sketching and dominance
(p. 6)

1D (a) There is a temptation here just to join up the crosses with a smooth curve; this would produce an *incorrect* graph.

(b) $y = -0.2$, $y = -40.04$, $y = -490.004$

These values show that y decreases very rapidly as x approaches 2.5 from below.

(c) When $x = 2.5$, $2x - 5 = 0$ and $\dfrac{1}{2x-5}$ is not defined.

At this point there is a **discontinuity** in the graph.

(d) The graph plotter shows the discontinuity at $x = 2.5$.

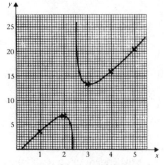

Important features of the graph can be missed if you simply plot points. It is therefore necessary to be able to recognise these features of a graph from its equation.

2 (b) All the graphs pass through $(0, 0)$ and $(1, 1)$.

(c) $y = x^5$ increases most rapidly and $y = x^2$ least rapidly. The graphs for the higher powers of x become steeper more rapidly than those for the lower powers of x as x increases above 1 or decreases below -1.

(d) The graphs of the even powers of x have line symmetry in the y-axis, and the graphs of odd powers have rotational symmetry of order 2 about the origin.

3 (b) When x is a large positive or negative number the graphs of $y = x^2$ and $y = x^2 + 4x$ look alike, in that, although they are not very close to each other, they increase at a similar rate. The x^2 term is said to be **dominant**.

(c) When x is a small positive or negative number the graphs of $y = 4x$ and $y = x^2 + 4x$ are very close together; the x^2 term has very little effect and the $4x$ term is said to be **dominant**.

4 The graph of $y = x^3 - 4x^2$ is similar to that of $y = -4x^2$ for small values of x and is similar to that of $y = x^3$ for large values of x.

5 The graph of $y = x^3 + x^2 - 2x + 1$ is similar to that of $y = -2x + 1$ for small values of x and is similar to that of $y = x^3$ for large values of x.

6 The graph crosses the x-axis at $x = 0, -1$ and 3. These values are related to the factors of $3x + 2x^2 - x^3$, i.e. x, $(x + 1)$ and $(3 - x)$. They are the solutions of $x = 0$, $x + 1 = 0$ and $3 - x = 0$.

In the expansion of $x(x + 1)(3 - x)$ the term of highest degree is $-x^3$ and the term of lowest degree is $3x$. So the graph of $y = x(x + 1)(3 - x)$ is similar to the graph of $y = -x^3$ for large positive and negative values of x, and similar to the graph of $y = 3x$ for small positive and negative values of x near the origin.

7 (a) $-x^3$ (b) x^2

(c) $2x^2 - x^3$ (You might have thought of trying $x^2 - x^3$ first.)

8 The relevant terms from each bracket are multiplied.

$f(0) = (-2)^2 \times 7 = 28$ and

$x^2 \times (2x) = 2x^3$

9 From the factorised form for $f(x)$, the graph can only cross (or touch) the x-axis at $-3\frac{1}{2}$ and 2.

Exercise C (p. 11)

1 The zeros are at $-3, 2, \frac{7}{3}$. The dominant parts of the graph are indicated by the line segments. The dashes indicate the completed sketch.

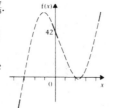

2 The zeros are at $-\frac{2}{5}, 1, 4$ and the graph is as illustrated here.

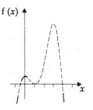

3 $x^3(x + 4)(x - 7) = x^5 - 3x^4 - 28x^3$

x^5 dominates for large x.

$-28x^3$ dominates for very small x.

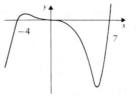

4 (a) The stone is level with the point of release when h is zero. This occurs when $t = 0$ or 2.4, and the relevant answer is 2.4 seconds.

(b) When $t = 4$ then $h = -32$. The point of release is 32 m above sea level and the height of the cliff will be a little less than this.

(c)

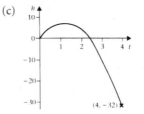

D Graph sketching using derivative functions (p. 11)

1 $f(x) = -x(x + 2)^2 = -x^3 - 4x^2 - 4x$

$f'(x) = -3x^2 - 8x - 4$

2 $f''(x) = -6x - 8$

(a) $f'(x)$ is increasing when $f''(x) > 0$.

$\Rightarrow -6x - 8 > 0 \Rightarrow x < -\frac{4}{3}$

(b) $f'(x)$ is decreasing when $x > -\frac{4}{3}$

3 At stationary points $f'(x) = 0$

$\Rightarrow -3x^2 - 8x - 4 = 0$

$\Rightarrow -(3x + 2)(x + 2) = 0$

$\Rightarrow x = -\frac{2}{3}$ or $x = -2$

$f''(-\frac{2}{3})$ is negative, hence $f(x)$ has a maximum at $x = -\frac{2}{3}$, where $f(x) = \frac{32}{27}$.

$f''(-2)$ is positive, hence $f(x)$ has a minimum at $x = -2$, where $f(x) = 0$.

4 (a) The point of inflexion for $f(x)$ is when $f''(x) = 0$.

$-6x - 8 = 0 \Longrightarrow x = -\frac{4}{3}$

The gradient function $f'(x)$ has a value $f'(-\frac{4}{3}) = +1.3$, hence $f(x)$ has a positive gradient point of inflexion at $(-\frac{4}{3}, \frac{16}{27})$.

(b) When you start to sketch the graph you can plot $(0, 0)$, and two further repeated zeros at $(-2, 0)$.

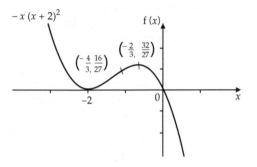

$-x(x+2)^2$

Exercise D (p. 14)

1 (a) $f'(x) = 15x^2 - 6x + 2 \Longrightarrow f''(x) = 30x - 6$

(b) $h'(x) = 5x^4 + 9x^2 - 4$
$\Longrightarrow h''(x) = 20x^3 + 18x$

(c) $\dfrac{dy}{dx} = 5 - 6x + 8x^3 \Longrightarrow \dfrac{d^2y}{dx^2} = -6 + 24x^2$

2 (a) $f'(x) = 5 - 2x \Longrightarrow f''(x) = -2$

Solve $f'(x) = 0$ to find stationary points

$5 - 2x = 0 \Longrightarrow x = 2.5$

$f''(2.5) = -2 \Longrightarrow$ this is a maximum point

$f(2.5) = 6.25$. Hence at $(2.5, 6.25)$ there is a maximum point.

(b) $f'(x) = 3x^2 - 24x \Longrightarrow f''(x) = 6x - 24$

$f'(x) = 0 \Longrightarrow x(3x - 24) = 0 \Longrightarrow x = 0$
or $x = \frac{24}{3} = 8$

$f''(0) = -24 \Longrightarrow$ maximum at
$x = 0, \qquad f(0) = 0$

$f''(8) = 24 \Longrightarrow$ minimum at
$x = 8, \qquad f(8) = -256$

Hence there is a maximum at $(0, 0)$ and a minimum at $(8, -256)$.

(c) $f'(x) = 15x^4 - 30x^2$
$\Longrightarrow f''(x) = 60x^3 - 60x$
$f'(x) = 0 \Longrightarrow 15x^2(x^2 - 2) = 0$
$\Longrightarrow x = 0 \text{ or } x = \pm\sqrt{2}$

$f''(0) = 0 \Longrightarrow$ point of inflexion at
$f(0) = -2$
$f''(+\sqrt{2}) = 84.8 \cdots \Longrightarrow$ minimum at
$f(\sqrt{2}) = -13.3$
$f''(-\sqrt{2}) = -84.8 \cdots \Longrightarrow$ maximum at
$f(-\sqrt{2}) = 9.3$

$(0, -2)$ is a point of inflexion
$(\sqrt{2}, -13.3)$ is a minimum and
$(-\sqrt{2}, 9.3)$ is a maximum.

3 (a) $f'(x) = -10x^4 + 20x^3 - 8$
$\Longrightarrow f''(x) = -40x^3 + 60x^2$
$f(2) = 0, \quad f'(2) = -8, \quad f''(2) = -80$

$(2, 0)$

(b) $f'(x) = 5x^4 - 40x^3 + 120x^2 - 120x$
$\Longrightarrow f''(x) = 20x^3 - 120x^2 + 240x - 120$
$f(2) = -58, \quad f'(2) = 0, \quad f''(2) = 40$

$(2, -58)$

4 (a) $f'(x) = 3x^2 - 6x \qquad f''(x) = 6x - 6$
$3x^2 - 6x = 0 \Longrightarrow x = 0 \text{ or } 2,$
$f(x) = 0 \text{ or } -4.$

At $x = 0, \qquad f''(0) = -6 \Longrightarrow$ maximum
at $(0, 0)$

At $x = 2, \qquad f''(2) = 6 \Longrightarrow$ minimum at
$(2, -4)$

At $x = 1, \qquad f''(x) = 0 \Longrightarrow$ point of
inflexion and $f'(1) = -3$
gives the gradient at
$(1, -2)$

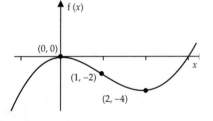

(b) $h'(x) = 4x^3 - 6x^2$ $h''(x) = 12x^2 - 12x$

Stationary point at $x = \frac{3}{2}$ and $h''(\frac{3}{2}) = 9$
so a minimum at $(\frac{3}{2}, -\frac{43}{16})$

Stationary point at $x = 0$ and $h''(0) = 0$
$\Rightarrow$ point of inflexion at $(0, -1)$

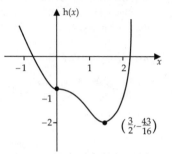

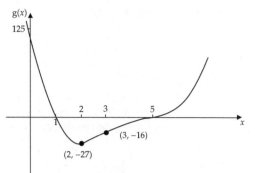

$g''(x) = 0$ also where $x = 3$, which can be
seen from the factorised form, and
$g'(3) = 16$, $g(3) = -16$, so there is a point of
inflexion at $(3, -16)$ with a gradient of 16.

5E   There is one zero at 1 and three zeros at 5,
giving the points $(1, 0)$ and $(5, 0)$.

$g(x) = (x-1)(x-5)(x^2 - 10x + 25)$

$\quad = (x-1)(x^3 - 15x^2 + 75x - 125)$

$\quad = x^4 - 16x^3 + 90x^2 - 200x + 125$

$g'(x) = 4x^3 - 48x^2 + 180x - 200$

$\quad = 4(x^3 - 12x^2 + 45x - 50)$

The repeated root at $x = 5$ indicates that
$(x-5)$ must be a factor of $g'(x)$, as well as 4.

So $g'(x) = 4(x-5)(x^2 - 7x + 10)$

$\quad = 4(x-5)(x-5)(x-2)$

$\quad = 4(x-2)(x-5)^2$

Stationary points are where $g'(x) = 0$

$4(x-2)(x-5)^2 = 0$

when $x = 2$, $x = 5$

$g''(x) = 12x^2 - 96x + 180 = 12(x^2 - 8x + 15)$
$\quad = 12(x-3)(x-5)$

$g''(2) = 36$ is positive, so $g'(x)$ is changing
from a negative to positive gradient at
$x = 2$. So $(2, -27)$ is a local minimum.

$g''(5) = 0$ indicates that $g'(x)$ is locally zero
and there is a point of inflexion. This
needs further investigation, and in this
case $g(x)$ has a stationary point at $x = 5$, so
we have a horizontal point of inflexion at
$(5, 0)$.

**E   Differentiating and integrating
inverse functions and x^n** (p. 15)

Exercise E (p. 16)

1   (a) $y = \dfrac{1}{x^2} = x^{-2} \Rightarrow \dfrac{dy}{dx} = -2x^{-3} = -\dfrac{2}{x^3}$

(b) An expression such as $(1 + x)\sqrt{x}$
should be multiplied out before
differentiation.

$\quad y = (1 + x)\sqrt{x} = \sqrt{x} + x\sqrt{x} = x^{\frac{1}{2}} + x^{\frac{3}{2}}$

$\quad$ Then $\dfrac{dy}{dx} = \dfrac{1}{2}x^{-\frac{1}{2}} + \dfrac{3}{2}x^{\frac{1}{2}} = \dfrac{1}{2\sqrt{x}} + \dfrac{3}{2}\sqrt{x}$

2   (a) $\frac{1}{3}x^{-\frac{2}{3}}$ (b) $-x^{-2}$ (c) $-3x^{-4}$

(d) $-2x^{-3} + \frac{1}{2}x^{-\frac{1}{2}}$

3 $y = x^{1/n} \Rightarrow \dfrac{dy}{dx} = \dfrac{1}{n}x^{(1/n)-1}$

4   (a) $\frac{10}{3}x^{\frac{3}{2}} + c$ (b) $3x^{\frac{2}{3}} + c$

(c) $-\dfrac{1}{2}x^{-2} + c = \dfrac{-1}{2x^2} + c$

(d) $-x^{-1} + \dfrac{2}{3}x^{\frac{3}{2}} + c = \dfrac{-1}{x} + \dfrac{2}{3}x^{\frac{3}{2}} + c$

(e) $\frac{2}{3}x^{\frac{3}{2}} + \frac{2}{5}x^{\frac{5}{2}} + c$

5 $y = x^{1/n} \Rightarrow \displaystyle\int x^{1/n}\,dx = \dfrac{1}{\left(\dfrac{1}{n} + 1\right)}x^{(1/n)+1} + c$

Note $\dfrac{1}{n} + 1 = \dfrac{1+n}{n}$

Hence $\displaystyle\int x^{1/n}\,dx = \dfrac{n}{n+1}x^{((n+1)/n)} + c$

F   Decimal search (p. 17)

1D (a) For $x^2 = x + 1$, draw the graphs $y = x^2$
and $y = x + 1$. The solutions are at the
points of intersection of the two
graphs.

For $x^2 - x - 1 = 0$, draw the graph of
$y = x^2 - x - 1$. The solutions are the
points where the graph cuts the x-axis.

(b) *Either*

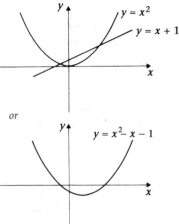

or

One root lies between -1 and 0. The
second root lies between 1 and 2.

(c) The roots are -0.618 and 1.618.

(d) Without a graph plotter, $x^2 = x + 1$
gives two simple graphs to sketch, but
care must be taken to ensure that *all*
solutions are obtained. Note that
approximate roots of *any* quadratic
equation can be found by sketching
$y = x^2$ and a straight line.

With $x^2 - x - 1 = 0$ it is simple to
check that no solutions have been
missed, but it is not so easy to sketch
the graph without a graph plotter.

2 (a) The interval $[3, 4]$

(b) $x = 1$ is one root; the other two lie in
$[-1, 0]$ and $[-4, -3]$.

(c) $[1, 2]$ (d) $[-3, -2], [2, 3]$

3D One way to speed up the method is to
estimate from the function values the most
likely interval. Since the value is -0.04 at
$x = 1.6$ and 0.19 at $x = 1.7$, the solution is
likely to be nearer 1.6 than 1.7.

The process could also be speeded up by
dividing the interval into two and
calculating the function value at 1.65 first.
Once this is known, it will only be
necessary to search one half of the interval.
You could continue to halve the interval at
each stage – this more efficient process is
known as **binary search**.

Exercise F (p. 21)

1 (a) 3.14 (b) $-3.41, -0.59,$
1.00 (c) 1.72 (d) $-2.32, 2.32$

2 (a) 1.77 (b) 3.33

G   Linear interpolation (p. 22)

Exercise G (p. 23)

1 (a) Integer bounds $4, 5$
$(4, -1)$ to $(5, 1.5)$

$$\text{root} \approx 4 + \frac{1}{2.5} \times 1 \approx 4.4$$

(b) Integer bounds $1, 2$
$(1, -\frac{2}{3})$ $(2, \frac{1}{3})$
$\text{root} \approx 1 + (\frac{2}{3} \div 1) \approx 1.67$
Also $x = -1$ is a root.

2 (a) 0.1449
(b) 0.1267

2 Sequences and series

A   Inductive definition (p. 24)

1D The population would be
$180.14 \times 1.024 = 184.46$ million.

2 (a) $u_1 = 2, u_4 = 20$
(b) $u_5 = 26, u_5 = u_4 + 6$
(c) $u_{i+1} = u_i + 6$

3 (a) $t_2 = 4 + 9 = 13, t_3 = 13 + 9 = 22,$
$t_4 = 31, t_5 = 40$
(b) $t_{20} = 4 + (19 \times 9) = 175$

4 (a) $u_1 = -5$

Putting $i = 1$ gives

$u_2 = u_1 + 2 = -5 + 2 = -3$,

putting $i = 2$ gives

$u_3 = u_2 + 2 = -3 + 2 = -1$ and so on.

$u_1 = -5, u_2 = -3, u_3 = -1, u_4 = 1,$

$u_5 = 3$

$u_{20} = -5 + (19 \times 2) = 33$

(b) $u_1 = 15, u_2 = 11, u_3 = 7, u_4 = 3,$

$u_5 = -1$

$u_{20} = 15 - (19 \times 4) = -61$

(c) $u_1 = 2, u_2 = 3 \times 2 = 6, u_3 = 3 \times 6 = 18,$

$u_4 = 3 \times 18 = 54, u_5 = 3 \times 54 = 162$

$u_{20} = 3^{19} \times 2 \approx 2.3 \times 10^9$

Note how *multiplying* by 3 gives a rapid increase in magnitude.

(d) $u_1 = 3, u_2 = \frac{1}{3}, u_3 = 3, u_4 = \frac{1}{3}, u_5 = 3,$

$u_{20} = \frac{1}{3}$

The sequence oscillates.

5 (a) The sequence alternates in sign. The magnitude of each term is twice that of the previous term.

With $u_1 = 3$ for example, the sequence is 3, −6, 12, −24, 48, −96, ...

(b) The sequence diverges rapidly unless $u_1 = -4$.

If $u_1 < -4$ the sequence approaches negative infinity.

If $u_1 > -4$ the sequence approaches infinity.

(c) If $u_1 > 0$ the sequence approaches infinity.

If $u_1 < 0$ the sequence approaches negative infinity.

(d) The sequence approaches zero.

(e) The sequence alternates between the values u_1 and u_2, for example $u_1 = 7$, $u_2 = \frac{2}{7}, u_3 = 7, u_4 = \frac{2}{7}, ...$

6E (a) If $u_1 = u_2 = 1$ the Fibonacci sequence 1, 1, 2, 3, 5, 8, 13, ... is obtained. Otherwise, a similar sequence where each term is the sum of the two preceding terms is obtained.

(b) The sequence eventually converges to a value of −4 unless $u_1 = 2.5$.

7E The sequence always appears to settle into the cycle 4, 2, 1, 4, 2, 1, ... This has never been proved and is known as Thwaites's conjecture.

Exercise A (p. 27)

1 $u_1 = 4, u_2 = 8, u_3 = 16, u_4 = 32, u_5 = 64$. The sequence is diverging.

2 (a) $u_1 = 9, u_2 = 6, u_3 = 4, u_4 = \frac{8}{3}$, converging

(b) $u_1 = 2, u_2 = \frac{1}{4}, u_3 = 16$; diverging

(c) $u_1 = 1, u_2 = 5, u_3 = 1, u_4 = 5$; oscillating

3 $u_1 = 1, u_2 = 1\frac{1}{2}, u_3 = 1\frac{3}{4}, u_4 = 1\frac{7}{8}, u_5 = 1\frac{15}{16}$

The sequence is converging, approaching the limit of 2.

4 The sequence is 1, 2, 3, 5, 8, 13, 21, 34, ... which diverges.

5 The sequence is 2, 6.75, 0.5926, 76.88, 0.0046, 1 294 319.3, ...

Odd terms approach zero, whilst the even terms become very large.

6 (a) $u_1 = 1, u_{i+1} = \frac{1}{2} u_i$

(b) $u_1 = 1, u_{i+1} = (-\frac{1}{2}) u_i$

B The general term (p. 27)

1 (a) $s_{50} = 300$ (b) $s_t = 6t$

(c) The inductive method requires every term in turn to be calculated, in this case a further forty-nine terms!

2 Each term is 3 times the previous term, so

$t_2 = 2 \times 3$

$t_3 = (2 \times 3) \times 3 = 2 \times 3^2$

$t_4 = (2 \times 3 \times 3) \times 3 = 2 \times 3^3$

To obtain t_n, t_1 must be multiplied by 3 a total of $n - 1$ times. Therefore, $t_n = 2 \times 3^{n-1}$.

3 $u_1 = (-1)^1 \frac{1}{1} = -1, u_2 = (-1)^2 \frac{1}{4} = \frac{1}{4},$ $u_3 = (-1)^3 \frac{1}{9} = -\frac{1}{9}, u_4 = (-1)^4 \frac{1}{16} = \frac{1}{16}$ and so on.

The $(-1)^i$ causes the sign to change for alternate terms.

Exercise B (p. 28)

1

Position in pattern	1	2	3	4	5	10	20	100	i

No. of dots

(a)	1	4	7	10	13	28	58	298	$3i-2$
(b)	4	8	12	16	20	40	80	400	$4i$
(c)	1	3	5	7	9	19	39	199	$2i-1$
(d)	1	4	9	16	25	100	400	10 000	i^2
(e)	2	8	18	32	50	200	800	20 000	$2i^2$
(f)	3	8	15	24	35	120	440	10 200	$i(i+2)$

2

No. of triangles	1	2	3	4	5	10	20	100	i
No. of matchsticks	3	5	7	9	11	21	41	201	$2i+1$

In this case the idea of adding on two matches each time helps you to find the first few terms of the sequence. In order to find the later terms you need to spot that the number of matches is found by doubling the number of triangles and adding 1.

3 (a) $i=1$: $u_1 = 3 \times 1 + 2 = 5$

$i=2$: $u_2 = 3 \times 2 + 2 = 8$

$u_3 = 3 \times 3 + 2 = 11$

$u_4 = 3 \times 4 + 2 = 14$

$u_5 = 3 \times 5 + 2 = 17$

(b) $u_1 = 5 \times 2^1 = 10$, $u_2 = 5 \times 2^2 = 20$, $u_3 = 5 \times 2^3 = 40$, $u_4 = 80$, $u_5 = 160$

(c) $u_1 = 3 \times 1^2 = 3$, $u_2 = 3 \times 2^2 = 12$, $u_3 = 27$, $u_4 = 48$, $u_5 = 75$

4 (a) (i) $-1, 1, -1, 1, -1, \dots$

(ii) $1, -1, 1, -1, 1, \dots$

(iii) $-1, 1, -1, 1, -1, \dots$

(iv) $-1, 2, -4, 8, -16, \dots$

(b) (i) $u_i = 3 \times (-1)^{i+1}$

(ii) $u_i = 3 \times (-1)^i$

5

			Term		
	5	6	9	100	i
A	10	12	18	200	$2i$
B	14	17	26	299	$3i-1$
C	32	64	512	2^{100}	2^i
D	96	192	1536	3×2^{100}	3×2^i
E	1	-1	1	-1	$(-1)^{i+1}$
F	-5	6	-9	100	$(-1)^i i$
G	5	-6	9	-100	$(-1)^{i+1} i$
H	10	-12	18	-200	$(-1)^{i+1} 2i$
I	$\dfrac{1}{6}$	$\dfrac{1}{7}$	$\dfrac{1}{10}$	$\dfrac{1}{101}$	$\dfrac{1}{i+1}$
J	25	-36	81	$-10\,000$	$(-1)^{i+1} i^2$

C Arithmetic series (p. 30)

1D The numbers from 1 to 100 can be paired up into 50 pairs, each with a total of 101, as shown.

$$1 + 2 + 3 + \cdots + 99 + 100$$

The total is therefore $50 \times 101 = 5050$.

2 (a) (i) Each pair of terms adds up to 21, so the total is $10 \times 21 = 210$.

(ii) Note that, because there is an odd number of terms, not all terms pair up. However, the same result may be obtained by finding the average of the first and last terms and multiplying by the number of terms.

The average of the first and last terms is

$$\frac{(1+9)}{2} = 5$$

so the total is $9 \times 5 = 45$.

(iii) $\dfrac{(1+29)}{2} \times 29 = 435$

(b) There are many possible ways. One way is to find the average of the first and last terms and multiply by the number of terms. This works for series with either an even or an odd number of terms.

3 There are many ways of doing this. For example, subtracting 4 from each term gives 1, 2, ..., 101 with 101 terms.

4 (a) 50; 1275   (b) 81; 4050

(c) 101; 15 150

5 The same principle applies here as in question 1. You can find the average of the first and last terms, and then multiply by the number of terms.

(a) $\dfrac{16}{2} \times 8 = 64$ (b) $\dfrac{104}{2} \times 33 = 1716$

(c) $\dfrac{267}{2} \times 26 = 3471$

6 (a) $1 + 2i$ (b) $2 + 4i$ (c) $17 - 5i$

7 (a) (i) 61   (ii) 495

(b) (i) $4i + 1$ (ii) $i(2i + 3)$

8 (a) $a + 4d$ (b) $a + 49d$

(c) $a + (n - 1)d$

(d) $\dfrac{a + (a + 49d)}{2} \times 50 = 25(2a + 49d)$

9 Your demonstration by substitution

Exercise C (p. 32)

1 (a) 4060   (b) 7500

(c) $10\,049\frac{1}{2}$ (d) 2356

2 (a) Last term $= 8 + 17 \times 2 = 42$;

$\text{sum} = \left(\dfrac{8 + 42}{2}\right) \times 18 = 450$

(b) Number of terms $= \dfrac{303 - 6}{9} + 1 = 34$;

$\text{sum} = \left(\dfrac{6 + 303}{2}\right) \times 34 = 5253$

(c) Common difference $= \dfrac{195 - 3}{24} = 8$;

$\text{sum} = \left(\dfrac{3 + 195}{2}\right) \times 25 = 2475$

3 The volume under the bottom step is

$V = 50 \times \frac{1}{4} \times \frac{3}{4}\,\text{m}^3$

Successive steps up have volumes $2V$, $3V$, ..., $15V$.

The total volume is therefore

$15 \times \dfrac{V + 15V}{2} = 120V = 1125\,\text{m}^3$

4 (a) $2n - 1$

(b) 7 (This uses 49 bricks.)

(c) $S = \frac{1}{2}n(2 + (n - 1)2)$

$= \frac{1}{2}n(2n)$

$= n^2$

5E (a) $4n - 2$

(b) $S = \frac{1}{2}n(4 + (n - 1)4) = 2n^2$

This is twice as many as in question 4.

6E (a) $£(5 + 10 + \cdots + 90) = £855$

(b) $\frac{5}{2}n(n + 1) > 500$

$\Rightarrow n(n + 1) > 200$

$\Rightarrow n = 14$

7E $8.2 + 8.3 + \cdots = 22\,000$

$\frac{1}{2}n(16.4 + (n - 1) \times 0.1) = 22\,000$

$n(n + 163) = 440\,000$

$n \approx 587$

D Loans and APR (p. 34)

1 £1200 is repaid, which includes £400 interest. This is a rate of 50%.

2 The outstanding debt after 12 months is £0 (approximately!) and so the debt is fully repaid.

3 $£100 \times 1.0165^{12} = £121.699$

The original £100 must be repaid together with interest of approximately 21.7%.

4 (a) 12.7%   (b) 26.8%   (c) 79.6%

5 Possibly the simplest algorithm is:

divide rate by 100,

add 1,

raise to the power 12,

subtract 1,

multiply by 100.

6 The reversed algorithm is:

divide APR by 100,

add 1,

find the 12th root,

subtract 1,

multiply by 100.

The rate is 5.95%.

7 Your computer demonstration

8E Monthly interest rate = 7.93%
(7.930 83%); APR = 149.9%

Exercise D (p. 36)

1 (a) $\frac{30}{100} \times 7292.86$

(b) $2187.86 + 36 \times 127.52 + 1786.75$

(c) 12 months and 52 weeks are assumed to be equivalent with
$29.43 = \frac{12}{52} \times 127.52$

(d) 0.979%

For normally structured loans, companies have printed charts for APR. More unusually structured loans like that for the car are often calculated using special financial calculators, with functions embodying the approved methods of calculating APR. The detailed regulations and prescribed financial formulas for APR calculation are governed by the Consumer Credit Act 1974.

E Sigma notation (p. 36)

1D (a) $£1000 \times 1.08^{10} = £2158.92$

(b) $£1000 \times 1.08^{9} = £1999.00$

(c) Continuing this pattern, the third investment will be worth $£1000 \times 1.08^{8}$ since it earns interest for eight years.

The final investment earns interest for one year and will be worth $£1000 \times 1.08^{1}$.

The total investment is therefore
$£(1000 \times 1.08^{1} + 1000 \times 1.08^{2}$
$+ \cdots + 1000 \times 1.08^{10})$
$= £1000(1.08 + 1.08^{2} + 1.08^{3}$
$+ \cdots + 1.08^{10})$

Exercise E (p. 38)

1 (a) $1 + \frac{1}{2} + \frac{1}{3} + \frac{1}{4} + \frac{1}{5}$

(b) $9 + 16 + 25 + 36 + 49$

(c) $\frac{1}{2} + \frac{1}{6} + \frac{1}{12} + \frac{1}{20} + \frac{1}{30}$

(d) $11 - 13 + 15 - 17 + 19$

(e) $1 + 8 + 27 + 64 + 125 + 216$

(f) $1 + 8 + 27 + 64 + 125 + 216$

Note that (e) and (f) are different representations of the same sum.

2 (a) $\sum_{i=1}^{50} \sqrt{i}$ (b) $\sum_{i=1}^{50} (2i)^2$

(c) $\sum_{i=1}^{49} \frac{1}{2i+1}$ (d) $\sum_{i=1}^{19} (-1)^{i+1} i^3$

(e) $\sum_{i=1}^{99} \frac{i}{i+1}$

3 (a) 400

(b) $35 + 33 + \cdots + (-3)$
$= 20 \times \frac{35-3}{2}$ (20 terms)
$= 320$

4 (a) $\sum_{1}^{25} (15 + 5i)$ (b) $\sum_{1}^{10} 10\,000 \times (\frac{1}{10})^i$

(c) $\sum_{0}^{14} 1.1^{i}$ (d) $\sum_{1}^{8} \frac{1}{i+(i+1)}$

(e) $\sum_{1}^{20} i \times 3^{i}$

5 (a) $1 \times 2 + 4 \times 3 + 9 \times 4 + 16 \times 5$
$+ 25 \times 6 + 36 \times 7$

(b) $(-1)^0 \times 1 + (-1)^1 \times 2 + (-1)^2 \times 3$
$+ (-1)^3 \times 4 + (-1)^4 \times 5$
(i.e. $1 - 2 + 3 - 4 + 5$)

(c) $1 + x + x^2 + x^3 + x^4 + x^5$

(d) $\frac{0}{1} + \frac{1}{2} + \frac{2}{3} + \frac{3}{4} + \frac{4}{5}$

(e) $f(x_1) + f(x_2) + f(x_3) + \cdots + f(x_6)$

F Geometric series (p. 39)

Exercise F (p. 40)

1 (a) $\frac{2(3^8 - 1)}{2} = 6560$ (b) 122 070 312

(c) 1 743 392 200 (d) 15.984 375

(e) 5.328 125

2 (a) $1 + 3 + 9 + 27 + 81 = 121$

(b) $1 + 8 + 8^2 + \ldots + 8^9 = 153\,391\,689$
$\approx 1.53 \times 10^8$, which is a more practical expression.

(c) $2 + 2^2 + \cdots + 2^7 = 2\left(\frac{2^7 - 1}{2 - 1}\right) = 254$

(d) $\frac{63}{256}$

(e) $\frac{1 - (-\frac{3}{4})^{20}}{1 - (-\frac{3}{4})} = 0.570$ (to 3 s.f.)

3 (a) He requested

$$1 + 2 + 4 + 8 + \cdots + 2^{63} = \frac{2^{64} - 1}{2 - 1}$$

$$\approx 1.84 \times 10^{19} \text{ grains!}$$

(b) 3.7×10^{17} g or 3.7×10^{11} tonnes!

4 $\dfrac{200 \times 1.05(1.05^{50} - 1)}{1.05 - 1} = £43\,963$ (to the nearest pound)

5 Taking the school leaver's salary as £8000, the total earnings over a 45-year period would be

$$£8000(1 + 1.05 + 1.05^2 + \cdots + 1.05^{44})$$

$$= £8000 \frac{(1.05^{45} - 1)}{1.05 - 1} = £1.28 \text{ million}$$

6 (a) $\dfrac{1000 \times 1.075(1.075^n - 1)}{1.075 - 1}$

(b) The conditions lead to the equation

$$\frac{1000 \times 1.075(1.075^n - 1)}{1.075 - 1} = 2000n$$

The conditions are met after 17 years.

G Sum to infinity (p. 41)

Exercise G (p. 42)

1 (a) $\dfrac{\frac{9}{10}}{1 - \frac{1}{10}} = 1$ (b) $\dfrac{4}{1 + \frac{3}{4}} = \dfrac{16}{7}$

(c) The sum diverges   (d) $\dfrac{5}{1 - \frac{1}{2}} = 10$

2 (a) $\frac{3}{2}$ (b) $\frac{4}{3}$ (c) 1

3 (a) The . sum is $\frac{1}{3}$.

(b) If you consider the diagram to be made up from a sequence of nested L shapes,

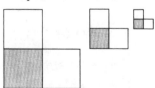

it can be seen that each L shape is made up of one shaded and two unshaded squares, i.e. $\frac{1}{3}$ of the diagram is shaded.

4 (a) 3 (b) 4 (c) $\frac{16}{3}$ (d) $3 \times (\frac{4}{3})^n$

$\frac{4}{3} > 1$, therefore $(\frac{4}{3})^n \to \infty$ as $n \to \infty$. This means $P_n \to \infty$ as $n \to \infty$.

The limiting curve is of infinite length, yet encloses a finite area!

5 The sum to n terms is

$$\frac{2(1 - (\frac{2}{5})^n)}{1 - \frac{2}{5}} = \tfrac{10}{3}(1 - (\frac{2}{5})^n)$$

The sum to infinity is $\frac{10}{3}$.

The difference, $\frac{10}{3}(\frac{2}{5})^n$, is less than 0.01 when $n = 7$.

H Manipulating series using sigma notation (p. 43)

1 (a) $\displaystyle\sum_1^n u_i$

(b) The sum is multiplied by the constant.

(c) $\displaystyle\sum_1^n au_i = au_1 + \cdots + au_n$

$$= a(u_1 + \cdots + u_n)$$

$$= a\sum_1^n u_i$$

2E (a) The sum is increased by n times the constant.

(b)

$$\sum_1^n (u_i + b) = u_1 + b + u_2 + b + \cdots + u_n + b$$

$$= u_1 + \cdots + u_n + nb$$

$$= \sum_1^n u_i + nb$$

(c) $\displaystyle\sum_1^n (au_i + b) = \sum_1^n au_i + nb$

$$= a\sum_1^n u_i + nb$$

3E (a) $2\displaystyle\sum_1^n i - 3n = n(n+1) - 3n$

$$= n^2 - 2n$$

(b) $5\displaystyle\sum_1^n i + n = \tfrac{5}{2}n(n+1) + n$

$$= \tfrac{5}{2}n^2 + \tfrac{7}{2}n$$

4E

$$\sum_{1}^{n} (u_i + v_i) = u_1 + v_1 + u_2 + v_2 + \cdots + u_n + v_n$$

$$= (u_1 + u_2 + \cdots + u_n)$$
$$\quad\quad + (v_1 + v_2 + \cdots + v_n)$$

$$= \sum_{1}^{n} u_i + \sum_{1}^{n} v_i$$

5E (a) $(n+1)^3 - 1^3$. The other terms cancel out in pairs.

(b) This is part (a) written in Σ notation.

(c) $(i+1)^3 - i^3 = 3i^2 + 3i + 1$

$$\sum_{1}^{n} (i+1)^3 - \sum_{1}^{n} i^3 = \sum_{1}^{n} [(i+1)^3 - i^3]$$

$$= \sum_{1}^{n} (3i^2 + 3i + 1)$$

$$= 3\sum_{1}^{n} i^2 + 3\sum_{1}^{n} i + n$$

(d) $3\sum_{1}^{n} i^2 + 3\sum_{1}^{n} i + n = (n+1)^3 - 1$

$$3\sum_{1}^{n} i^2 + \frac{3n(n+1)}{2} + n = n^3 + 3n^2 + 3n$$

$$3\sum_{1}^{n} i^2 = n^3 + \frac{3n^2}{2} + \frac{n}{2}$$

$$\sum_{1}^{n} i^2 = \frac{(2n^3 + 3n^2 + n)}{6}$$

$$\sum_{1}^{n} i^2 = \frac{n(n+1)(2n+1)}{6}$$

6E $\dfrac{99 \times 100 \times 199}{6} = 328\,350$

7E (a) $2\sum_{1}^{n} i^2 - 6\sum_{1}^{n} i + 4n$

$$= \frac{n(n+1)(2n+1)}{3} - 3n(n+1) + 4n$$

$$= \frac{n(2n^2 - 6n + 4)}{3}$$

$$= \frac{2n(n-1)(n-2)}{3}$$

(b)

$$\sum_{1}^{n} (2i-1)^2 = \sum_{1}^{n} (4i^2 - 4i + 1)$$

$$= 4\sum_{1}^{n} i^2 - 4\sum_{1}^{n} i + n$$

$$= \frac{2n(n+1)(2n+1)}{3} - 2n(n+1) + n$$

$$= \frac{n(4n^2 - 1)}{3}$$

$$= \frac{n(2n-1)(2n+1)}{3}$$

3   Algebra of functions

A   Composition of functions (p. 46)

Exercise A (p. 47)

1 (a) (i) $2x^3 + 3$ (ii) $(2x+3)^3$

(b) (i) $\dfrac{2}{x} + 1$

(ii) $\dfrac{1}{2x+1}$

(c) (i) $3(5-x) + 2 = 17 - 3x$

(ii) $5 - (3x+2) = 3 - 3x$

(d) (i) $1 - (1-2x)^2 = 4x - 4x^2$

(ii) $1 - 2(1-x^2) = 2x^2 - 1$

2 (a) $ch(x) = 9 + 0.4 \times (1.034x)$
$$= 9 + 0.4136x$$

(b) The cost in pounds of x cubic feet of gas.

3 There are alternative answers for all of the following questions.

(a) $f(x) = \dfrac{1}{x}$, $g(x) = x + 2$

(b) $f(x) = x + 2$, $g(x) = \dfrac{1}{x}$

(c) $f(x) = \dfrac{1}{x}$, $g(x) = 2x + 3$

(d) $f(x) = 2x - 1$, $g(x) = \sqrt{x}$

(e) $f(x) = \dfrac{1}{x} + 3$, $g(x) = x^2$

(f) $f(x) = x^4$, $g(x) = 2x + 1$

(g) $f(x) = x^2 - 4x - 3$, $g(x) = x^4$

4 (a) $x+4$ (b) x^4 (c) $4x-9$

(d) x (e) $\sin(\sin x)$ (f) x

5 (a) $f(g(f(x))) = f(g(x-3))$
$= f((x-3)^2) = (x-3)^2 - 3$

(b) (i) $fg(x)$ (ii) $gfg(x)$ (iii) $ff(x)$
(iv) $fggg(x)$ (v) $ffggf(x)$

6 (a) $qs(x)$ (b) $sq(x)$ (c) $ss(x)$

7 (a) $fg(x) = (x+3)^2$, $gf(x) = x^2 + 3$, $x = -1$

(b) $fg(x) = x - 3$, $gf(x) = x - 3$,
all values of x

(c) $fg(x) = 6x + 1$, $gf(x) = 6x - 2$,
no values of x

(d) $fg(x) = \dfrac{1}{x^3}$, $gf(x) = \dfrac{1}{x^3}$, all values of x

(e) $fg(x) = x + 2$, $gf(x) = x + 1$,
no values of x

(f) $fg(x) = \sqrt{x-1}$, $gf(x) = \sqrt{x} - 1$,
$x = 1$

8

	e	f	g	h
e	e	f	g	h
f	f	e	h	g
g	g	h	e	f
h	h	g	f	e

B Range, domain and inverse functions (p. 49)

1D Domain $\{x \in \mathbb{R}: x \neq 0\}$
Range $\{y \in \mathbb{R}: y > 0\}$

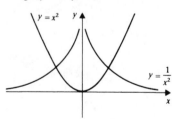

2D (a) $\{x \in \mathbb{R}^+\}$ (x can be any real number
that is positive)
or $\{x \geqslant 0: x \in \mathbb{R}\}$ or $\{x \leqslant 0: x \in \mathbb{R}\}$

(b) $\{0 \leqslant x < 180: x \in \mathbb{R}\}$

(c) $\{-90 \leqslant x < 90: x \in \mathbb{R}\}$

3 (a) f^{-1} reverses the effect of f and so
$f^{-1}(f(x)) = x$.

(b) If $f(x) = y$, then $f^{-1}(y) = x$. Any point
in the domain of f is therefore in the
range of f^{-1} and vice versa.

(c)

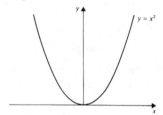

(d) If a function is many-to-one (as is
$y = x^2$ in (c)), then the inverse is not a
function because it is one-to-many.

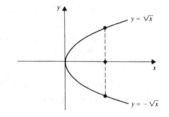

4 (a)

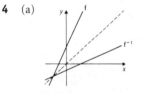

$f^{-1}(x) = \frac{1}{3}(x - 5)$
Domain of f = $\{x \in \mathbb{R}\}$

(b)

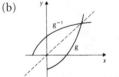

$g^{-1}(x) = \sqrt{x+7}$
Domain of g = $\{x \in \mathbb{R}: x \geqslant 0\}$

(c)

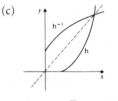

$h^{-1}(x) = \sqrt{x+7}$
Domain of h = $\{x \in \mathbb{R}: x \geqslant 7\}$

(d)

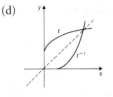

$r^{-1}(x) = (x-6)^2$

Domain of $r = \{x \in \mathbb{R}: x \geqslant 0\}$

5   Reflection in $y = x$ (resulting in interchange of x and y in the equation)

6   (a) $y = \pm\sqrt{x+3} - 5$ (b) $y = \frac{1}{2}(\frac{1}{3}x + 1)$

7   (a) (i)   The reciprocal sequence alternates between two values, except when $x_1 = 0$ (x_2 undefined) or $x_1 = \pm1$ (constant sequence).

    (ii)   The 'charge sign' sequence behaves similarly; it is constant for $x_1 = 0$.

   (b)   Both functions are self-inverse and hence $ff(x) = x$ in each case.

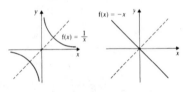

The graphs of both functions reflect in the line $y = x$ onto themselves.

8   (a) $\dfrac{1-x}{2x}$ (b) $12 - x$ (c) $\dfrac{1}{x+1}$

   (d) $\sqrt{\dfrac{8}{x} - 1}$ (e) $\sqrt{1 - x^2}$

   (f) $\sqrt{4 - x} + 2$

   (b) and (e) are self-inverse.

Exercise B (p. 57)

1   (a) $x = \frac{1}{5}(2y + 3)$ (b) $x = \frac{4}{3}y + 5$

   (c) $x = 5 \pm \sqrt{y - 4}$ (d) $x = 3 + \dfrac{1}{y}$

2   (a) $f^{-1}(x) = \frac{1}{5}(2x + 3)$;
       f has domain and range $\{x \in \mathbb{R}\}$

   (b) $f^{-1}(x) = \frac{4}{3}x + 5$;
       f has domain and range $\{x \in \mathbb{R}\}$

   (c) $f^{-1}(x) = 5 + \sqrt{x - 4}$;
       f has domain $x \geqslant 5$, and range $y \geqslant 4$
       or $f^{-1}(x) = 5 - \sqrt{x - 4}$;
       f has domain $x \leqslant 5$ and range $y \geqslant 4$

   (d) $f^{-1}(x) = 3 + \dfrac{1}{x}$;
       f has domain $x \neq 3$, and range $y \neq 0$

3   (a) $a = \dfrac{2y}{900 - y}$

   (b) Since a and y are both positive, the denominator $(900 - y)$ must be positive.

4   (a) $x = \dfrac{1 + y}{1 - y}$ (b) $x = \dfrac{2 - 3y}{1 + y}$

5   The image will be $y = f^{-1}(x) = \dfrac{x}{1 - 2x}$.

6 $f^{-1}(x) = -\sqrt{\dfrac{x-1}{x+1}}$ $(x < -1)$

7   (a) $W = \dfrac{P - b}{a}$ or $\dfrac{1}{a}(P - b)$

   (b) $r = \dfrac{C}{2\pi}$

   (c) $l = \dfrac{2s}{n} - a$ (d) $r = 1 - \dfrac{a}{s}$ or $\dfrac{s - a}{s}$

   (e) $x = \dfrac{yR}{y - R}\left(\text{since } \dfrac{1}{x} = \dfrac{1}{R} - \dfrac{1}{y} = \dfrac{y - R}{yR}\right)$

8   (a) (i) 75 feet   (ii) 175 feet
       (iii) 315 feet

   (b) $v = \sqrt{20(d + 5)} - 10$ (c) 61.4 m.p.h.

9 $a = 1.7 \times 10^{-5}$

10 $c = \sqrt{\dfrac{E}{m}}$

11 $v = \sqrt{\dfrac{2E + mu^2}{m}}$ $\left[\text{or } v = \sqrt{\dfrac{2E}{m} + u^2}\right]$

12 $T = 2\pi\sqrt{\dfrac{l}{g}}$

   $\Rightarrow \dfrac{T}{2\pi} = \sqrt{\dfrac{l}{g}}$

   $\Rightarrow \dfrac{T^2}{4\pi^2} = \dfrac{l}{g}$

   $\Rightarrow \dfrac{T^2 g}{4\pi^2} = l$

   $l = \dfrac{2^2 \times 9.81}{4\pi^2} = 0.9940$

13 (a) Area of cylindrical surface $= 2\pi rh$
Area of ends $= 2\pi r^2$
Total surface area $= 2\pi rh + 2\pi r^2$

$$S = 2\pi r(h + r)$$

(b) $h = \dfrac{S}{2\pi r} - r$

14 (a) $r = \sqrt{\dfrac{3V}{\pi h}}$ (b) $r = \dfrac{100I}{Pn}$

15 (a) $I = \dfrac{nE}{R + nr} \Rightarrow I(R + nr) = nE$

$$\Rightarrow IR = nE - nrI$$

$$\Rightarrow R = \dfrac{n(E - rI)}{I}$$

(b) $E = \frac{1}{2}mv^2 \Rightarrow 2E = mv^2$

$$\Rightarrow \dfrac{2E}{m} = v^2$$

$$\Rightarrow v = \sqrt{\dfrac{2E}{m}}$$

C Functions and transformations of graphs (p. 60)

1 Graphs b, c and e can be mapped onto each other. Graphs a and d can be mapped onto each other.

2 (a) The translation through $\begin{bmatrix} 5\frac{1}{2} \\ -2\frac{3}{4} \end{bmatrix}$

(b) The translation through $\begin{bmatrix} 7 \\ -2 \end{bmatrix}$

(c) The translation through $\begin{bmatrix} 11 \\ 0 \end{bmatrix}$

3 b can be mapped onto e by a reflection in the y-axis.

4 (a) $f(x) = x^4$, $f(x) + 2 = x^4 + 2$,
$f(x + 3) = (x + 3)^4$

(b) The three graphs are congruent and the transformations needed are:

(i) translation $\begin{bmatrix} 0 \\ 2 \end{bmatrix}$

(ii) translation $\begin{bmatrix} -3 \\ 0 \end{bmatrix}$

5 (a) $g(x) = \dfrac{1}{x}$, $g(x + 4) = \dfrac{1}{x + 4}$,

$$g(x + 4) + 3 = \dfrac{1}{x + 4} + 3$$

(b) The three graphs are congruent and the transformations needed are:

(i) translation $\begin{bmatrix} -4 \\ 0 \end{bmatrix}$

(ii) translation $\begin{bmatrix} -4 \\ 3 \end{bmatrix}$

6 In questions 4 and 5 you saw that replacing 'x' by '$x - 5$' resulted in a translation of 5 parallel to the x-axis; and that adding 2 to the function was equivalent to a translation of 2 parallel to the y-axis.

So it is reasonable to suggest that the image of

$$y = \dfrac{3}{x^2} \text{ under a translation } \begin{bmatrix} 5 \\ 2 \end{bmatrix} \text{ is}$$

$$y = \dfrac{3}{(x - 5)^2} + 2$$

7 $y = (x + 2)^2 - 1$, a translation by $\begin{bmatrix} -2 \\ -1 \end{bmatrix}$

8 (a) $f(x) = x^2 - x$, $f(-x) = x^2 + x$,
$-f(x) = -x^2 + x$

(b) (i) Reflection in y-axis
(ii) Reflection in x-axis

(c) Yes

(i) If (a, b) is a point on the graph of $y = f(x)$, then $(-a, b)$ will be a point on the graph of $y = f(-x)$.

(ii) Similarly, if (a, b) is on the graph of $y = f(x)$, then $(a, -b)$ is on the graph of $y = -f(x)$.

9 (a) The equation of the reflected graph
will be $y = -f(x) = -x^4 + 2x^3$.

(b) The equation of the reflected graph
will be $y = f(-x) = x^4 + 2x^3$.

10 (a) $f(-x) = 3x^2 - x^4$

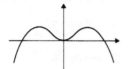

The graphs of $f(x)$ and $f(-x)$ coincide,
since $(-x)^2 = x^2$ and $(-x)^4 = x^4$.

(b) $f(-x) = -x^3 + 5x = -f(x)$

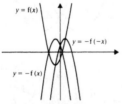

Here $f(-x) = -f(x)$, since $(-x)^3 = -x^3$
and $5(-x) = -5x$.

11 (a) Even   (b) Odd   (c) Neither

12 (a) Even   (b) Neither   (c) Neither
(d) Odd   (e) Odd   (f) Even

13 (a) After the first reflection,
$$y = -f(x) = -x^2 - 3x + 2 = g(x)$$
After the second reflection,
$$y = g(-x) = -x^2 + 3x + 2$$

(b) A single equivalent transformation is
a 180° rotation about the origin.

14 The equation of the curve obtained by
reflection is
$$y = f(-x) = 2x^2 + \frac{1}{x} = g(x)$$
The equation of the curve obtained after
translation is
$$y = g(x - 4) + 3$$
$$= 2(x - 4)^2 + \frac{1}{x - 4} + 3$$

Exercise C (p. 65)

1 (a)

$y = x^2$ translated through $\begin{bmatrix} 0 \\ 9 \end{bmatrix}$

(b) $y = x^3$ translated through $\begin{bmatrix} 0 \\ -2 \end{bmatrix}$

(c)

$y = x^2$ translated through $\begin{bmatrix} 1 \\ 0 \end{bmatrix}$

(d)

$y = 5x^2$ translated through $\begin{bmatrix} 3 \\ 6 \end{bmatrix}$

(e) $y = \dfrac{3}{x}$ translated through $\begin{bmatrix} -\frac{1}{2} \\ 0 \end{bmatrix}$

(f)

$y = x^2 + 2x = (x + 1)^2 - 1$

i.e. $y = x^2$ translated through $\begin{bmatrix} -1 \\ -1 \end{bmatrix}$

2 (a) $y = (x - 4)^2$ (b) $y = \dfrac{1}{(x - 3)^2}$

(c) $y = -2 - |x|$ (d) $y = 3 - 2(x - 4)^2$

(e) $y = (x + 3)^3 + 2$

(f) $y = (x + 3 - 4)\sqrt{x + 3} + 1$
$= (x - 1)\sqrt{x + 3} + 1$

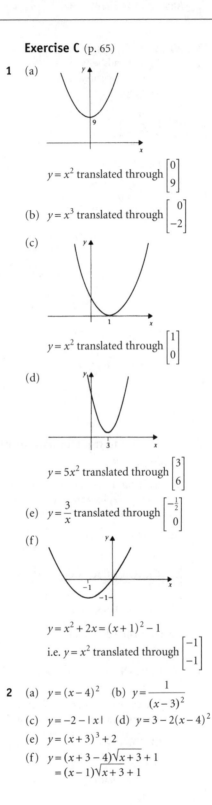

3 (a) $y = \dfrac{-1}{x+6} - 7$ (b) $y = 3x + 7$

(c) $y = 3 - \dfrac{1}{(x-2)^2}$

D   The modulus function: using graphs
(p. 67)

1 (a) 2 (b) 3 (c) 0 (d) 12 (e) 0.5

2D (a) 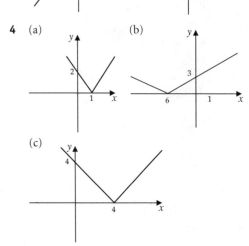 (b)

(c) (d)

3 (a) (b)

4 (a) (b)

(c)

5 (a) 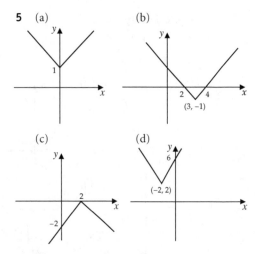 (b)

(3, −1)

(c) (d)

(−2, 2)

6 (a) $x = 1$ or 5 (b) $1 < x < 5$

7D (a) 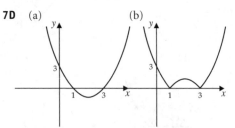 (b)

8 1 matches Q, 2 matches P, 3 matches R.

9 (a) 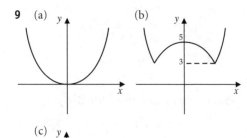 (b)

5

3

(c)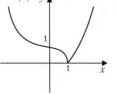

1

Exercise D (p. 71)

1   (a) 16   (b) 9   (c) 1   (d) 64
(e) −5   (f) −4

2   (a) (b) (c) (d) (e) (f)

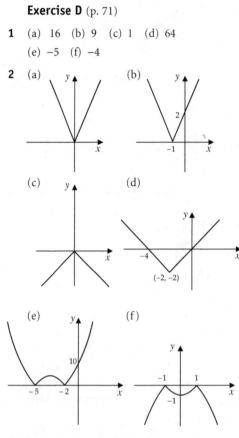

3   (a) $x = 1.5$ or 3 (b) $x < 1.5$ or $x > 3$

4E $x = -1.37, 0, 1$ or 4.37

S3.1   Composition of functions (p. 72)

(a) (i) $f(4) = 4^2 = 16$

(ii) $g(16) = 3 \times 16 + 1 = 49$

(b) $g(f(4)) = g(16) = 49$

(c) (i) $g(f(2)) = g(4) = 13$

(ii) $g(f(-3)) = g(9) = 28$

(iii) $f(g(-2)) = f(-5) = 25$

(d)

$$x \longrightarrow \boxed{f} \xrightarrow{x^2} \boxed{g} \xrightarrow{3(x^2) + 1 = g\,(f(x))}$$

(e)   For example, from (a) $g(f(2)) = 13$, and $3(2^2) + 1 = 13$

(f)

$$x \longrightarrow \boxed{g} \xrightarrow{3x + 1} \boxed{f} \xrightarrow{(3x + 1)^2} \; f(g(x)) = (3x + 1)^2$$

2   (a) (i) $gf(x) = \dfrac{1}{x} - 3,\ fg(x) = \dfrac{1}{x - 3}$

(ii) $gf(x) = \sqrt{2x},\ fg(x) = 2\sqrt{x}$

(iii) $gf(x) = (x + 5) - 9 = x - 4$,
$fg(x) = (x - 9) + 5 = x - 4$

(iv) $gf(x) = fg(x) = 10 - (10 - x) = x$

(v) $gf(x) = fg(x) = \dfrac{1}{1/x} = x$

(b)   When $fg(x) = gf(x)$, the order in which the functions are applied does not matter.

In (iii), the order in which successive addition and subtraction is carried out does not matter.

In (iv) and (v), the composite function is in both cases the identity function. Since functions f and g are the same in each example, they are both **self-inverse** functions.

3   (a) $x + 2$ (b) x^2 (c) $\dfrac{1}{x}$ (d) $\sqrt{x}$

4   (a) $x + 8$ (b) x^2 (c) $3x + 1$

(d) $\dfrac{12}{x}$ (e) $\sqrt[3]{x}$ (f) $4x - x^2$

S3.2   Rearranging formulas (p. 73)

1 $x = \pm\sqrt{\dfrac{y}{5} + 7}$

2   (a) $x = \pm\sqrt{\dfrac{y + 7}{3}}$

(b) $x = \tfrac{1}{2}(\pm\sqrt{9y} - 1)$

(c) $x = \tfrac{1}{9}(y + 1)^2$

3 $x = \dfrac{3}{y + 4}$

4 (a) $x = \dfrac{1}{2 - y}$

   (b) $x = \pm \sqrt{\dfrac{3}{y}}$

   (c) $x = \dfrac{1}{4(y - 5)^2}$

   (d) $x = \dfrac{2}{y} - 1$

   (e) $x = \dfrac{1}{2}\left(\dfrac{4}{y} - 1\right)$

   (f) $x = \dfrac{1}{2}\left(1 - \dfrac{7}{y}\right)$

   (g) $x = \pm\sqrt{y} - 1$

   (h) $x = \tfrac{1}{2}(1 \pm \sqrt{y})$

   (i) $x = \pm 2\sqrt{1 - y}$

4 Circular functions

A Graphs of the sine and cosine functions (p. 74)

1 (a) $\sin 50° = 0.77$

   (b) $-230°,\ 130°,\ 410°,\ 490°$

2 (a) $\cos 163° = -0.96$

   (b) $-197°,\ -163°,\ 197°,\ 523°,\ 557°$

3 (a) $\sin 339° = -0.36$

   (b) $-21°,\ -159°,\ 201°$

4 $y = \sin \theta°$ maps onto $y = a \sin \theta°$ by a stretch of factor a in the y-direction.

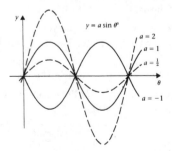

5 (a) $y = \sin \theta°$ maps onto $y = \sin b\theta°$ by a stretch of factor $\dfrac{1}{b}$ in the θ-direction.

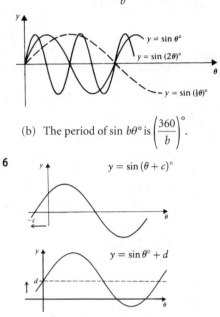

   (b) The period of $\sin b\theta°$ is $\left(\dfrac{360}{b}\right)°$.

6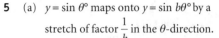

$y = \sin(\theta + c)°$ is obtained by a translation of $-c$ in the θ-direction. $-c$ is known as the phase shift.

$y = \sin \theta° + d$ is obtained by a translation of d in the y-direction.

$y = \sin(\theta + c)° + d$ is obtained by a translation of $\begin{bmatrix} -c \\ d \end{bmatrix}$.

7 (a) As in question 5, $y = \cos b\theta°$ has period $\dfrac{360}{b}$.

   (b) $y = \cos \theta°$ is mapped onto $y = \cos(b\theta + c)°$ by a stretch of $\dfrac{1}{b}$ in the θ-direction, followed by a translation of $-\dfrac{c}{b}$ in the θ-direction.

   Thus $y = \cos(b\theta + c)°$ has period $\dfrac{360}{b}$, and phase shift $-\dfrac{c}{b}$.

   This is not surprising, since the maximum value of $\cos(b\theta + c)°$ is 1, which occurs when $b\theta + c = 0$, i.e. when $\theta = -\dfrac{c}{b}$.

8 $a = 2$, $b = 3$, $c = 30$ (there are other possible values of c)

9 $y = \cos \theta°$ is mapped onto $y = a \cos(b\theta + c)° + d$ by stretches of a and $\dfrac{1}{b}$ in the y- and θ-directions followed by a translation $\begin{bmatrix} -c/b \\ d \end{bmatrix}$. Note that the stretches have been done before the translation.

Exercise A (p. 80)

1 In each case there are alternative correct answers.
(a) $y = 2 \cos \theta°$ (b) $y = -3 \sin \theta°$
(c) $y = 10 \cos \theta°$ (d) $y = 4 \cos \theta° + 4$
(e) $y = \sin \theta° + 2$ (f) $y = 3 \sin 2\theta°$
(g) $y = 2 \cos 60\theta° + 1$
(h) $y = 4 \sin(3\theta + 30)° + 3$

2

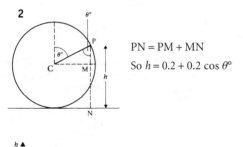

$PN = PM + MN$
So $h = 0.2 + 0.2 \cos \theta°$

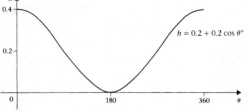

$h = 0.2 + 0.2 \cos \theta°$

3 (a) A one-way stretch of scale factor $\frac{1}{3}$ parallel to the x-axis, followed by a translation $\begin{bmatrix} -20 \\ 0 \end{bmatrix}$ and then a one-way stretch of scale factor 2 parallel to the y-axis.

(b) (i) $(180°, 0) \rightarrow (60°, 0) \rightarrow (40°, 0)$
      $\rightarrow (40°, 0)$
(ii) $(90°, 1) \rightarrow (30°, 1) \rightarrow (10°, 1)$
      $\rightarrow (10°, 2)$

B Modelling periodic behaviour (p. 81)

1 (a) $\theta = 6t$

(b)

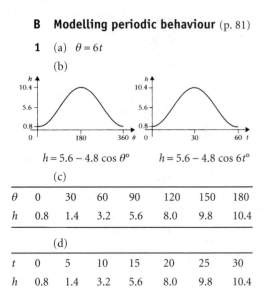

$h = 5.6 - 4.8 \cos \theta°$ $h = 5.6 - 4.8 \cos 6t°$

(c)

θ	0	30	60	90	120	150	180
h	0.8	1.4	3.2	5.6	8.0	9.8	10.4

(d)

t	0	5	10	15	20	25	30
h	0.8	1.4	3.2	5.6	8.0	9.8	10.4

Exercise B (p. 83)

1 (a) (i)

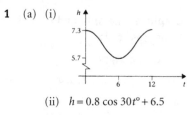

(ii) $h = 0.8 \cos 30t° + 6.5$
(b) $h = 0.65 \cos 30t° + 4.25$

2 From your first graph you will see that the points from April to October, inclusive, do not conform because of the British Summer Time adjustment. To make the data easier to graph you might proceed as follows:

• subtract 1 hour from sunset times in BST,

• change from hours and minutes to hours written in decimal form,

• count days from 12 December (when sunset is earliest).

This should give the table shown below, where t is the number of days after 12 December and s is the sunset hour.

t	20	48	76	103	131	159	187
s	16.05	16.75	17.60	18.40	19.18	19.92	20.35

t	215	243	261	299	327	355
s	20.17	19.45	18.43	17.37	16.43	15.90

The graph of s against t is an approximate sine or cosine curve, having amplitude about 2.28 (hours). A possible equation is

$$s = 18.11 - 2.28 \cos\left(\frac{360t°}{365}\right)$$

3 $l = 12 + 2.5 \cos 360t°$

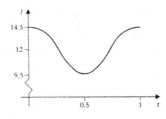

C Inverses and equations (p. 84)

1D (a) $x = 36.9°$

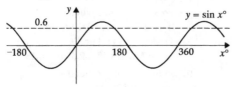

(b) From the graph there is clearly an infinite number of solutions. They include

$180 - 36.9 = 143.1$, $360 + 36.9 = 396.9$,
$360 + 143.1 = 503.1$,
$36.9 - 360 = -323.1$,
$143.1 - 360 = -216.9$

The **general solution** is $180n + (-1)^n 36.9$. The idea of a general solution is further developed in question 6E.

(c) In general, a mapping from a set A to a set B is a function if and only if every element a of set A has a unique image in set B. For continuous functions of real numbers, this means that a vertical line drawn on the graph must cut the graph at exactly one point.

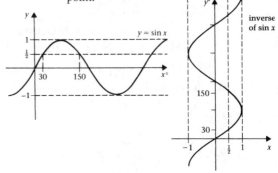

$\sin x$ **is** a function. It is a many-to-one mapping.

From the graph you can see that the inverse of sine is **not** a function. For example, the image of $\frac{1}{2}$ includes 30, 150, 390, ... indicating a one-to-many mapping.

The function called $\sin^{-1}$ later in this section is sometimes called arcsin.

2D The range $-90 \leqslant \cos^{-1} x \leqslant 90$ is no longer appropriate since cos is an even function.

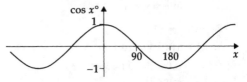

It is conventional to choose the range $0 \leqslant \cos^{-1} x \leqslant 180$ as giving all positive and negative values of $\cos x°$.

3 (a) $\cos x° = \frac{3}{4} = 0.75$

(b) One solution is $x = 41.4$

(c), (d) The other solution between 0 and 360 is $x = 360 - 41.4 = 318.6$

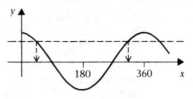

4 (a) $\cos x° = 0.56 \Rightarrow x = 55.9, 304.1$

   (b) $\sin x° = -0.23 \Rightarrow x = 193.3, 346.7$

   (c) $\cos x° = -0.5 \Rightarrow x = 120, 240$

5 $5 \sin(3t + 40)° = 4$

   $\Rightarrow \sin(3t + 40)° = \frac{4}{5}$

   $\Rightarrow \sin x° = 0.8$, where $x = 3t + 40$

   From a calculator, $x = 53.1$

   $x = 53.1, 126.9, 413.1, 486.9, 773.1, 846.9$

   $t = 4.37, 28.97, 124.37, 148.97, 244.37,$
   268.97

6E (a) $x = 23.6$

   (b)

sin x°

   From the graph the other solutions
   are: $180 - 23.6 = 156.4$,
   $360 + 23.6 = 383.6, 540 - 23.6 = 516.4$

   (c) $3600 + 23.6 = 3623.6$,
   $3600 + 156.4 = 3756.4$

   (d) $360n + 23.6, 360n + 156.4$

   (e) Yes. For example, if $n = -1$, the
   solutions $23.6 - 360$ and $156.4 - 360$
   are generated. The graph has period
   360 in both positive and negative
   directions.

7E (a) $p = 30$

   (b) $540 - 30, 720 + 30$

   (c) $180 \times 20 + 30 = 3600 + 30$,
   $180 \times 21 - 30 = 3780 - 30$

   (d) $180n + 30$ if n is even, $180n - 30$ if n is
   odd.

   Using the $(-1)^n$ notation,
   $x = 180n + (-1)^n 30$.

8E (a) The principal value is 44.4
   The general solution is
   $180n + (-1)^n 44.4$

   (b) The principal value is −44.4
   The general solution is
   $180n - (-1)^n 44.4$

   (c) The principal value is 45.6
   Other solutions are $360 - 45.6$,
   $360 + 45.6, 720 + 45.6, 720 - 45.6$, etc.
   The general solution is $360n \pm 45.6$

Exercise C (p. 87)

1 (a) 11.5°   (b) 25.8°   (c) −21.1°
   (d) 137.7°   (e) 90°   (f) 180°

2 (a) 17.5, 162.5, 377.5, 522.5, −197.5,
                                    −342.5

   (b) 36.9, 323.1, 396.9, 683.1, −36.9,
                                    −323.1

   (c) 107.5, 252.5, 467.5, 612.5, −107.5,
                                    −252.5

   (d) −30, −150, 210, 330, 570, 690

   (e) −180, 180, 540

   (f) 19.5, 160.5, 379.5, 520.5, −199.5,
                                    −340.5

3 (a) $\sin x° = 0.65 \Rightarrow x = 40.5, 139.5$

   (b) $\cos x° = -0.38 \Rightarrow x = 112.3, -112.3$

   (c) $\sin x° = -0.47 \Rightarrow x = -28.0, -152.0$

4 (a) $3 \sin x° = 2 \Rightarrow x = 41.8, 138.2$

   (b) $5 \cos x° + 2 = 0 \Rightarrow x = 113.6, 246.4$

   (c) $2 \cos x° + 5 = 0$ No solution for x

5 (a) $\sin 2t° = 0.7 \Rightarrow t = 22.2, 67.8, 202.2,$
                                    247.8

   (b) $2 \cos 3t° = 1 \Rightarrow t = 20, 100, 140, 220,$
                                    260, 340

   (c) $3 \cos(0.5t + 20)° = 2 \Rightarrow t = 56.4$

6 (a) $8 \sin 10t° = 5 \Rightarrow \sin 10t° = 0.625$
   $\Rightarrow \sin x° = 0.625$ where $x = 10t$
   If $0 \leqslant t \leqslant 60$, then $0 \leqslant x \leqslant 600$
   $x = 38.7$ or 141.3 or 398.7 or 501.3
   $\Rightarrow t = 3.87, 14.13, 39.87$ or 50.13

   (b) $7 \cos(t + 35)° = 4$. So, if $x = t + 35$,
   $\cos x° = 0.571$
   $\Rightarrow x = 55.2$ or 304.8
   $\Rightarrow t + 35 = 55.2$ (or 304.8)
   $\Rightarrow t = 20.2$, since remaining solutions
   are not in the required interval.

   (c) $t = 31.2$ or 41.6

   (d) $t = 51.6$

7E (a) $\sin x° = 0.2$
   Calculator value for $x = 11.5$ (to 3 s.f.)
   Solutions are $90 \pm 78.5 \pm 360n$.

   (b) Calculator value for $x = 143$ (to 3 s.f.)
   General solution $x = \pm 143 \pm 360n$

   Other forms are possible in both (a) and
   (b).

8E (a) −23.6°   (b) 143.1°   (c) −92.9°
   (d) 25.8°   (e) 163.3°   (f) 168.5°

D Solving problems with sine and cosine (p. 88)

1 (a) If $h = 6$,

$6 = 2.5 \sin 30t + 5 \Rightarrow \sin 30t = 0.4$

Using a calculator,
$\sin x° = 0.4 \Rightarrow x = 23.58$ and, using the symmetry of the sine graph,
$x = 156.42$ is also a solution. So

$30t = 23.58$ or 156.42

$\Rightarrow \quad t = 0.786$ hours or 5.214 hours

The height is 6 m at 0047 hours and 0513 hours.

You could find subsequent times by extending the range of values of x beyond 360. The next two are

$x = 383.58$ and 516.42

$\Rightarrow \quad 30t = 383.58$ and 516.42

$\Rightarrow \quad t = 12.786$ and 17.214

giving, as expected, 1247 and 1713.

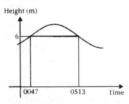

Height (m)

(b) From the graph, the depth is greater than 6 m between 0047 and 0513 and again between 1247 and 1713 for a total of 8 hours 52 min each day.

Exercise D (p. 90)

1 $5.6 - 4.8 \cos 6t° = 9 \Rightarrow \cos 6t° = \dfrac{-3.4}{4.8}$

$\Rightarrow t = 22.5, 37.5$

The chair is above 9 metres for
$37.5 - 22.5 = 15$ seconds.

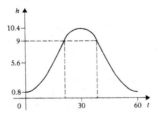

2 (a) $5 + 2.5 \sin 30t° = 6.7 \Rightarrow \sin 30t° = \dfrac{1.7}{2.5}$

$\Rightarrow t = 1.43, 4.57, 13.43, 16.57$

Times: 0126, 0434, 1326, 1634

(b) $5 + 2.5 \sin 30t° = 4.5 \Rightarrow \sin 30t° =$

$\dfrac{-0.5}{2.5} \Rightarrow t = 6.38, 11.62, 18.38, 23.62$

Times: 0623, 1137, 1823, 2337

3 (a) $2 + 1.5 \sin 500t° = 2.75 \Rightarrow \sin 500t°$
$= 0.5 \Rightarrow t = 0.06, 0.3$

0.06 and 0.3 seconds from the start and repeatedly every 0.72 seconds

(b) $2 + 1.5 \sin 500t° = 2 \Rightarrow \sin 500t° = 0$
$\Rightarrow t = 0, 0.36, 0.72, ...$

Every 0.36 seconds from the start

(c) $2 + 1.5 \sin 500t° = 3.5 \Rightarrow \sin 500t° = 1$
$\Rightarrow t = 0.18$

0.18 seconds from the start and every 0.72 seconds thereafter

4 (a) 61 cm

(b) $56 - 10$ when
$\sin(130t) = \sin(270°) = 46$ cm

(c) $56 + 10$ when
$\sin(130t) = \sin(90°) = 66$ cm

(d) $10 \sin(130t) = 6$
$\Rightarrow 130t = \sin^{-1}(0.6)$
$= 36.87°, 143.13°$
$\Rightarrow \quad t = 0.283 ..., 1.101$
$= 0.28$ and 1.10 seconds

(e) $360 ÷ 130 = 2.77$ seconds

E The tangent function (p. 91)

1D (a) (i) $5 \tan θ°$

(ii) the acute angle whose tangent is 3; $\tan^{-1} 3 \approx 71.6°$

(b) (i) 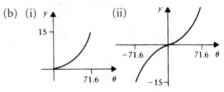 (ii)

(c) $\tan θ° = \dfrac{a}{b}$

$\dfrac{\sin θ°}{\cos θ°} = \dfrac{a}{c} ÷ \dfrac{b}{c} = \dfrac{a}{b}$

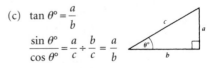

(d) All real numbers θ for which
     $\cos \theta° \neq 0$

(e) $-90° < \tan^{-1} x < 90°$

2 (a) -1 (b) -1 (c) 1 (d) -1

Exercise E (p. 93)

1 (a) $45°$ (b) $-80.5°$ (c) $0°$

2 (a)

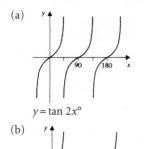

$y = \tan 2x°$

(b)

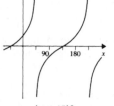

$y = \tan(x + 45)°$

3 (a) $x = 71.6$ or $180 + 71.6 = 251.6$

(b) $\tan(2x + 30)° = 0.8$

$\Rightarrow 2x + 30 = 38.7$ or 218.7 or 398.7
         or 578.7

$\Rightarrow x = 4.4$ or 94.4 or 184.4 or 274.4

(c) $\tan x° = \pm 1$

$\tan x° = +1 \Rightarrow x = 45$ or 225

$\tan x° = -1 \Rightarrow x = 135$ or 315

(d) $4 \sin x° = 3 \cos x°$

$\Rightarrow \dfrac{4 \sin x°}{\cos x°} = 3$

$\Rightarrow \tan x° = \dfrac{3}{4}$

$\Rightarrow x = 36.9$ or 216.9

4 (a) (i) $60°$ (ii) $\dfrac{40°}{3}$

(b) (i) $1080°$ (ii) $-288°$

(c) (i) $270°$ (ii) $-45°$

S4.1 Sine and cosine of angles greater than 90° (p. 94)

1 (b) (i) $(45, 0.71)$ (ii) $(60, 0.87)$
          (iii) $(0, 0)$ (iv) $(90, 1)$
          (v) $(20, 0.34)$ (vi) $(70, 0.94)$

2 (b) $(135, 0.71)$ $(120, 0.87)$ $(180, 0)$
          $(170, 0.17)$ $(110, 0.94)$

3 (b) $(225, -0.71)$ $(240, -0.87)$ $(270, -1)$
          $(200, -0.34)$ $(260, -0.98)$

4 (b) $(315, -0.71)$ $(300, -0.87)$ $(360, 0)$
          $(350, -0.17)$ $(280, -0.98)$

5 $(390, 0.5)$ $(405, 0.71)$ $(420, 0.87)$ $(450, 1)$
      $(480, 0.87)$ $(495, 0.71)$ $(510, 0.5)$ $(540, 0)$

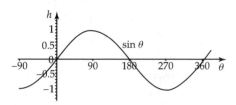

6 $(45, 0.71)$ $(60, 0.5)$ $(0, 1)$ $(90, 0)$ $(20, 0.94)$
      $(70, 0.34)$

8 $(135, -0.71)$ $(120, -0.5)$ $(180, -1)$
      $(170, -0.98)$ $(110, -0.34)$ $(225, -0.71)$
      $(240, -0.5)$ $(270, 0)$ $(200, -0.93)$
      $(260, -0.17)$ $(315, 0.71)$ $(300, 0.5)$ $(360, 1)$
      $(350, 0.98)$ $(280, 0.17)$

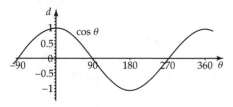

5 Growth functions

A Exponential growth (p. 98)

1D (a) From the graph there were 4000 bacteria after approximately 2 hours and 8000 after 7 hours.

(b) There were 5000 bacteria after approximately 3.7 hours and 10 000 after 8.7 hours.

(c) Notice that in each of the cases above it takes 5 hours to double the number of bacteria. If the number of bacteria doubles in any period of 5 hours, you could use this to estimate the time for 24 000 bacteria. Doubling does appear to take place in all 5-hour intervals.

Since there are 12 000 bacteria after 10 hours it is reasonable to suggest that there will be 24 000 after 15 hours.

(d) Similarly, since there are 3000 bacteria after 0 hours there would have been 1500 bacteria 5 hours earlier, when $t = -5$.

The number of bacteria doubles every 5 hours. It can also be seen that the number of bacteria trebles approximately every 8 hours. For example, 3000 after 0 hours, 9000 after 8 hours; 4000 after 2 hours, 12 000 after 10 hours. Given any fixed time period, the number of bacteria will always increase by the same factor during that time, independent of the number at the start of the period.

Exercise A (p. 100)

1 Although the growth factors show slight variations, they are all 1.20 to 3 s.f. Allowing for the error introduced in rounding the profit figures, the profit is growing exponentially.

2 In each case the annual growth factor is 1.09. This means that the amount in the account at the end of the year is 109% of that at the beginning, so the increase or interest rate is 9%.

Since the growth factor is constant, the growth is exponential.

3

Age	Pocket money (£)	Growth factor
0	50	
1	60	1.2
2	70	1.17
3	80	1.14
4	90	1.13
5	100	1.11

Since the yearly growth factor is not constant, this is not exponential growth.

4 Notice that the time intervals are sometimes 4 years and sometimes 8 years.

Over the 4-year intervals, the growth factor is approximately 1.12 in each case.

Over the 8-year intervals, the growth factor is approximately 1.24 in each case.

Over two 4-year intervals the population would increase by a factor of 1.12 twice, giving an 8-year factor of $1.12 \times 1.12 \approx 1.25$.

The growth is therefore approximately exponential.

5 (a)

Time (s)	0	1	2	3	4	5
Charge (V)	9	8	7	6	5	4
Growth factor		0.89	0.88	0.86	0.83	0.80

Time (s)	6	7	8	9
Charge (V)	3	2	1	0
Growth factor	0.75	0.67	0.50	0

The decay is not exponential.

(b)

Time (s)	0	1	2	3	4	5
Charge (V)	9	6.75	5.063	3.797	2.848	2.136
Growth factor		0.75	0.75	0.75	0.75	0.75

The decay is exponential with growth factor 0.75.

B   Growth factors (p. 101)

1   (a)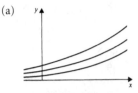

The family of graphs is as shown. The graph of the function cuts the y-axis where $y = K$.

(b)   If $y = K \times a^x$, $y = K$ when $x = 0$.

2   (a) $y = 1$ when $t = 0$ (b) $y = K$ when $t = 0$

3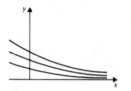

This time the graph shows exponential decay. The graph of $y = K \times \left(\frac{1}{2}\right)^x$ is obtained by reflecting that of $y = K \times 2^x$ in the y-axis.

Again, K is the value of y when $x = 0$.

4   (a) $y = 5 \times 3^t$ (b)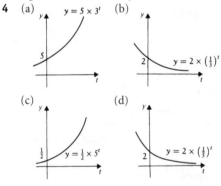

(c) $y = \frac{1}{2} \times 5^t$ (d) $y = 2 \times \left(\frac{1}{3}\right)^t$

the other graphs: $y = 2 \times \left(\frac{1}{3}\right)^t$

5   (a) $K = 1.5 \times 10^6$, i.e. the initial value.

(b)   In 1700, $P = 6.1 \times 10^6 = Ka^{634}$, since $t = 634$

i.e. $6.1 \times 10^6 = 1.5 \times 10^6 a^{634}$

$\Rightarrow a^{634} = \dfrac{6.1}{1.5}$

$\Rightarrow a = \left(\dfrac{6.1}{1.5}\right)^{\frac{1}{634}} = 1.002\,22$

(c)   In 1990, $t = 924$

$P = Ka^{924}$

$= 1.5 \times 10^6 \times 1.002\,22^{924}$

$= 11.59 \times 10^6$

(d)   The annual growth factor since 1700 has been considerably greater than 1.002 22, since the population of the United Kingdom is approximately 55 million.

Exercise B (p. 103)

1   (a)   There will be 14 400 bacteria after 2 hours.

(b)   There will be 1 000 000 bacteria after 4–5 hours.

(c)   Since the growth factor is constant, a growth function can be used.

Number of bacteria $= 400 \times 6^t$

2   (a)   1.08

(b)   The value of the investment after n years is £4000 $\times$ 1.08^n. When the value is £5000,

$5000 = 4000 \times 1.08^n$

Dividing by 4000,

$1.25 = 1.08^n$

(c) $n \approx 2.899$. In practice, there would be £5000 at the end of the third year.

3   (a)   The growth factor over the 10 days is

$\dfrac{2.48}{10} = 0.248$.

The daily growth factor is $(0.248)^{\frac{1}{10}} = 0.87$.

(b) $M = 10 \times 0.87^t$

(c)

t (days)	0	2	3	6	7	10
Mass (kg)	10	7.57	6.57	4.34	3.77	2.48
M	10	7.57	6.59	4.34	3.77	2.48

(d)   After 3 weeks, when $t = 21$ the mass is 0.54 kg.

(e)   Approximately 5 days

4   If $V = Ka^t$,

$V = 15$ when $t = 0 \Rightarrow K = 15$

Growth factor $a = \left(\frac{6}{15}\right)^{\frac{1}{12}} \approx 0.93$

$V = 15 \times \left(\frac{6}{15}\right)^{\frac{1}{12}t} \approx 15 \times 0.93^t$

C   Logarithms (p. 104)

1   (a) $2^6 = 64 \Longrightarrow \log_2 64 = 6$

(b) $2^{-3} = \frac{1}{8} \Longrightarrow \log_2 \frac{1}{8} = -3$

(c) $2^1 = 2 \Longrightarrow \log_2 2 = 1$

(d) $2^{\frac{1}{2}} = \sqrt{2} \Longrightarrow \log_2 \sqrt{2} = \frac{1}{2}$

2   (a) $3^2 = 9 \Longrightarrow \log_3 9 = 2$ (b) 3

(c) -2 (d) 0   (e) -3

(f) $\frac{1}{4}$, since $\sqrt[4]{3} = 3^{\frac{1}{4}}$

(g) $\frac{1}{2}$, since $2 = 4^{\frac{1}{2}}$ (h) 1

(i) This cannot be found since 3^x is always positive.

3   (a) $a^0 = 1 \Longrightarrow \log_a 1 = 0$

(b) $a^1 = a \Longrightarrow \log_a a = 1$

(c) $a^{-1} = \frac{1}{a} \Longrightarrow \log_a \frac{1}{a} = -1$

(d) $\log_a a^2 = 2$

4   (a) $\log_{10} 10^{3.7} = 3.7$ (b) $10^{\log_{10} 3.7} = 3.7$

This is to be expected, since $\log_{10} x$ and 10^x are inverse functions. In each case 3.7 is operated on by the function and its inverse and so is its own image.

5   (a) (i) $\log_2 8 = 3$ (ii) $\log_2 16 = 4$

(iii) $\log_2 128 = 7$

(b) $8 \times 16 = 128$ becomes $2^3 \times 2^4 = 2^7$ so $a = 3, b = 4, c = 7$ and $a + b = c$.

(c) Since $a = \log_2 8, b = \log_2 16$, $c = \log_2 128$ it follows that $\log_2 8 + \log_2 16 = \log_2 128$.

6   As with question 5, $2 + 3 = 5$, but $2 = \log_3 9, 3 = \log_3 27$ and $5 = \log_3 243 = \log_3 (9 \times 27)$ so $\log_3 9 + \log_3 27 = \log_3 (9 \times 27)$.

7   (b) (i) $\log_{10} 3 = 0.4771$

(ii) $\log_{10} 5 = 0.6990$

(c) $\log_{10} 15 = \log_{10} (3 \times 5)$
$= \log_{10} 3 + \log_{10} 5 = 0.4771 + 0.6990$
$= 1.1761$

8 $\log_{10} 9 = 0.954, \log_{10} 8 = 0.903$,
$\log_{10} 72 = 1.857 = 0.954 + 0.903$

9 $\log_a m + \log_a \dfrac{l}{m} = \log_a m \times \dfrac{l}{m} = \log_a l$

$\Longrightarrow \log_a l - \log_a m = \log_a \dfrac{l}{m}$

10 $\log_{10} \frac{1}{2} = \log_{10} 1 - \log_{10} 2 = 0 - 0.3010$
$= -0.3010$

$\log_{10} 1.5 = \log_{10} \frac{3}{2} = \log_{10} 3 - \log_{10} 2$
$= 0.4771 - 0.3010 = 0.1761$

$\log_{10} 2.5 = \log_{10} \frac{10}{4} = \log_{10} \dfrac{10}{2 \times 2}$

$= \log_{10} 10 - \log_{10} 2 - \log_{10} 2$
$= 1 - 2 \times 0.3010 = 0.398$

$\log_{10} 4 = 0.6020$ $\log_{10} 5 = 0.6990$

$\log_{10} 6 = 0.7781$ $\log_{10} 8 = 0.9030$

$\log_{10} 9 = 0.9542$

11D   From the table,

$\log_{10} 1.17 = 0.0682$

$\log_{10} 1.091 = 0.0378$ (add on the amount given for 1 in the end columns).

Since $\log_{10} \left(\dfrac{a}{b} \right) = \log_{10} a - \log_{10} b$,

$\log_{10} (1.17 \div 1.091) = \log_{10} 1.17 - \log_{10} 1.091$
$= 0.0682 - 0.0378$
$= 0.0304$

Using the table in reverse,

$\log_{10}(1.073) = 0.0304$

So

$1.17 \div 1.091 = 1.073$

Exercise C (p. 108)

1   (a) $\log_3 9 = 2$ (b) $\log_4(\frac{1}{64}) = -3$

(c) $\log_{0.5} 4 = -2$ (d) $\log_{\frac{1}{8}} 2 = -\frac{1}{3}$

(e) $\log_{27} 9 = \frac{2}{3}$

2   (a) -2 (b) 3   (c) -1 (d) $-\frac{2}{3}$

3   (a) By the laws of logarithms,

$\log_3 9 + \log_3 27 - \log_3 81$

$= \log_3 \left(\dfrac{9 \times 27}{81} \right) = \log_3 3 = 1$

(b) $\log_5 15 - \log_5 3 = \log_5 \left(\dfrac{15}{3} \right) = \log_5 5 = 1$

(c) $2 \log_7 \sqrt{7} = \log_7 \sqrt{7} + \log_7 \sqrt{7}$

$= \log_7 (\sqrt{7} \times \sqrt{7}) = \log_7 7 = 1$

4

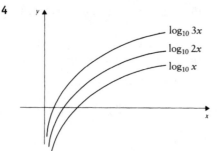

The graphs of $\log_{10} 2x$ and $\log_{10} 3x$ can be considered *either* as scalings of $\log_{10} x$ by factors of $\frac{1}{2}, \frac{1}{3}$ from the y-axis *or* as translations in the y direction.

By the laws of logs,

$\log_{10} 2x = \log_{10} 2 + \log_{10} x$

$\qquad = \log_{10} x + 0.3010$

$\log_{10} 3x = \log_{10} 3 + \log_{10} x$

$\qquad = \log_{10} x + 0.4771$

5 (a) $\log 1.05 = 0.0212$, $\log 1.267 = 0.1028$

$\log(1.05 \times 1.267) = 0.0212 + 0.1028$

$\qquad\qquad\qquad\quad = 0.1240$

Using the table in reverse,

$\qquad \log 1.330 = 0.1240,$

so $1.05 \times 1.267 = 1.330$

(b) $\log_{10} 10.5 = \log_{10}(10 \times 1.05)$

$\qquad\qquad = \log_{10} 10 + \log_{10} 1.05$

$\qquad\qquad = 1 + 0.0212 = 1.0212$

$\log_{10} 1267 = \log_{10}(10^3 \times 1.267)$

$\qquad\qquad = 3 + 0.1028 = 3.1028$

$\log_{10}(10.5 \times 1267) = 1.0212 + 3.1028$

$\qquad\qquad\qquad\qquad = 4.1240$

Now, since $\log 1.330 = 0.1240$

$4.1240 = 4 + \log 1.330$

$\qquad = \log 10^4 + \log 1.330$

$\qquad = \log 13\,300$

$10.5 \times 1267 \approx 13\,300$

6 $\log_5 5! = \log_5(5 \times 4 \times 3 \times 2 \times 1)$

$\qquad = \log_5 5 + \log_5(4 \times 3 \times 2 \times 1)$

$\qquad = \log_5 5 + \log_5 4!$

$\qquad = 1 + 1.9746$

$\qquad = 2.9746$

7 $t = \log_2 1000$

$2^9 = 512,\quad 2^{10} = 1024 \quad 9 < t < 10$

$t = 9.97$

D   Equation of the form $a^x = b$ (p. 108)

1 (a) (i) $\log_{10} 49 = 1.6902,$
$\qquad\qquad \log_{10} 7 = 0.8451,$
$\qquad\qquad \log_{10} 49 = 2\log_{10} 7$

$\qquad$(ii) $\log_{10} 64 = 1.806$, $\log_{10} 2 = 0.301,$
$\qquad\qquad \log_{10} 64 = 6 \times \log_{10} 2$

$\qquad$(iii) $\log_{10} 125 = 2.0969,$
$\qquad\qquad \log_{10} 5 = 0.6990,$
$\qquad\qquad \log_{10} 125 = 3 \times \log_{10} 5$

(b) The results above suggest that
$\qquad \log_{10} m^p = p\log_{10} m.$

2 (a) $\log_a m^2 = \log_a(m \times m)$

$\qquad\qquad\quad = \log_a m + \log_a m + \log_a m$

$\qquad\qquad\quad = 2\log_a m$

(b) For any positive index,
$\qquad \log_a m^p = \log_a \underbrace{(m \times m \times \cdots \times m)}_{p\text{ factors}}$

$\qquad\quad = \underbrace{\log_a m + \log_a m + \cdots + \log_a m}_{p\text{ terms}}$

$\qquad\quad = p\log_a m$

3D (a) $\log 2^x = x\log 2$

(b) If $2^x = 7$, then $\log 2^x = \log 7$

$\qquad\qquad \Longrightarrow x\log 2 = \log 7$

$\qquad\qquad \Longrightarrow x = \dfrac{\log 7}{\log 2} = 2.807$

4 (a) 1% interest represents a monthly growth factor of 1.01. After m months the amount in the account will be 1000×1.01^m. There will be £2000 in the account when $1000 \times 1.01^m = 2000$. Dividing by 1000,

$\qquad\qquad 1.01^m = 2$

(b) $\qquad\quad 1.01^m = 2$

$\qquad \log(1.01^m) = \log 2$

$\qquad m\log 1.01 = \log 2$

$\qquad m = \dfrac{\log 2}{\log 1.01} = 69.66$

The amount will be a little over £2000 (£2006.76) after 70 months.

5 $t = 4.98$

The half-life is 5.0 days.

Exercise D (p. 111)

1   (a) $x = 5$ (b) $x = 2.5$ (c) $x = 2.67$

     (d) $x = 2.10$ (e) $x = 1.38$ (f) $x = 2.71$

2   (a) $2 \times 2 \times 2 \times 2 \times 2 = 32 \Longrightarrow 2^5 = 32$

     (b) $9 \times 9 \times 3 = 243$

          $\Longrightarrow 9^2 \times 9^{\frac{1}{2}} = 243 \Longrightarrow 9^{2.5} = 243$

     (c) $8 \times 8 \times 2 \times 2 = 256$

          $\Longrightarrow \quad 8^2 \times 2^2 = 256$

          $\Longrightarrow 8^2 \times (8^{\frac{1}{3}})^2 = 256$

          $\Longrightarrow \quad 8^2 \times 8^{\frac{2}{3}} = 256$

          $\Longrightarrow \quad\quad 8^{2.67} = 256$

3   (a)   The number of bacteria after t hours is given by 250×3.7^t.

     (b)   There will be 10 000 bacteria when

         $2.50 \times 3.7^t = 10\ 000$

         $\Longrightarrow \quad\quad 3.7^t = 40$

         $\Longrightarrow \quad\quad\quad t = 2.82$

         i.e. after 2 hours 49 minutes.

4   The time when there is $\frac{1}{5}$ of the original charge is given by the solution of

     $0.9^t = 0.2$

     i.e. $t = 15.28$ (seconds)

5   The equation used was $1.08^n = 1.25$.

     $n = 2.90$ (years).

6 $1000 = 470 \times 1.029^t$

     $\Longrightarrow 1.029^t = \dfrac{1000}{470} = 2.128$

     $\Longrightarrow \quad t = \dfrac{\log 2.128}{\log 1.029} = 26.4$

     i.e. the population will reach one thousand million in 2006.

7   They will be equal t years after 1980, where

     $t = \dfrac{\log 995 - \log 470}{\log 1.029 - \log 1.014} = 51$

8E   (a)   Use $\log a^x = x \log a$

        $(x - 1) \log 3 = \log 5$

            $x = \dfrac{\log 5}{\log 3} + 1$

            $x = 2.465$

     (b) $(2x + 1) \log 7 = \log 5$

            $2x = 0.8271 - 1$

            $x = -0.0865$

     (c) $5(3^x) = 2$

         $x \log 3 = \log 0.4$

            $x = -0.8340$

     (d) $2^{2x} = 2^x 2^x$ or $(2^x)^2$ hence we have a quadratic equation

         $(2^x + 5)(2^x - 2) = 0$

         $\Longrightarrow$ $2^x = -5$ not possible

         or $2^x = 2$

         $\Longrightarrow$ $x = 1$

E   **Using logarithms in experimental work** (p. 112)

Exercise E (p. 113)

1   3

2 $Q = 65 \times 0.35^t$

(There may be some variation in answers to questions 2 and 3, depending on the graphs drawn.)

3 $P = 3.2\sqrt{L}$;   8.7 should be 7.8

4   13.2

F   **Differentiating growth functions** (p. 114)

1   (a)

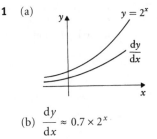

     (b) $\dfrac{dy}{dx} \approx 0.7 \times 2^x$

2 (a)

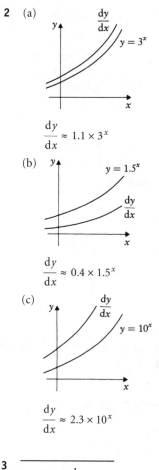

$$\frac{dy}{dx} \approx 1.1 \times 3^x$$

(b)

$$\frac{dy}{dx} \approx 0.4 \times 1.5^x$$

(c)

$$\frac{dy}{dx} \approx 2.3 \times 10^x$$

3

a	$\dfrac{d}{dx}(a^x)$
1.5	0.4×1.5^x
2	0.7×2^x
3	1.1×3^x
10	2.3×10^x

The value of a will lie somewhere between 2 and 3, probably around 2.7.

4 Since multiplication by k represents a scaling by a factor of k in the y-direction, the gradient will also be multiplied by k.

$$\frac{d}{dx}(ke^x) = ke^x$$

5 (a) The x-coordinate of Q is $x + 0.001$
$\Rightarrow$ the y-coordinate of Q is
$$2^{x+0.001} = 2^{0.001} \times 2^x.$$

(b) The gradient is
$$\frac{\text{change in } y}{\text{change in } x} = \frac{2^{0.001} \times 2^x - 2^x}{0.001}$$

(c) $\dfrac{2^{0.001} \times 2^x - 2^x}{0.001} = \dfrac{(2^{0.001} - 1)2^x}{0.001}$
$$\approx 0.693 \times 2^x$$

(d) You could zoom in even more so that the difference in x between P and Q is even less than 0.001. For example,
$$\frac{2^{0.000\,01} - 1}{0.000\,01} \times 2^x \approx 0.6931 \times 2^x$$

6 $\dfrac{5^{0.000\,01} - 1}{0.000\,01} \times 5^x \approx 1.6094 \times 5^x$

Exercise F (p. 116)

1 (a) 20.09 (b) 164.0 (c) 0.1353
(d) 0.249 (c) 1.649

2 (a)

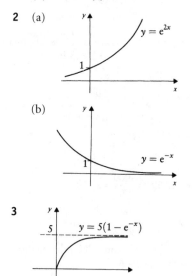

(b)

3

4 (a) (i) When $t = 0, y = 5$ (ii) 0.677
(iii)

The graph exhibits exponential decay.

(b) Since $0.5 > 0.2$, it decays more rapidly.

5 $y = 4e^t \Rightarrow \dfrac{dy}{dt} = 4e^t = y$

The rate of growth is equal to the size of the colony. It is growing at a rate equal to its size, i.e. at 500 bacteria per hour.

G Differentiating e^{ax} (p. 117)

1 (b) (i) $a = 1.46$ (ii) $a = 1.77$

(iii) $a = 0.63$

2 (a) (i) $a > 0$

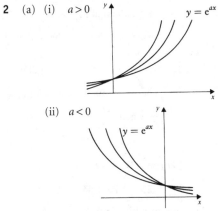

(ii) $a < 0$

If $a = 0$, $y = e^0 = 1$. The graph is a straight line.

(b) If $a > b > 0$ then e^{ax} lies above e^{bx} for positive values of x and below e^{bx} for negative values.

3 (a) 1.61 (b) 2.08 (c) 0.69

4 (a) $\dfrac{d}{dx}(e^{0.69x}) = \dfrac{d}{dx}(2^x) = 0.69 \times 2^x$
$$= 0.69 \times e^{0.69x}$$

(b) As in (a), $\dfrac{d}{dx}(e^{5x}) = 5e^{5x}$

5 (a) e^{2q} (b) q

(c) It multiplies the gradient of the graph by 2.

(d) $2g$, from part (c)

(e) The gradient is e^x, which at R is e^{2q}. Therefore the gradient at Q is $2 \times e^{2q}$.

(f) $\dfrac{d}{dx}(e^{2x}) = 2 \times e^{2x}$

6D $\displaystyle\int e^{ax}\,dx = \dfrac{1}{a}e^{ax} + \text{constant}$

Exercise G (p. 120)

1 (a) $4e^{4x}$ (d) $-2e^{-2x}$

(c) $\dfrac{d}{dx}(e^x)^5 = \dfrac{d}{dx}(e^{5x}) = 5e^{5x}$

(d) $\dfrac{d}{dx}\left(\dfrac{1}{e^{3x}}\right) = \dfrac{d}{dx}(e^{-3x}) = -3e^{-3x}$

(e) $20e^{4x}$ (f) $e^x - \dfrac{1}{e^x}$

(g) $\dfrac{1}{2}e^{\frac{1}{2}x}$ (h) $-45e^{-9x} = -\dfrac{45}{e^{9x}}$

2 (a) $\dfrac{1}{4}e^{4x}$ (b) $-\dfrac{1}{2}e^{-2x}$ (c) $\dfrac{1}{5}e^{5x}$

(d) $-\dfrac{1}{3}e^{-3x}$ (e) $\dfrac{5}{4}e^{4x}$ (f) $e^x - \dfrac{1}{e^x}$

(g) $2\sqrt{e^x}$ (h) $-\dfrac{5}{9e^{9x}}$

The constant of integration has been omitted in all cases.

3 (a)   (b)

(c)

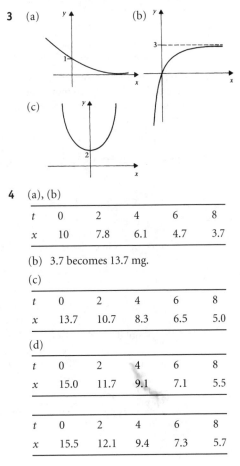

4 (a), (b)

t	0	2	4	6	8
x	10	7.8	6.1	4.7	3.7

(b) 3.7 becomes 13.7 mg.

(c)

t	0	2	4	6	8
x	13.7	10.7	8.3	6.5	5.0

(d)

t	0	2	4	6	8
x	15.0	11.7	9.1	7.1	5.5

t	0	2	4	6	8
x	15.5	12.1	9.4	7.3	5.7

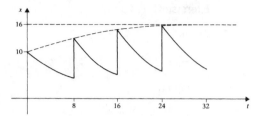

The maximum level of the drug in the body approaches 16 mg, which is approximately 1.6 times the administered dose. (In fact, you can show that it is $\dfrac{10e}{e-1}$ = 15.82 mg.)

5

t	0	2	4	6	8	
x	16	12.5	9.7	7.6	5.9	$\to 15.9$

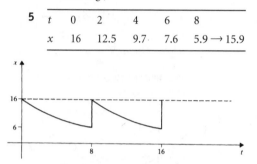

Thus, with a single booster dose, the required level is reached immediately and subsequent doses of 10 mg give a stable level of 16 mg.

H   Natural logarithms (p. 121)

1   (a) (i) $x = \ln 1 \Rightarrow e^x = 1 \Rightarrow x = 0$

(ii) $\ln e = \ln e^1 = 1$

(iii) $\ln e^2 = 2$

(iv) $\ln \dfrac{1}{e} = \ln e^{-1} = -1$

(v) $\ln \dfrac{1}{e^5} = \ln e^{-5} = -5$

(vi) $\ln(-1) = x \Rightarrow e^x = -1$, which has no solution. That is, $\ln(-1)$ is not defined.

(b)

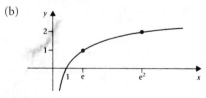

2D   (a) $b = e^a$ (b) (b, a)

(c) From the triangle 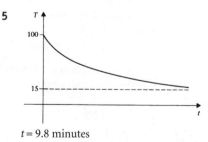 , the gradient

of $y = e^x$ at P is $\dfrac{\beta}{\alpha}$. From the triangle

, the gradient of $y = \ln x$ at

Q is $\dfrac{\alpha}{\beta}$. With x and y interchanged, the gradient at Q is the reciprocal of the gradient at P.

(d) Using a result in (c), the gradient is $\dfrac{1}{e^a}$.

(e) The gradient of $y = \ln x$ at Q is $\dfrac{1}{e^a} = \dfrac{1}{b}$.
The x-coordinate of Q is b and so
$$\frac{d}{dx}(\ln x) = \frac{1}{x}.$$

Exercise H (p. 123)

1   (a) 1.25   (b) −1.05   (c) 1.95

2   (a) $\ln 3 + \ln 4 = \ln(3 \times 4) = \ln 12$

(b) $\ln 10 - \ln 2 = \ln \frac{10}{2} = \ln 5$

(c) $3 \ln 5 = \ln 5^3 = \ln 125$

3   (a) $\ln x^3 = 3 \ln x$

(b) $\ln 4x = \ln 4 + \ln x$

(c) $\ln \frac{1}{3} x = \ln x - \ln 3$

4   (a) $\dfrac{4}{x}$

(b) $\dfrac{d}{dx}(\ln x^3) = \dfrac{d}{dx}(3 \ln x) = \dfrac{3}{x}$

(c) $\dfrac{d}{dx}(\ln 4x) = \dfrac{d}{dx}(\ln 4 + \ln x) = \dfrac{1}{x}$

5

$t = 9.8$ minutes

6 (a) $\frac{1}{2}m_0 = m_0 e^{-5570K}$

$\Rightarrow \quad e^{-5570K} = \frac{1}{2}$

$\Rightarrow \quad -5570K = \ln \frac{1}{2}$

$\Rightarrow \quad K = \frac{-1}{5570} \ln \frac{1}{2} = 1.24 \times 10^{-4}$

(b) $\frac{9}{10}m_0 = m_0 e^{-Kt}$

$\Rightarrow \quad 0.9 = e^{-Kt}$

$\Rightarrow \quad t = -\dfrac{1}{1.24 \times 10^{-4}} \ln 0.9 = 847 \text{ years}$

6 Radians and trigonometry

A Rates of change and radians (p. 125)

1D (a) The tide rises most rapidly after 0 and
12 hours, at the points where the
gradient of the graph is greatest.

(b) The tide falls most rapidly after 6
hours, when the gradient of the graph
is most negative.

(c) The rate of change is zero at high and
low tides, i.e. After 3, 9 and 15 hours.

2 (a) (i)

θ	10	5	2	1	0.1
$\dfrac{\sin \theta°}{\theta}$	0.01736	0.01743	0.01745	0.01745	0.01745

(ii) The sequence tends to a value of
0.017 45 rounded to five decimal
places.

3 (a)

θ	10	5	2	1	01
(i) BC	0.1736	0.0872	0.0349	0.01745	0.001745
(ii) arc BA	0.1745	0.0873	0.0349	0.01745	0.001745

(b) The lengths of BC and arc BA become
close in value as θ gets smaller. Both
tend to $0.01745 \times \theta$, the same limit as
question 1.

4 Length BC = $\sin \theta°$

$$\text{Arc BA} = \frac{\theta}{360} \times 2\pi = \frac{\pi\theta}{180}$$

Since the lengths are approximately equal
for small values of θ,

$$\sin \theta° \approx \frac{\pi\theta}{180} \Rightarrow \frac{\sin \theta°}{\theta} \approx \frac{\pi}{180}$$

5 $\dfrac{\pi}{180} = 0.017\,45$, rounded to five decimal
places.

6 The gradient of $\sin \theta°$ at the origin is $\dfrac{\pi}{180}$.

7 $y = \sin \theta° \Rightarrow \dfrac{dy}{d\theta} = \dfrac{\pi}{180}\cos\theta°$

8D (a) Sketching the gradient graph of
$y = \cos x°$ gives the graph of
$\dfrac{dy}{dx} = -k\sin x°$.

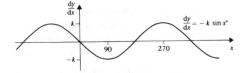

(b) (i) Working in radians, you can
make the maximum gradient
(i.e. the value of k) equal to 1. So

$$y = \cos x^c \Rightarrow \frac{dy}{dx} = -\sin x^c$$

So, if x is measured in radians,

$$\frac{d}{dx}(\cos x) = -\sin x$$

(ii) If x is in degrees, then

$$\frac{d}{dx}(\cos x°) = -\frac{\pi}{180}\sin x°$$

9D (a) 2π

(b) $360° \div 2\pi = \dfrac{180°}{\pi}$

$= 57.295\ldots°$

10 (a) 0.841   (b) 0.017   (c) 0.996

(d) 0.284   (e) 1.000   (f) 0.014

11 (a) $\sin 30° = \sin(\frac{1}{6}\pi)^c = 0.5$

(b)

Radians	π	$\frac{1}{2}\pi$	$\frac{1}{3}\pi$	$\frac{1}{4}\pi$	$\frac{1}{6}\pi$	$\frac{3}{2}\pi$	2π
Degrees	180	90	60	45	30	270	360

(c) To convert $\theta°$ to radians, multiply by
$$\frac{\pi}{180}.$$

(d) To convert θ^c to degrees, multiply by
$$\frac{180}{\pi}.$$

12 (a) 1.047 (b) 0.866 (c) 0.018

13 $\sin 60° = 0.866$. In radian mode, this will probably give an error on a calculator. In fact, $\sin 60^c = -0.305$.

14 Plotting a graph of $y = \sin x$ with x in radians, using simple numerical values rather than multiples of π, helps to emphasise that multiples of π are not the only way to express angles measured in radians.

Exercise A (p. 129)

1 (a) $\frac{1}{2}\pi$ (b) 2π (c) $\frac{1}{4}\pi$

(d) $\frac{2}{3}\pi$ (e) $\frac{1}{3}\pi$ (f) 4π

(g) $-\frac{1}{6}\pi$ (h) $\frac{3}{4}\pi$

2 (a) 45° (b) 540° (c) −180°

(d) 270° (e) −360° (f) 30°

(g) 150° (h) −135°

B Area and arc length (p. 130)

Exercise B (p. 130)

1 (a) $\frac{1}{2} \times 2^2 \times \frac{1}{4}\pi = \frac{1}{2}\pi$

(b) $2 \times \frac{1}{4}\pi = \frac{1}{2}\pi$ (c) $4 + \frac{1}{2}\pi$

2 The perimeter of CDE $= 3r$
Area CDE $= \frac{1}{2}r^2$
So $3r = \frac{1}{2}r^2$, giving $r = 6$ (since $r \neq 0$).

3 (a) 1600 m

(b) Area $= 160\,000$ m^2
The largest crowd is 80 000.

4 (a) $BC = r \sin \theta$ (b) $\frac{1}{2}r^2 \sin \theta$ (c) $\frac{1}{2}r^2\theta$

(d) Area of segment = area of sector OAB
$\qquad\qquad$ − area of triangle OAB
$$= \tfrac{1}{2}r^2\theta - \tfrac{1}{2}r^2 \sin \theta$$
$$= \tfrac{1}{2}r^2(\theta - \sin \theta)$$

5 104.7 cm^2, 43.3 cm^2, 61.4 cm^2

C Pythagoras and circular functions (p. 132)

1D

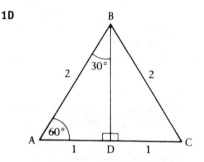

By Pythagoras's theorem, $BD^2 = 4 - 1 = 3$

i.e. $BD = \sqrt{3}$

You can then read off the required trigonometric ratios.

	30°	60°
sin	$\dfrac{1}{2}$	$\dfrac{\sqrt{3}}{2}$
cos	$\dfrac{\sqrt{3}}{2}$	$\dfrac{1}{2}$
tan	$\dfrac{1}{\sqrt{3}}$	$\sqrt{3}$

2

Radians	Degrees	Sin θ	Cos θ	Tan θ
$\dfrac{\pi}{6}$	30	0.5	$\dfrac{\sqrt{3}}{2}$	$\dfrac{1}{\sqrt{3}}$
$\dfrac{2\pi}{3}$	120	$\dfrac{\sqrt{3}}{2}$	-0.5	$\sqrt{3}$
$\dfrac{3\pi}{4}$	135	$\dfrac{1}{\sqrt{2}}$	$\dfrac{-1}{\sqrt{2}}$	-1
$\dfrac{5\pi}{6}$	150	0.5	$\dfrac{-\sqrt{3}}{2}$	$\dfrac{1}{\sqrt{3}}$
$\dfrac{7\pi}{6}$	210	-0.5	$\dfrac{-\sqrt{3}}{2}$	$\dfrac{1}{\sqrt{3}}$
$\dfrac{5\pi}{4}$	225	$\dfrac{-1}{\sqrt{2}}$	$\dfrac{-1}{\sqrt{2}}$	1
$\dfrac{4\pi}{3}$	240	$\dfrac{-\sqrt{3}}{2}$	$\dfrac{-1}{2}$	$\sqrt{3}$
$\dfrac{3\pi}{2}$	270	-1	0	Not defined
$\dfrac{4\pi}{3}$	240	$\dfrac{-\sqrt{3}}{2}$	$\dfrac{-1}{2}$	$\sqrt{3}$
$\dfrac{7\pi}{4}$	315	$\dfrac{-1}{\sqrt{2}}$	$\dfrac{1}{\sqrt{2}}$	-1
$\dfrac{11\pi}{6}$	330	-0.5	$\dfrac{\sqrt{3}}{2}$	$\dfrac{-1}{\sqrt{3}}$

3

Radians	Degrees	Sin θ	Cos θ	Tan θ
$\dfrac{13\pi}{6}$	390	0.5	$\dfrac{\sqrt{3}}{2}$	$\dfrac{1}{\sqrt{3}}$
$\dfrac{-2\pi}{3}$	-120	$\dfrac{-\sqrt{3}}{2}$	-0.5	$\sqrt{3}$
$\dfrac{5\pi}{2}$	450	1	0	Not defined
$\dfrac{-5\pi}{6}$	-150	-0.5	$\dfrac{-\sqrt{3}}{2}$	$\dfrac{+1}{\sqrt{3}}$
$\dfrac{15\pi}{4}$	675	$\dfrac{-1}{\sqrt{2}}$	$\dfrac{1}{\sqrt{2}}$	-1
$\dfrac{7\pi}{3}$	420	$\dfrac{\sqrt{3}}{2}$	0.5	$\sqrt{3}$
$\dfrac{-11\pi}{6}$	-330	0.5	$\dfrac{\sqrt{3}}{2}$	$\dfrac{1}{\sqrt{3}}$

Exercise C (p. 136)

1 (a) $1 + \cos x = 3(1 - \cos^2 x)$
        $\Rightarrow 3\cos^2 x + \cos x - 2 = 0$

   (b) $(3c - 2)(c + 1)$

   (c) 48.2°, 180°, 311.8°

2 (a) $\tan \theta = \frac{2}{3}$, $\theta = 33.7°, 213.7°$

   (b) $\tan \theta = 1.6$, $\theta = 58.0°, 238.0°$

   (c) $\tan 2\theta = 1.4$, $\theta = 27.2°, 117.2°, 207.2°,$
        297.2°

3 (a) $0, \dfrac{2\pi}{3}, \dfrac{4\pi}{3}, 2\pi$ (b) $\dfrac{\pi}{3}, \dfrac{4\pi}{3}$

   (c) $1.05\left(=\dfrac{\pi}{3}\right)$, 1.82, 4.46, 5.24, $\left(=\dfrac{5\pi}{3}\right)$

4 (a) 0.52, 2.62, 3.67, 5.76 (b) $0, \pi, 2\pi$

   (c) 0.46, 2.68, 3.61, 5.82

   (d) 0.34, 2.80, 4.71

5E (a) Let N be the foot of the perpendicular
         from C to OP.
         Then $PC^2 = NC^2 + PN^2$, where
         $NC = 100 \sin \theta$ and
         $PN = 130 - 100 \cos \theta$.

    (b) $PC^2 = 100^2 \sin^2 \theta + 100^2 \cos^2 \theta$
              $-2 \times 130 \times 100 \cos \theta + 130^2$
              $= 26\,900 - 26\,000 \cos \theta$

    (c) $-32.2° \leqslant \theta \leqslant 32.2°$

6E $4x^2 + 9y^2 = 36$ or $\left(\dfrac{x}{3}\right)^2 + \left(\dfrac{y}{2}\right)^2 = 1$

The curve is a stretched circle (i.e. an
ellipse).

7E The student's proof.

8E The student's proof.

**D   Solution of non-right-angled
     triangles: the cosine rule** (p. 137)

1D Plymouth

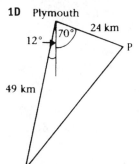

From the drawing
it is clear that the
distance between
the two boats is
approximately
50 km, the limit of
the radio range.

2 $h = b \sin A$

$y = b \cos A$

3 $x = c - y$, because $x + y = c$

$x = c - b \cos A$

4 $a^2 = h^2 + x^2$

$= (b \sin A)^2 + (c - b \cos A)^2$

5 $a^2 = b^2 \sin^2 A + c^2 - 2bc \cos A + b^2 \cos^2 A$

$= b^2 + c^2 - 2bc \cos A,$

since $\cos^2 A + \sin^2 A = 1$

$\Rightarrow a^2 = b^2 + c^2 - 2bc \cos A$

6 If $A = 90°$, $\cos A = 0$ and the cosine rule gives $a^2 = b^2 + c^2$, which is Pythagoras's theorem.

If $A < 90°$, then $a^2 < b^2 + c^2$, which corresponds with the result given by the cosine rule.

7 (a) $c^2 = a^2 + b^2 - 2ab \cos C$

(b) $b^2 = a^2 + c^2 - 2ac \cos B$

8D

$MB = c \cos B$

$MC = c \cos B - a$

In triangle ACM,

$b^2 = h^2 + (c \cos B - a)^2$ (1)

and in triangle ABM,

$c^2 = h^2 + (c \cos B)^2$ (2)

Eliminating h^2 from (1) and (2) leads to the result.

9 The distance between the boats was 51.5 km, beyond the range of the radio.

Exercise D (p. 139)

1 5.76 cm

2 (a) $\cos A = \dfrac{b^2 + c^2 - a^2}{2bc}$

(b) 34.0°, 44.4°, 101.5°

3 (a) $a^2 = 10^2 + 7^2 - 2 \times 10 \times 7 \cos 45°$

$a = 7.1$ cm

(b) $a^2 = 10^2 + 7^2 - 2 \times 10 \times 7 \cos 120°$

$a = 14.8$ cm

(c) $a = 17$ cm

4 5.15

5 5.41 km

E Solution of non-right-angled triangles: the sine rule (p. 139)

1 $h_1 = c \sin A$

$\frac{1}{2}bh_1 = \frac{1}{2}bc \sin A$

Note: This is a more useful

expression for the area of a triangle than $\frac{1}{2}bh_1$, since it is given in terms of sides and angles.

Area of triangle $= \frac{1}{2}bc \sin A$

$= \frac{1}{2} \times$ product of two sides $\times$ sine of included angle.

2 $h_2 = b \sin C$

Area $= \frac{1}{2}ab \sin C$

3 $\frac{1}{2}bc \sin A = \frac{1}{2}ab \sin C$

$\Rightarrow c \sin A = a \sin C$

$\Rightarrow \dfrac{a}{\sin A} = \dfrac{c}{\sin C}$

4 By symmetry, if c is the base, area $= \frac{1}{2}ac \sin B$

5 $\frac{1}{2}ac \sin B = \frac{1}{2}bc \sin A$

$\Rightarrow \dfrac{b}{\sin B} = \dfrac{a}{\sin A}, \quad \dfrac{c}{\sin C} = \dfrac{b}{\sin B}$

So, combining this result with that obtained in question 3 gives the sine rule:

$\dfrac{a}{\sin A} = \dfrac{b}{\sin B} = \dfrac{c}{\sin C}$

6 Area $= \frac{1}{2} \times 4 \times 7 \times \sin 30° = 7$ cm^2

Exercise E (p. 141)

1 (a) $\dfrac{8}{\sin 80°} = \dfrac{5}{\sin \theta}$

$\Rightarrow \sin \theta = \dfrac{5 \sin 80°}{8} = 0.6155,$

giving $\theta = 38°$

Thus the third angle is 62° and

$\dfrac{8}{\sin 80°} = \dfrac{x}{\sin 62°}$, where x is the length of the unknown side

giving $x = \dfrac{8 \sin 62°}{\sin 80°} = 7.17$ cm

(b) $\theta = 27.4°$, the third angle is 22.6° and $x = 10.05$ mm

2 (a) $x^2 = 18^2 + 10^2 - 2 \times 18 \times 10 \cos 35°$

$\Rightarrow x = 11.4$ cm

$\dfrac{\sin \theta}{10} = \dfrac{\sin 35°}{11.4} \Rightarrow \theta = 30.2°$

(θ must be acute)

The remaining angles are 30.2° and 114.8°.

(b) $x = 100.3$ m

The remaining angles are 49.3° and 58.7°.

3 (a) 51.6 cm^2 (b) 3420 m^2 (to 3 s.f.)

4 (a) 43.2 m, 33.2° and 46.8°

(b) 24 mm, 16.3° and 73.7°

(c) 41.9° and 73.1°, 40.1 cm

(d) 48.2°, 58.4°, 73.4°

5 437 km, 050°

Index